PENGUIN BUSINESS

DEMONETIZATION AND THE BLACK ECONOMY

Arun Kumar is the country's leading authority on the black economy. He has written, studied and lectured extensively on this subject for nearly four decades. He was educated at Delhi University, Jawaharlal Nehru University (JNU) and Princeton University. He taught economics at JNU for three decades and retired in 2015.

Kumar's focus areas include public finance, development economics, public policy and macroeconomics. His work has been published widely in these areas, both in the popular press and academic journals. He is currently the Malcolm Adiseshiah chair professor at the Institute of Social Sciences, New Delhi.

T0017716

BY THE SAME AUTHOR

The Black Economy in India

DEMONETIZATION
and the
BLACK ECONOMY

ARUN KUMAR

BUSINESS

An imprint of Penguin Random House

PENGUIN BUSINESS

USA | Canada | UK | Ireland | Australia
New Zealand | India | South Africa | China

Penguin Business is part of the Penguin Random House group of companies
whose addresses can be found at global.penguinrandomhouse.com

Published by Penguin Books India Pvt. Ltd
4th Floor, Capital Tower 1, MG Road,
Gurugram 122 002, Haryana, India

Penguin
Random House
India

First published in Portfolio by Penguin Random House India 2017
Published in Penguin Business 2021

Copyright © Arun Kumar 2017

10 9 8 7 6 5 4 3 2 1

ISBN 9780143456407

Typeset in Adobe Caslon Pro by Manipal Digital Systems, Manipal
Printed at Replika Press Pvt. Ltd, India

www.penguin.co.in

To Nakul, my son, a constant reminder of why we need to strive for a better world

Contents

Preface   *xiii*

Introduction   *xix*

What the PM Said   xx

Major Questions Thrown Up by Demonetization 2016   xxi

Why Demonetization in a Well-functioning Economy?   xxii

    Demonetization Preceded by Preparation Elsewhere:
       India, a Case Study

    India's Economic Performance Preceding
       Demonetization 2016

Were the Goals Achieved?   xxviii

Economic Aspect: Slowing Economy, Deepening Divide   xxx

Political Aspects   xxxiii

Institutional Damage   xxxvi

Chapter Outline   xxxviii

I. DEMONETIZATIONS IN INDIA: THE NUTS AND BOLTS   **1**

Legal Aspects of Demonetization 2016   2

The Demonetizations of 1978 and 1946   6

    Why Demonetization of High-denomination Notes?

Lessons from the 1978 Demonetization   11

Demonetization 2016: Build-up of a Crisis   11
    The Genesis of the Decision
    Crisis Management, Rapid Changes in Announcements
    Most Cash Returned to Banks, Data Release Stopped
    Demonetization and 'Pain': For How Long?
    Coping with the 'Pain'

II. THE ROLE OF MONEY   30

Money in the Economy   30
Money Creation and Different Forms of Money   33
    Money Is a Multiple of Cash Released by
      the Central Bank
    The RBI, the Lender of Last Resort
    Different Forms of Money, Liquidity
    Money Supply during Demonetization 2016
Quantity of Money Needed in the Economy:
    Transactions and Incomes   40
    Velocity of Circulation and Money
The RBI's Role and Its Autonomy   45
Implications of Shortage of Money in an Economy   48

III. ASPECTS OF THE BLACK ECONOMY RELEVANT TO
    DEMONETIZATION   51

Black Economy and Cash   52
Nomenclature and Definitional Aspects   55
    Is Indian Black Money Held Abroad?
Some Not-so-obvious but Common Misconceptions   58
    Corruption Only a Small Part of the Black Economy
    Real Estate Is Not the Biggest Generator of Black

Simple Remedies Have Not Worked

More Laws and Regulations Have Not Helped

Terrorism and Counterfeiting of Currency   64

Impact of the Black Economy   67

   Black Economy, Inefficiency and Slow Growth

   Black Economy, Policy Failure, Poverty
    and Inequality

   Black Economy and Shortage of Resources for Development

Steps to Curb the Black Economy   73

Conclusion   76

IV. SOME SECTORAL ASPECTS OF DEMONETIZATION 2016   77

Who Holds the Cash?   78

Black Not Affected by Demonetization   81

Shortage of Money, Output and Emergence of
   Near-money Forms   84

Impact on the RBI and Its Operations   86

   The RBI and Currency Printing

   Impact on the RBI's Balance Sheet

   Windfall Gain for the RBI Unlikely

Impact on Banks   92

   Deposits in Jan Dhan Accounts

   Lower Interest Rates Did Not Help

Impact on Government Finances   96

   Increased Tax Collection Unlikely

   Difficulty in Budget Making

Impact on Agriculture   100

Conclusion   102

V. DEMONETIZATION: THE MACROECONOMIC COST 105

Demonetization: A Shock to the Economy 105
Government Data on the Impact of Demonetization 109
  Higher Tax Collections in November
  Increase in Acreage under Rabi Sowing
New Black Incomes 113
Transactions Difficult: Demand Hit 114
Impact on Economic Growth 116
  Measuring the Quarterly Rate of Growth of
    the Economy
  The Likely Rate of Growth
Recessionary Conditions Taking Hold 120
  Uncertainty, NPAs and Credit Off-take
  V-shaped Recovery Not in Sight
Conclusion 126

VI. SHIFTING GOALPOSTS 127

Moving Towards a Cashless Economy 127
  'Less Cash' Economy, a Difficult Objective
Other Steps—Raids and *Benami* Property 132
Conclusion 135

VII. WIDER SOCIAL IMPACT 136

Increasing Marginalization of the Marginalized 136
Impact on Institutions 138
  The RBI and the Banks
  Parliament and Politics

Political Aspects 142
  Opposition Means Black and Anti-national
  Politics by Slogans: Creating a Robin Hood Image
  Opposition Confused: Unable to Mobilize
  Would a Benevolent Dictator Deliver?
Inclusiveness Undermined: Unorganized Sector Hit 150
  Push for Technology and Rising Unemployment
Social Aspects 154
  Impact on the Marginalized Sections
  Agitating Youth
Conclusion 158

Conclusion 161

The Principal Argument 161
Changing Goalposts: Cashless Economy and Digitization 164
Shortage of Money in an Economy Is a Serious Matter 165
Economic Costs 166
Steps to Tackle the Black Economy: Demonetization
  Not the First 170
Political Gambit 171

Acknowledgements 175
Bibliography 179
Annexures 197

Preface

I heard the prime minister's speech on demonetization on the Internet while in the US. On the same day the *Hindustan Times* approached me for a quick and short article on the announcement, so I immediately got to work, producing the first piece in a few hours' time.[1] For me, demonetization was not a new subject as I had been teaching it since 1985 in the context of the black economy in India as a small part of my black economy module in my course on public finance. There is also a section devoted to this topic in my book, *The Black Economy in India*,[2] where I had argued why demonetization would not help tackle the black economy. So it was a subject I had given thought to for a long time, and I knew precisely what this move would imply for India.

The initial response of the media was welcoming. So, I was an outlier. I understood why the move was welcomed. There is a common (mis)understanding among the public that 'black' means 'cash', so if cash is squeezed out, the black economy would be eliminated. I realized that the PM too believed this to be true, which was why he announced the move. Everything I argued in my article for the *Hindustan Times* on 9 November 2016 has since turned out to be correct. According to data presented in the book in Chapter VII, based on the Reserve Bank of India (RBI) data, by 13 January 2017, 98.8 per cent of the old currency had

---

[1] Kumar, 2016b.
[2] Kumar, 1999.

come back into the banks.[3,4] So, the government's expectations were belied.

This article led to a deluge of calls to me in the US, requesting interviews and analyses. I had gone to the US to deliver lectures in Columbia and Yale. Apart from fulfilling these commitments, the last seven days of my stay in the US were spent glued to my laptop following the developments in India, giving interviews and writing articles from time to time. The short vacation I thought I would have with family and friends had come to an abrupt end on 9 November. Since then, between talks, interviews, writing articles and books, I have had little respite.

There was so much disruption in the Indian economy that until the focus shifted to the Uttar Pradesh elections in the second week of February, the media was full of stories of the adverse impact of demonetization on the society. I could have given a lot more references since a large number of people have written on the subject, but I have kept this to a minimum so as to not clutter the text.

Since demonetization was linked to the control of black money, I have had to repeatedly clarify why the black economy is not impacted by it. To explain this, I have had to describe the nature of the Indian black economy and clear the many misconceptions about it (and demonetization). For most Indians, including economists and public policy experts, the black economy has been a black box. It is an irritant that can be ignored, except in anecdotal terms when a big scam bursts on the scene. Even then, the scam is the focus and not the system that leads to the scams, which have been bursting on the Indian landscape at an increasingly fast pace. So in this book I have explained the essentials of the black economy in

---

[3] Kumar and Verma, 2017.
[4] RBI on 1 September 2017, in its Annual Report 2016–17, confirmed that 99 per cent of the old notes are back.

addition to explicating the various aspects of demonetization, banking and money.

I started my research on the black economy in 1978; I first wrote on bearer bonds in 1979. I quickly realized why the black economy is the single biggest problem confronting India. I have tried to get others interested in researching the subject but failed in spite of giving hundreds of talks all over the country and publishing a large number of papers on the topic in the last thirty-nine years. Now, in just a single day, the PM had got a lot of people interested in the subject; something that I could not achieve in four decades. This, I hope, will help bring a better understanding of the black economy in India which touches the lives of everyone in the country. The black economy is actually familiar to all but remains a mystery since it is perceived in bits but not as a whole.

This book is a relatively simple exposition of the economic, social and political aspects of demonetization. While there are some technical aspects that need to be understood, the attempt is to present them in simple language while keeping the jargon to a minimum. In other words, I wanted to use simple terms but without compromising on their correct use. There is some repetition for the sake of readability. Cross-references have been put in footnotes so as to not disturb the flow of the reader. Supporting data have been provided by way of annexures so that the text does not get cluttered with tables and diagrams which some people find distracting. The data work took quite a while, delaying the completion of the book.

The social, political and institutional aspects of demonetization are also important and have been presented in this volume. In fact, if demonetization had been undertaken with full preparation, it would not have led to the crisis that it has created in the society. Even if, after it was realized that demonetization would not help eliminate the black economy, the government had admitted its mistake, reversed its decision and allowed the use of the then existing high-denomination notes, the crisis would have reversed quickly. The long-term impact of demonetization would not have been felt, in the same way that the 1978 demonetization did not produce any long-term impact on society.[5]

The book points out that there was a shock to the economy resulting from demonetization, and that its most severe impact was on the sector that depends on cash for its transactions—and that is the unorganized sector of the economy. It produces 45 per cent of the country's output and employs 93 per cent of its workforce.[6] Production in the non-farm component of this sector came to a standstill, and unemployment followed because the units in this sector employ people on a casual basis. The rate of growth of the economy turned negative and impacted the rest of the economy too.[7] Investment fell, and this led to a recessionary situation.

It is explained in the book that the official data do not reflect this downturn. It still talks of a 6 per cent to 7 per cent rate of growth. The reason for this is that data for the unorganized sectors come with a lag of one to three years, until which time it is assumed that the unorganized sector is growing at the same rate as the organized sector. Thus, there is a methodological problem with the way growth is calculated when there is a severe shock to the economy.

The split between the organized and the unorganized sectors has led to a further marginalization of the weakest in society. This is aggravated by the push for digitization, which is supposed to follow from demonetization. The government sought to change

---

[5] See Chapter I.
[6] See Annexure 16, Table 24.
[7] See Chapter V. Official data now released by the government points to a slowing down of the economy but this is also due to the implementation of GST from 1 July 2017.

the goalpost—from one of tackling the black economy to one of creating a cashless society—but even that is difficult to realize.

Demonetization has also led to a weakening of the institutions of democracy. The brute majority in Parliament has meant that the ruling dispensation need not admit its mistake and can bulldoze its way with its views. The upper house of Parliament was bypassed in the decision, and anyone opposing the move was branded as anti-national or as one in possession of black money. The undermining of democratic processes also weakens the marginalized sections further because then the well-off and the powerful can more easily have their way and push for policies that are favourable to them.

In brief, this book attempts to present demonetization in a more holistic and long-term perspective. The idea that Demonetization 2016 was only a short-term phenomenon is sought to be debunked. The hope is to create a wider debate on Demonetization 2016 and its consequences.

Introduction

Demonetization is the term widely used for the denotification of high-denomination currency notes, as was done in India on 9 November 2016. These notes would no longer be legal tender, it was announced the previous evening.

When currency notes are issued they are notified as legal tender, otherwise they would not be valid. So if they are to be removed from currency they have to be denotified. Since the denotification of 9 November 2016 affected 86 per cent of the currency then in circulation, it dealt a huge shock to the economy, setting into motion months of turmoil—still playing out—in the country. It is as if 86 per cent of the blood from a person's body was quickly taken out but only slowly replaced. That body would die from lack of oxygen and other nutrients. Currency is the means of circulation of incomes in the economy, so its shortage leads to an adverse impact on the economy.

Demonetization became the single biggest economic event of the fiscal year 2016-17 for India. It impacted life all round, and the media was full of stories about it for at least three months till political news on the UP elections took over. However, demonetization has remained in the news since then too. The impact of this shock to the economy is still being felt and appears to be long-lasting. Given all this, the demonetization raises many questions, and this book will try to address them. But the first thing is to know what exactly was announced that set into motion this long chain of events and their consequences.

What the PM Said

In his famous speech[1] (GoI, 2016), the PM said:

> *To break the grip of corruption and black money, we have decided
> that the 500 rupee and 1,000 rupee currency notes presently in use
> will no longer be legal tender from midnight tonight, that is 8th
> November 2016. This means that these notes will not be acceptable
> for transactions from midnight onwards. The 500 and 1,000
> rupee notes hoarded by anti-national and anti-social elements will
> become just worthless pieces of paper.*

He exhorted every citizen to participate in this '*mahayagna*':

> *So, in this fight against corruption, black money, fake notes and
> terrorism, in this movement for purifying our country, will our
> people not put up with difficulties for some days? I have full
> confidence that every citizen will stand up and participate in this*
> mahayagna. *My dear countrymen, after the festivity of Diwali,
> now join the nation and extend your hand in this* Imandaari ka
> Utsav, *this* Pramanikta ka Parv, *this celebration of integrity, this
> festival of credibility.*

Demonetization was no doubt considered by the PM as a war
on corruption and black money, and he exhorted every honest
citizen to not only participate in this national endeavour but also
sacrifice for it in case it resulted in any difficulties.

He forcefully stated the purpose of demonetization in the
following words:

> *There comes a time in the history of a country's development when
> a need is felt for a strong and decisive step. For years, this country*

---

[1] The text of the speech is given in Annexure 1.

has felt that corruption, black money and terrorism are festering sores, holding us back in the race towards development . . . fight against corruption, black money, fake notes and terrorism . . .

The questions here are: How effective has demonetization been in achieving its objectives of tackling black money, terrorism and counterfeit currency? And, irrespective of failure or success in achieving its objectives, what has the demonetization cost the society? The cost has to be assessed, both in the short run when demonetization led to a shortage of currency, and in the long run, in terms of its economic consequences.

In this book, I try to answer both these questions. I found that as time went by, analysts, both in the government and outside, kept discovering new aspects of demonetization. These are presented and analysed here.

Major Questions Thrown Up by Demonetization 2016

1. Did the public bear hardships, accepting demonetization as necessary for the wider good?
2. What has its impact been on the black economy?
3. What would be the cost to society, both in the short term and over time?
4. Was the decision legally valid?
5. What is the difference between money and cash, and what is their importance in an economy?
6. Who holds how much cash in an economy, and how much of it could be black money?
7. Can there be a one-shot solution to the problem of black money?
8. What was the nature of the shock to the economy?
9. The PM said that there will be pain; how long will this last?
10. Is there an increasing marginalization of the already marginalized, widening the social divide?

11. Did the government shift its goalposts?
12. In a democracy, is it desirable to place more faith in technology than in human beings?
13. Was demonetization driven by a political or a business conspiracy?
14. Is the Opposition being targeted to curb dissent?
15. What has been the impact on institutions of democracy, like Parliament, political parties, RBI, the Cabinet, decision-making, and so on?

I am highlighting a few of the issues here to give a background to the discussion that is to follow in this book.

Why Demonetization in a Well-functioning Economy?

It is often asked why the government went in for demonetization when the economy was functioning well. When demonetization was carried out in the past in other countries, it was either because there was an economic crisis, as was the case in Russia after the Soviet Union collapsed, or because the currency had to be replaced, as in the case of the introduction of the euro. There was adequate preparation for replacing the currency in the case of the euro.

Demonetization Preceded by Preparation Elsewhere: India, a Case Study

Up to 8 November 2016, the Indian government was saying that the country's economy was growing at above 7 per cent, making it the fastest growing economy in the world. There was no deep crisis of any kind facing the economy that required the demonetization that was announced. There was no hyper-inflation, as in Germany immediately after World War II or as in Venezuela at present. The government had not tired of stating how good the macroeconomic situation was. I have listed below some of the countries which carried out demonetization in the last 100 years, most of them after World War II.

Germany introduced a new currency (the Rentenmark) on 20 November 1923 to replace all the old papiermark (mark) notes, which ceased to be legal tender. The mark itself had replaced the goldmark in August 1914 at the start of World War I. The reason for these changes was high levels of inflation. In 1924, when the Rentenmark came into circulation, 1 Rentenmark was exchanged for 1 trillion papiermark. Notes of value 1 trillion, 10 trillion, 50 trillion and 100 trillion papiermark had been issued during the hyper-inflation phase. The Rentenmark was replaced by the Reichsmark in 1924. From 1944 to 1948, there was also the 'allied militàrmark'. In 1948, these were replaced in West Germany by the Deutsche mark. In brief, the two World Wars produced an economic crisis in Germany calling for currency replacement.

Some of the countries which have demonetized their currencies since World War II:

A. Economies facing high inflation,[2] which went in for demonetization:

1. Ghana, in 1982
2. Nigeria, in 1984
3. Myanmar, in 1987
4. Russia and former constituents of the Soviet Union, changing their currency in 1991
5. Zaire, in 1993
6. Zimbabwe, in 2015

---

[2] For a list of countries that have faced hyper-inflation since 1900, see p. 42 of Ray, 2013.

7. Venezuela. This country presents an example of a failed demonetization. On 12 November 2016, it announced demonetization of the 100 bolivar notes to check raging inflation. A massive shortage of currency followed, and there was rioting, etc., leading to a quick reversal of the decision.

B. Economies not facing a crisis that implemented demonetization:

1. The United States. In 1969 it took out of circulation the existing $10,000, $5000, $1000 and $500 notes (called bills in the USA). The high-denomination bills were not in general use, and it was feared that they were being used by criminals for nefarious purposes.

2. The United Kingdom. In 1971 it phased out its old currency in favour of the new one so that it could decimalize its currency. Preparation for it began in March 1966, and it took eighteen months to make the change to decimal currency.

3. Europe. The euro replaced national currencies in Europe on 1 January 2002. Time was given till 30 June 2002 for exchange of old currency at banks. For several years afterwards the currency could still be exchanged in the Central Banks. The preparation for this took three years, from 1999 onwards.

India went in for demonetization on 8 November 2016 without preparation. The PM did not consult the Cabinet, and the ministers were told of the decision just before the PM's speech to the nation. According to reports, RBI was asked the day before the announcement, on 7 November, to recommend the decision. The RBI board met on 8 November and 'recommended' demonetization to the government. It appears to have simply carried out the orders of the government. It is unclear that it applied its mind in the short time it was given to figure out the pros and cons of the policy. It is also not known if it warned the government about the possible pitfalls of such a move and the precautions that needed to be taken in advance.

In his speech, the PM said:

> *It is only now, as I speak to you, that various agencies like banks, post offices, railways, hospitals and others are being informed. The Reserve Bank, banks and post offices have to make many arrangements at very short notice. Obviously, time will be needed. Therefore all banks will be closed to the public on 9th November.*

Thus, everyone who should have prepared for the demonetization was unprepared. Enough new currency had not been readied to replace the demonetized notes. ATMs were not recalibrated to dispense the new notes, which were of a different size from the old notes. There were repeated changes in the notifications, and new notifications were issued as more and more problems cropped up.[3] This led to a lot of confusion, intensifying the uncertainty people were already facing and aggravating the sense of crisis in the society.

Demonetization as it was implemented in India led to an immediate crisis, as I will explain later in Chapter II. Economics seldom presents instances such as this one, which are akin to an experiment in the sciences. The impact of demonetization continues to play out, and I will explain that in Chapter VI and in the Conclusion. Now India has become a case study for economists all over the world to understand what happens when an unplanned demonetization is carried out in a large, well-functioning economy.[4]

---

[3] See Annexures 2, 3 and 4.
[4] Birch, 2017; Sunder, 2016.

India's Economic Performance Preceding Demonetization 2016

So, how was the Indian economy performing at the time of the announcement of demonetization on 8 November 2016?[5]

Graph 2 shows that the Indian economy's high-growth phase began in 2003-04, when the economy started to grow at about 8 per cent per annum. The average since then has been 7.5 per cent annually, though the rate of growth has been declining overall. After the global crisis beginning 2007-08, the economy recovered for two years before again recording a declining rate of growth.

This was a result of the decline in the rate of investment in the economy after its peak in 2008, which in turn had resulted from a decline in demand in the economy, leading to low capacity utilization in industry. The government encouraged the private sector to invest heavily in high-cost infrastructure, such as highways, airports, power and so on. India, with the majority of its population being poor, can ill afford such high-cost infrastructure because its population does not have the purchasing power to make these investments viable. So, many infrastructure projects have languished or have not been able to generate the profits they should have. This led to losses for many companies, making it difficult for them to repay their loans to the banks, which in turn ended up with large non-performing assets (NPAs).

An important reason underlying the low demand in the economy is that after 2002, inequality in the economy has risen. A surge in the propensity to save and direct tax collections indicate that the rich are getting richer. The rise in the number of billionaires in a country with such a large poor

---

[5] The economic situation is depicted in detail through Graphs 2 to 5 in Annexure 5.

population also suggests the same. As inequality rises, more and more income is concentrated in the hands of the rich, and since they proportionally consume less than the non-rich, the share of consumption in the economy tends to fall, leading to a shortage of demand.

It is easy to understand this in the following way. If I give Rs 100 to a rich person she would save most of it since she is already consuming most of what she wants. However, if I give Rs 100 to a poor person she/he would consume most of it by buying more clothing, utensils, footwear, food and many other things she/he does not have. One can see that demand will rise more if we transfer incomes to the poor rather than to the rich.

Be that as it may, a slowdown in demand led to the decline in the growth rate of the economy.

Another factor responsible for the slowdown was the international situation, which deteriorated again after some green shoots became visible in 2009 after the global financial crisis. This led to a decline in India's exports and a rise in its current account deficit.

This was also accompanied by high fiscal deficit and inflation. In other words, there was a macroeconomic crisis confronting the economy from 2012 onwards. This crisis started to moderate from 2013, but other problems arose in the economy—such as lack of growth in the industrial sector, inadequate investment, inadequate employment generation, two droughts and decline in agriculture.

However, the NDA government, since coming to power in 2014, has claimed that the rate of growth of the economy has increased and that India, by 2016, had become the fastest-growing economy in the world. Since China's rate of growth has fallen below 7 per cent per annum, India now stood ahead of China in terms of growth rate. However, given the continuing problems in the economy, many analysts have doubted India's claim to a 7 per cent-plus rate of growth. Ten years back, when the economy was growing at over 7 per cent, the 'feel' was entirely different.

The sudden increase in India's rate of growth in 2013 announced in 2015 was a result of a change in the base year. Also, a different method was used to calculate the growth rate. The government has claimed that it now uses more complete and more appropriate data to calculate growth so the latest data is better and more robust. This new method of calculation has also meant that during the last two years of UPA rule the rate of growth was higher than what was calculated earlier.

So in October 2016, just before demonetization was announced, the economy was doing well, according to government statistics,[6] with the second and third quarter data showing all sectors growing at 6 per cent to 7 per cent per annum.

Clearly, India's demonetization was not forced by any crisis in the economy. There was no hyper-inflation to tackle; it was not that India's currency had become worthless; and it was not that people had lost faith in the currency and were switching to dollars, etc.

Naturally, the question uppermost in the minds of many analysts has been—then why such a move? The demonetization looks like an experiment conducted to find out what happens in a well-running economy in which a sudden shortage of cash is engineered by policy. And it is turning out to be a test case of what not to do.

Were the Goals Achieved?

In his speech, the PM linked cash to black money:

> Which honest citizen would not be pained by reports of crores worth of currency notes stashed under the beds of government officers? Or by reports of cash found in gunny bags?

---

[6] Graphs 3 to 5 in Annexure 5.

The magnitude of cash in circulation is directly linked to the level of corruption.

It was expected that a lot of the money with the public would not be surrendered since it was black. This hope has been belied. The government and the RBI announced how many of the old notes in circulation had been returned up to 10 December 2016; but after that, under one pretext or the other, they stopped providing the figures altogether. However, I will show later, in Chapter II, that 98.8 per cent of the old notes had been relinquished by the people by 13 January 2017. Only Rs 18,000 crore worth of old notes had still not come back to the RBI by that date. One can barely call this small amount black money, because Rs 8000 crore of this was with the cooperative banks who were not allowed to return the money to the RBI. The rest is most likely in the neighbouring countries or lying with people who have forgotten about it or is lying abroad with those who are no longer Indian nationals and who, under the rules, cannot return it any more. There have been cases of people who were sick and were left holding their old notes and of people in jail who could not return their currency, etc.

Thus, most of the white and black cash had come back into the banking system by the time of the deadline of 30 December 2016. The government realized by mid-December that most of the cash was back and that its attempt to extinguish 'black money' had failed.

Not only that, it became clear to the government that it had confused the yearly flow of black income with the stock of black money collected over the years lying with those who generate black incomes. Lack of this theoretical clarity on the part of the government is what made them go for demonetization. They thought that by surprising everyone, they would, in one stroke, get rid of the black money in the economy.

The other objective—of eliminating counterfeit currency—was also not fulfilled; new counterfeit currency started to appear soon after the new notes were introduced. And the final objective of checking terrorist financing was not achieved as terrorist activity continued, with maybe a temporary lull in November and December.

It must be appreciated that terrorists also finance themselves with dollars, drugs and so on. That part of their financing has continued. Also, foreign state actors are supposed to be involved in the counterfeiting of notes, and that India cannot stop.

With its demonetization goals not achieved, the government shifted the goalposts. It started talking of achieving the goal of a cashless economy via digitization and of formalizing the informal economy, and began swooping down on *benami* property, conducting raids and so on. However, all this required advance preparation and could be done independent of demonetization. These new pronouncements only further confused the picture, both for the public and the policymakers.

Economic Aspect: Slowing Economy, Deepening Divide

Not only were the goals of demonetization not achieved, but the economy also started to suffer intensely. But the impact of demonetization was not uniform, as discussed below. On its part, the government put up a brave front; rather than reverse the step quickly so that its ill effects disappeared, it gave the spin of demonetization being useful to achieve these new objectives (which were not stated in the PM's speech of 8 November 2016). This, rather than solving the problem, led to even more confusion.

The Indian economy, consisting of an elite organized sector and the unorganized sector, is deeply divided. The former offers well-paid jobs with those in this sector enjoying a high lifestyle, comparable to that of the average citizen in middle-income countries and even the rich anywhere in the world. Those in the unorganized sectors have low incomes, often only 10 per cent to 20 per cent of what the organized-sector worker in a corresponding job earns.

The organized-sector employees are able to use all the formal-sector structures, such as banks, credit and debit cards, and electronic means of money transfer. The unorganized sector consists of the small, cottage and other informal businesses, which work on cash and have little access to banks and the formal structures of the economy. If cash is short the organized sector can quickly switch to using other means of payment. That is not the case with the unorganized sector.

So a cash shortage in the economy immediately affects the income-generation process of the unorganized sector, while it impacts the organized sector much less. This has increased the existing divide between the two sectors even more. The move to a cashless society will further enhance the divide, given the poor infrastructure and training available to the marginalized sections of society.

The unorganized sector collapsed after demonetization, and reports from ground zero said many businesses had almost shut down so that this sector showed negative growth. Its workers were left unemployed. This in turn adversely affected demand for the organized sector. As will be shown later, discretionary demand fell. What this means is that I would postpone a purchase if I could, to save on cash which was in short supply. I could always buy that thing later once the situation eased. Business profitability, which was already low because of lack of adequate demand for industrial goods, suffered further because of the decline in demand for goods. This led to a decline in investments because industry could not utilize the capital it had already installed so that any additional investment would have only added to the idle capital. The economy faced a recessionary situation, in which output falls and so do investment and employment.

The official data does not show a fall in the rate of growth following the demonetization of late 2016. This is because the government does not routinely collect data on the unorganized sector, which could show its decline. On the contrary, it assumes that the unorganized sector grew exactly as much as the organized sector. So there was a methodological flaw in estimating the economy's rate of growth. The method applicable in normal times is not valid when there has been a big shock to the economy.

The shock to the economy was that the well-running economy was expected to speed up, but instead its rate of growth fell. Agriculture was expected to do well because of a good monsoon after two years. But the rise in production was not as sharp as it could have been, and the farmers were in a crisis because the prices of commodities collapsed as demand declined consequent to the fall in incomes in major parts of the economy. It is no wonder then that farmers have been demanding loan waiver and better support prices, etc. This crisis has also brought the urban-rural divide into sharp focus.

As will be discussed in Chapters I, IV and VII, the crisis was different in different sectors. But the common thread is that money is needed to carry forward transactions, and when it is short it leads to an economic crisis. If enough currency had been printed in advance there would have been no problem.

The government argued that if those with black money had got wind of the decision, they would have taken steps to convert their black money to white. The PM said, 'Secrecy was essential for this action.'

However, the secrecy was not required, since if I had black money and was also forewarned, I would try to pass it on to someone else and that person would be left holding the black money. My black money becomes someone else's black money. But it remains black money. Yes, I could pass it on to a business that could show it as cash in hand and working capital. But secrecy and the surprise element cannot prevent me from still doing this. So the effort at secrecy was futile, and the resulting lack of preparation causing disruption to the economy and dislocation in the lives of citizens was needless.

The government reiterated times without number that there would be temporary pain. The PM first said the pain would last fifty days, but later said the pain would begin to lessen after fifty days. He even said that if he had made a mistake he was willing to accept any punishment the public would deal him.

What was the pain the PM was talking about when according to the government the economic growth rate had not fallen sharply? The government expected a V-shaped recovery—a fast decline and an equally sharp rise. What it did not factor in was that no economy is like a science experiment, where when the conditions are reversed the situation reverses too. Often, there is hysteresis. Material remembers the stages through which it passed. (That is, it remembers its history.) This is strongly true of societies. People are not automatons—that is, machines without consciousness—who do things mechanically. Unemployment, decline in investment, etc., have a big effect on society, and the situation does not automatically return to what it was. The economy has suffered long-lasting damage, as will be made clear in this book.

Political Aspects

Apart from the economic aspect of demonetization, there was also a political aspect to it. It is hardly ever the case that there is a purely economic angle to a policy. Good economics should also make for good politics. In the case of demonetization, the economic fallout was not what the government thought it would be, but the political aspect of the policy turned out to be positive.

There was the conspiracy theory that the move was well timed for the elections in Uttar Pradesh in March 2017.[7] The

---

[7] The Opposition in UP lost the election badly, strengthening the conspiracy theory. But it must be remembered that compared to 2014, BJP's vote share fell by 2 per cent, while that of BSP increased by 2 per cent. Hence, the victory can be interpreted as a result of division of Opposition vote.

theory was that most of the opposition parties had collected a large chest of funds for expenditure in the elections and that demonetization in one fell swoop had reduced that to zero, giving an advantage to the ruling dispensation.[8]

Be that as it may, from the reports of rallies and electioneering, all the parties appear to have spent a lot of money in the UP elections, and none of them seem to have been short of funds. So, this could not have been the main reason for demonetization.

The PM, in his speech on 8 November 2016, had spelt out the reason for demonetization. He said the government, since its coming to power in May 2014, had tried various steps to control the black economy. He listed the salient features of the fight against black money. But it was clear that these steps did not yield the expected results, said the PM. What he did not list was the promise he had made during the 2014 election campaign that huge sums of black money were lying abroad and that he would bring them back and that would be enough to give each Indian family Rs 15 lakh. He was repeatedly reminded of this by the media. In election campaigns the Opposition taunted him about this promise, especially during the campaigns for the Bihar elections, which he lost comprehensively. In spite of Amit Shah, the BJP president, admitting that this promise was a 'chunavi jumla'[9] and should not be taken seriously, people were not willing to forget it. The PM was also taunted for being a government for the corporates (Rahul Gandhi's 'suit boot ki sarkar') and anti-poor. Before the next general elections in 2019, Modi needed to correct these two images.

Demonetization was the political masterstroke that he thought would serve this purpose of correcting his image of being pro-large businesses and anti-poor. He was clear that it would be

---

[8] Assuming that it had converted its black funds in advance or that it would continue to get funds because it is in power.

[9] PTI, 2015.

seen by the people as the boldest step ever taken in the country against black money. The public also believed that 'black' means 'cash', and that if cash is squeezed out of the system, black money would be extinguished. Modi assessed correctly that people would think he was attempting to take from the bad rich guys and give to the poor via demonetization, creating for himself a Robin Hood image. This is borne out by the statement in the PM's speech of 8 November 2016:

> The evil of corruption has been spread by certain sections of society for their selfish interest. They have ignored the poor and cornered benefits. Some people have misused their office for personal gain. On the other hand, honest people have fought against this evil.

At the end of the speech, he said:

> Let us ensure that the nation's wealth benefits the poor.
> Let us enable law-abiding citizens to get their due share.

On another occasion, when it became apparent that the accounts of the poor (Jan Dhan accounts or other bank accounts they had) were being used by black money holders to recycle their black wealth, he exhorted the poor to not return this money, even offering them the protection of the state for this. The government also announced an email ID where anonymous complaints could be lodged by the poor about such laundering of money. It is clear that the PM tried in every way to use demonetization to appear to be against the rich bad guys who had been harming the nation.

The opposition parties were confused by the demonetization and could not mobilize the people against its obviously deleterious impact on them. Anyone who opposed the move was branded as a holder of black money. By implication, they would also be considered anti-poor. Since most of the political leaders get black money for their party's day-to-day operations, for financing elections, and for getting rich, none dared to come forward to consistently mobilize the people, who suffered severely. In India, the poor are used to suffering in silence; they rise up against injustice only when they are mobilized by some political or social forces. The PM's gambit thus paid off.

Institutional Damage

Demonetization severely impacted the many institutions of democracy in India. This will weaken the structure of democracy in the country.

The Cabinet was not consulted in the name of secrecy. It was told at the last minute. The PM did not answer any questions about demonetization. He made a large number of announcements in public speeches but did not answer questions either in a press conference or in Parliament. If the PM does not think it proper to make a statement and answer questions, then one can imagine what the situation would be when lesser issues are taken up for discussion.

Accountability is attached to the PM responding to questions in Parliament. The erosion of this accountability of his office is a warning signal for democracy.

The RBI was told by the government to approve demonetization the day before (7 November 2016) it was announced. While a board meeting was called on 8 November 2016, it is unclear what discussion took place before the government was 'advised' to go ahead with demonetization. RBI has not given the public the information crucial to a proper analysis of the impact of demonetization.

The RBI governor chose to remain quiet when he was supposed to have clarified matters. He did not answer questions regarding advance preparations for execution of demonetization.

For instance, information on how much of the new currency had been printed in advance was not revealed. Before the Rajya Sabha Committee he did not divulge information on how much of the denotified currency had come back to its vaults and so on.

The banking system came under huge stress. Banks were busy collecting old notes, managing serpentine queues of customers, dispensing new notes in dribbles and so on. They had no time to do their normal banking operations. Customers were repeatedly turned away and ATMs did not function properly or did not have cash for several months. To top it all, some corrupt bankers gave large sums of new currency notes to black money holders, probably having made money out of being in league with them. This aggravated the shortage of cash for the general public. The image of Indian banking and its credibility took a beating because the public were incensed that they could not withdraw their own money. This will have a long-term impact on the people's perception of Indian banks.

The credibility of the government's statistical department and NITI Aayog has also come under question. These institutions repeatedly tried to justify demonetization by arguing that it had no impact on the economy. They said there had been no adverse impact on employment or any drop in output due to it. This flew in the face of ground reports. Reports in the media and surveys by industry and business groups showed a sharp drop in economic activity right from November 2016.[10]

The budget for 2017-18 was made on the assumption that demonetization had no impact on the economy. It was assumed that revenues would remain buoyant and that expenditures could therefore be increased without creating a larger fiscal deficit. If data were not available to the government, as the statistical department has said, how were these assumptions made?

---

[10] See Annexure 20.

Demonetization has thus brought into question the credibility of the Union budget too.

In brief, demonetization not only had an economic impact but also social and political implications, all of which have served to dent the various institutions of democracy in the country. The divide between the marginalized sections and the elite has widened. The implementation of GST without taking into account the interests of the unorganized sectors is another sign of the marginalization of these sections of citizens.

This book presents Demonetization 2016 and the black economy, and their implications in the sequence described below.

Chapter Outline

The book consists of nine chapters, including Introduction and Conclusion. The Introduction gives the overall perspective underlying the sudden Demonetization 2016.

The first chapter describes the demonetizations of 1978 and 2016 and how different they have been. Chapter II analyses the importance of money in a modern-day economy, since demonetization is all about impacting its circulation. In this, the role of banks and the RBI is important, which is discussed in this chapter. How money plays a different role in different sectors is also described here. Chapter III presents the analytics of the black economy for an understanding of how demonetization may or may not impact it. It discusses the various misconceptions about the black economy and its overall impact on the society. The chapter contains an analysis of terrorism and counterfeiting in India and discusses whether demonetization would impact these activities. In the end, the chapter mentions the other steps available to policymakers to tackle the black economy in India.

Chapter IV presents some important features of the 2016 demonetization, including its impact on RBI, banking, government finances, budget making and agriculture. Chapter V discusses the impact of demonetization on the Indian economy at the macro level, including its impact on the growth rate of the economy. It shows why a V-shaped recovery did not take place and why the economy has instead gone into a recessionary phase with a negative rate of growth in the immediate aftermath of the demonetization. It argues that it will take a long time for the country to get out of this situation. Chapter VI describes how the government shifted the goalposts as it realized soon enough that the original goals set in the PM's speech were not likely to be achieved. The prospects of a cashless economy, and dealing with *benami* property and the gold economy, are discussed here.

Chapter VII looks at the wider social impact of demonetization; how it has affected institutions, and what its political and social ramifications are. It is argued that the PM managed to create a Robin Hood image for himself which has paid political dividend. The question is whether it would last given the exclusionary character of demonetization and digitization. The concluding chapter presents the findings emerging from the book regarding demonetization, the import of such a shock to an economy, why a sudden shortage of cash leads to an economic crisis, the importance of dealing with the black economy, why demonetization does not impact it, and the political and social aspects of policies like demonetization and digitization, which are basically exclusionary policies. The plea is that reforms should be such as to transform the lives of people and not to exclude them.

1

Demonetizations in India:
The Nuts and Bolts

Demonetization in India in 2016 is not the first time it has been resorted to in the world as mentioned in the introduction. First, it was done in times of economic crisis, e.g. due to hyper-inflation. Second, recourse was taken to it when currency was changed, e.g. the introduction of the euro in place of currencies of individual European nations.

The demonetization of 2016 was by no means the first in India. There have been demonetizations earlier, in 1946 and in 1978. The first demonetization was announced on 12 January 1946. It removed from circulation the existing notes of Rs 500, Rs 1000 and Rs 10,000. The second demonetization was announced on 16 January 1978, and denotified the currency notes of values Rs 1000, Rs 5000 and Rs 10,000. Both times, the intention was to check black income generation and the use of high-denomination notes in illegal activities. Neither demonetization undermined the black economy or illegalities, nor did it have any major impact on the Indian economy. The questions that naturally arise are, can we learn anything from these past episodes, and how did the 2016 scheme unravel?

Legal Aspects of Demonetization 2016

Demonetization makes currency that was valid at one point in time invalid. As the prime minister put it in his speech of 8 November 2016:

> . . . *we have decided that the 500 rupee and 1,000 rupee currency notes presently in use will no longer be legal tender from midnight tonight, that is 8th November 2016. This means that these notes will not be acceptable for transactions from midnight onwards. The 500 and 1,000 rupee notes hoarded by anti-national and anti-social elements will become just worthless pieces of paper.*

Currency is issued by a country's Central Bank (in India's case, the RBI) and has legal sanctity, which is provided by the government. If that legal sanctity is withdrawn, currency becomes worthless pieces of paper. So, the money that was once used for exchange or could be stored for its value cannot be used for these purposes after it is demonetized. In fact, it is no longer money. Demonetization strips a currency unit of its status as legal tender.

The Attorney General of India, Mukul Rohatgi, arguing in the Supreme Court on 15 November 2016, made a distinction between demonetization and the withdrawal of legal status for old notes. In the former case, he said, possession of the old notes would be illegal, while in the latter case the notes could still be owned, though they were no longer legal tender. And, while the former would require an Act of Parliament, the latter could be done via a Gazette Notification. It may be noted that the demonetization of 2016 was done via a Gazette Notification on 8 November. It may also be noted that neither the Government of India nor the RBI used the term 'demonetization' in their notifications. Instead, they have said, '. . . specified bank notes [SBN] shall cease to be legal tender . . .'

It has also been argued that the government notification was 'issued in exercise of the powers conferred by sub-section (2) of section 26 of the Reserve Bank of India Act, 1934 (2 of 1934)'. This sub-section of section 26 reads, '. . . with effect from such date as may be specified in the notification, any series of bank notes of any denomination shall cease to be legal tender . . .'

Critics have argued that the use of the term 'any series' does not imply an entire denomination (like Rs 1000). Hence, Demonetization 2016 should have been done via a law passed in Parliament or via an Ordinance later approved by Parliament. This is what was done in 1978. First an Ordinance was passed, and then an Act was approved by Parliament. It is argued that for such a major step as demonetization, parliamentary discussion and approval are crucial.

On 30 December 2016, the last day for surrender of old notes by the public, the Specified Bank Notes (Cessation of Liabilities) Ordinance, 2016 was promulgated. The Bill for replacing this Ordinance was introduced in the Lok Sabha on 3 February 2017 and notified on 1 March 2017. This Act has made possession of more than ten of the old notes illegal. If anyone is caught with more than this number, they can be prosecuted.

Another criticism is that wiping out 86 per cent of the country's currency overnight caused harassment and loss of work to a large number of people, thus constituting a violation of the fundamental right under Article 19(1)(g) of the Constitution, allowing any citizen to practise any profession . . . The suddenness of the move led to adverse consequences for a lot of people. It has even been argued that one cannot say that only those with black money were affected. The government, of course, cites Article 19(6), which implies that it can override Article 19(1)(g) in the interest of the general public, by placing reasonable restrictions on the exercise of that article.

The question this naturally throws up is, what is in the interest of the general public? And, what are reasonable restrictions? To bring to heel a few, can a very large number of people be put to inconvenience, especially when other measures were available and when this measure has been known not to have curbed the black economy in the past? An illustration that this argument made no sense was the release of even larger-denomination notes, of Rs 2000, after Demonetization 2016, the critics pointed out.

That the government asked the RBI to recommend demonetization one day before the announcement showed that it was not an independent process and there was little deliberation on the matter, went another argument. Article 26(2) of the RBI Act implies proper deliberation before a recommendation by its board, and not a perfunctory decision. It has also been argued that the recommendation should have been based on public consultation, given the importance of the matter. It was further argued that there should be 'a correlation between reasonableness of a legislation and its immediate effect'. In this case, the impact was drastically negative, so this step was not desirable.[1] For example, what business could be done with a withdrawal limit in early days of Demonetization 2016 of Rs 20,000 per week, which was later raised to Rs 50,000 and then to Rs 1 lakh? Even these sums were not easily available because of the tremendous shortage of cash at the banks.

Critics have further argued that the rules for exchange of old currency were repeatedly changed. Assurances given were suddenly withdrawn.[2] It was initially said that the old notes would be accepted for change until 31 March 2017. Citizens were repeatedly told that there was no need to panic and to rush to join queues since there was enough time to exchange old notes. These and many other promises were revoked without notice, and many people were left holding their old notes which

---

[1] For more details of these arguments see, The Wire, 2016.
[2] See Annexures 3 and 4.

they could not get exchanged for new ones. This is akin to appropriation of someone else's property. The critics point out that this move amounted to wiping out the public's wealth, since a currency note is an asset of the person holding it. This kind of action should have been undertaken via an Act of Parliament.

The government has given the argument of secrecy for the suddenness of demonetization and its resort to a Gazette Notification. It was argued by the government that if secrecy was not maintained, then those holding black money would have converted their black hoards into other assets and escaped the net.

But it has been known theoretically that demonetization does not stop black income generation and cannot unearth any significant portion of black wealth.[3] In reality too,[4] the old notes yet to be returned to RBI[5] are worth only around Rs 18,000 crore. Of this amount, Rs 8000 crore were lying with the cooperative banks.[6] This amounted to less than 0.1 per cent of the black wealth in 2016-17. Secrecy neither worked in 1978 nor in 2016. It was the wrong premise to go by, and brings into doubt the 'reasonableness of the decision'. Further, an Ordinance, as in 1978, could also have achieved secrecy, if it was absolutely required. So the entire intent appears to have been to bypass Parliament. This damages the institution of democracy in India and strengthens authoritarian tendencies, as discussed in Chapter VII.

In brief, while the power to demonetize rests with the Government of India, the issue is, should it be done bypassing Parliament? Even if what was done is technically and legally correct, was it desirable in a democracy? Was the RBI given

---

[3] Kumar, 1999.
[4] See Chapter II.
[5] See Annexure 7, Tables 7 and 8.
[6] Kumar, 2017h.

complete autonomy to make its decision on this issue? Parliament should have been brought into the picture. The issue of remonetization needs to be separated from demonetization. As the government has not tired of saying, it would not want to reissue new notes of the same value as the old demonetized notes because it wants to ensure there is less cash in the economy. Finally, the issue of black money should be analysed separately from both the demonetization carried out in 2016 and its legality. The two are not directly linked, even though the government erroneously linked them.

The Demonetizations of 1978 and 1946

The 1978 scheme is the more relevant one to draw lessons from about the implications of the 2016 demonetization. The high-denomination notes then in existence were of Rs 10,000, Rs 5000 and Rs 1000. These were demonetized. As shown in a recent article,[7] the high-denomination currency notes then accounted for about 0.6 per cent of the total currency with the public. So the removal of this small amount from circulation hardly had any impact on the economy.

The article also showed that 45 per cent of these notes were with the banks and the government, and consequently the impact of their withdrawal on the public was even less than it might otherwise have been. The effect of that demonetization on availability of cash was negligible. Further, 85.6 per cent of the Rs 145.42 crore of high-denomination notes in existence was returned to the RBI for conversion to new currency. So there was hardly any dent on the black economy either. But crucially, the demonetization of 1978 hardly impacted the public.

The annual per capita income (at current prices) in 1977-78 was Rs 1550, or in monthly terms Rs 130. Most people only

---

[7] Rajakumar and Shetty, 2016.

carried a few rupees in their pocket. Hardly anyone had seen the high-denomination notes, and even fewer used them.

In 1950-51, the annual per capita income (at current prices) was Rs 274. In 1946 it must have been even less. This implies a monthly average income of less than Rs 23. Again, there was no question that citizens, except the extremely wealthy, would have kept or used or even seen the high-denomination notes. Again, there was no impact on the public. Further, of the Rs 143.97 crore of these notes in circulation, only Rs 9.07 crore did not come back.

The economy was much smaller in 1978 than it is now, and was even smaller in 1946. In 1950-51, the gross domestic product (GDP, a measure of production in the economy) was Rs 10,401 crore. It was even lower in 1946. The data for 1946 is for the undivided India, including data for Pakistan and Bangladesh, and is hence not comparable with the later figures for India. The 1950-51 figure is a good proxy for gauging the size of GDP for 1946. In 1977-78, the GDP was Rs 1,05,848 crore, ten times larger than in 1950-51. In 2016-17 it has become Rs 1,50,00,000 crore, about fourteen times larger than in 1977-78. That is why high-denomination notes were in common use in 2016 but not in 1978 or in 1946.

Why Demonetization of High-denomination Notes?

A nation's GDP expands because of two reasons. One is increase in real production—there is greater production of food, industrial goods and services. The other is inflation, when prices rise so that the consumer has to pay more for the same thing. Higher production and higher prices together lead to a higher GDP.

How do consumers buy products and producers sell what they make? Both use money to do so. The money is not just in the form of cash, but also consists of bank accounts, cheques, credit cards and electronic transfers. This will be discussed in greater detail in the next chapter. Cash has been an important component of money and is carted around by the public to carry out their transactions. As the GDP increases, more and more transactions take place and are of larger and larger value. So, in the 1950s, a rupee was enough to cover a middle-class family's daily transactions; in the 1970s, ten rupees were required for this purpose. In 2016, one needed a few hundred rupees to carry out the day-to-day transactions of such a family.

Another development is that the economy sees much larger financial transactions today than earlier. Savings have increased, and are invested in various assets. These require much larger volumes of money for their transaction. This requirement is aggravated by the rise in the size of the black economy, where cash transactions are preferred. It is not that black economy transactions cannot be carried out in non-cash ways, but it is easier to do them using cash.

If cash exists only in small denominations—say, in Rs 10, Rs 20 and Rs 50 notes—then citizens would have to carry around a lot of notes. Businesses would collect a huge quantity of notes daily, and this would be a big inconvenience. A petrol station with a daily transaction of Rs 10 lakh would collect a lakh of Rs 10 notes. Their storage and transportation would pose huge problems. If the payment was in Rs 500 notes the station would have to deal with only 2000 notes, and if it had collected money in Rs 1000 notes it would have to deal with only 1000 notes. This is manageable. What is true for a petrol station is true for other businesses too.

This is the reason why, as the GDP has expanded, the RBI has printed more and more large-denomination currency notes. In 1978,[8] high-denomination currency notes accounted for 0.6 per cent of the total notes in the country. By 2000-01 it became 26.7 per cent, by 2010-11, 78.7 per cent, and by 2015-16, 86

---

[8] Rajakumar and Shetty, 2016.

per cent. Is there anything unusual about this? Not if one takes into account the fact that transactions exceed the GDP itself, and their ratio to GDP has been increasing at a fast rate as financialization of the economy has taken place.

Since 1950-51,[9] the rate of growth of currency in circulation and the rate of growth of nominal GDP have, more or less, been in tandem. Even if the decadal average is taken, the two have grown together, except in the decade of the 2000s. This was due to the faster growth in currency in the early part of the decade. However, if an average of the last ten years—that is, 2006-07 to 2016-17—is taken, then the rates of growth are again similar. From 2001-02 to 2016-17, up to the time of demonetization, the growth rate of currency in circulation, at 14.1 per cent, was not very different from the growth rate of the nominal GDP of the country, which rose 13.3 per cent.[10] What data does show is that the growth in high-denomination notes was much higher. In fact, because the printing of high-denomination notes began on a small base with the printing of Rs 1000 notes from 2001, most of the notes that were printed were of this and Rs 500 denominations.[11] This is likely to have resulted from a growing demand on RBI for more high-denomination notes.

In his 8 November 2016 speech, the prime minister also said:

> In 2014, the Reserve Bank sent a recommendation for issue of 5,000 and 10,000 rupee notes. After careful consideration, this was not accepted. Now as part of this exercise, RBI's recommendation to issue 2,000 rupee notes has been accepted.

---

[9] Annexure 6, Table 5 and Graph 6.
[10] Table 6.
[11] Graphs 7, 8 and 9.

So the RBI had felt the need for notes of even higher denominations to ease transactions in the economy. Finally, the government did accept the need for the higher-denomination Rs 2000 notes. That would make big-value transactions easier.

The need for cash can be curtailed if people begin to use cheques, plastic cards and electronic means of money transfer. But in India, these modes of payment have been slow to take off because of large-scale fraud in such means of money transaction. In spite of the legal provisions that exist against cheques that bounce, this phenomenon is so widespread that businesses largely do not accept cheques. The other means of transaction are picking up, but slowly.[12] There is fraud in the use of plastic cards too. However, till all these means of payment pick up, the need for notes of higher denominations will continue.

People compare the availability of notes of higher denomination domestically with their availability in other economies. It is said that in the USA, the highest denomination of currency is $100, and in Europe, €500. As fractions of the per capita incomes in those economies, these amount to 0.002 per cent and 0.0014 per cent, respectively. In the case of India, this ratio for the Rs 1000 note is 0.01. It has been suggested that for India to equal the US economy's ratio, the highest denomination of currency should be Rs 200. Proponents of this suggestion also suggest scrapping the Rs 500 and Rs 1000 currency notes.

The comparison of India with the US or Europe is not a valid one. People transact differently in different countries based on their customs and experiences. Financial literacy, levels of general literacy and technological capabilities are different across countries, and so is the level of fraud. Taking all this into account is crucial if we are to move towards alternative means of transaction.

---

[12] See Chapter VI.

Lessons from the 1978 Demonetization

The 1946 demonetization is not really relevant from today's perspective as the economy has transformed considerably since then. The 1978 demonetization is closer to the present. It is clear that the two earlier demonetizations neither impacted the black economy nor the common person on the streets. The regular economy too was not affected by those demonetizations. As I explain in the next chapter, the lesson to learn is that if demonetization affects the money supply only marginally, there is no adverse impact on the economy.

It is clear that high-denomination notes are needed as the economy grows and transactions become increasingly larger. By itself, the presence of high-denomination currency notes is not the cause of black income generation, though it may facilitate it.

Demonetization 2016 was unlike the earlier Indian demonetizations, in the sense that the high-denomination notes that were denotified were in common use and, at the point of demonetization, constituted 86 per cent of the currency in circulation. This demonetization was also done without any preparation, leading to extreme cash shortage.

Demonetization 2016: Build-up of a Crisis

The Genesis of the Decision

How did such a momentous decision come about? The prime minister has explained that partially in his speech, but the full story needs to be told. He said the government, when it came to power in May 2014, had immediately embarked on steps to tackle the black economy, and to this end had set up the Supreme Court-ordered Special Investigation Team (SIT), introduced the Income Declaration Scheme (IDS), 2016, the Foreign Money Bill, and so on, but none of them had yielded the expected results. The creation of the SIT under orders of the Supreme Court was the first decision of the Modi-led government in May 2014. This team was to investigate the black money held abroad by Indian citizens. The IDS was designed to enable holders of black money to come clean by paying a small fine. The government was constantly being taunted in the media and by the Opposition for its failure to tackle the black economy—an important electoral promise made by Modi in the 2014 general elections. So something big had to be done.

An organization called Arthakranti, based in Pune and headed by Anil Bokil, had been proposing various tax reforms to tackle the black economy.[13] One of the steps they had suggested was to demonetize high-denomination currency notes. They argued that black transactions take place through cash, so if cash was squeezed out then these transactions would become difficult. They suggested other steps too, such as abolition of all taxes and their replacement by a tax on bank transactions. They worked this out in 2013 and made a presentation to Modi, who was then the chief minister of Gujarat.[14] He apparently liked the suggestion.

Arthakranti also convinced Ramdev of the desirability of their suggestions, and Ramdev started campaigning for these ideas.[15] He was close to Modi and he put his weight behind the scheme. Thus Modi, looking for something big to counter the Opposition, saw this as something that could change his image.

There were newspaper reports that Raghuram Rajan, the former governor of RBI, was asked for his advice on demonetization, but he was negative about it.[16] He had to leave

---

[13] Arthakranti, 2016.
[14] Menon, 2016.
[15] Dash, 2016.
[16] DNA, 2017.

at the end of his term in September 2016 since there was a lot of controversy around him, given his outspokenness.

It is unclear at what point the decision was taken. If the decision had been taken well in advance of the announcement, then preparation could have commenced to contain the consequences. But the shortage of new notes, and their size, which was different from the old ones, suggest that the decision was a last-minute one. The decision to introduce new Rs 2000 notes is likely to have been taken independent of the move to demonetize, otherwise they could have been made the same size as the Rs 1000 notes that were to be withdrawn. That would have helped the ATMs to function. The printing of the Rs 2000 notes started after Patel took over as RBI governor, and that is why the new notes bore his signature and not Rajan's.

It is also clear that unlike in 1978, when the then governor of RBI, I.G. Patel, had advised the government against demonetization, in 2016, the RBI governor did not take an independent stand. Perhaps he has to work under the direction of the Government of India, but he could have put in a note of caution. Patel had been clear that demonetization would not be able to tackle the black economy. All this is recorded in the history of the RBI. Perhaps if the present RBI governor had put down in writing his discomfiture at the idea, the Indian economy's trajectory might have been different.

It is obvious from the PM's speech that consultation for the move was carried out among a narrow circle of bureaucrats. The Cabinet was not taken into confidence. Even the ministry of finance was not in the loop as a whole, and that is why so many later developments were unanticipated, leading to much distress. Similarly, if the RBI had been consulted in advance, some steps could have been taken by it to reduce the confusion that prevailed once the decision was implemented.

Bokil, in an interview on 22 November 2016, said demonetization as it was done was not what Arthakranti had suggested.[17] This step should have been the last of the four steps his organization had suggested. He too thought that the step would have adverse effects on the economy. Anyhow, it was too late.

Crisis Management, Rapid Changes in Announcements

Demonetization came unexpectedly, and for the next few months was the only topic of conversation in the country—where was money available, how long were the queues, which sectors of the economy were suffering, how many changes the government was making in the rules, how the goalpost was shifting and so on.

The government issued several Gazette Notifications in quick succession, correcting some of its earlier announcements.

Demonetization 2016 need not have been characterized as one of the biggest economic decisions of the Government of India if it had been well planned and prepared for. However, as earlier described, in the name of secrecy, those who should have been consulted were hardly in the picture. The entity that should have been the main actor in this move—the banking sector with the RBI at its pinnacle—was unprepared for it. It is this lack of planning that led to the large number of problems that followed the announcement, making the demonetization of 2016 one of the most cataclysmic economic decisions in the country's history. Since its implications were so widespread, it was bound to have political, social and institutional impact.

In Annexure 2, Table 1, I have listed the various steps the government was forced to announce to rectify or correct what was going wrong. Table 2 shows the frequency of the notifications issued by the government on the matter. Of course, the government spokespersons put a spin on this by arguing that the flurry of notifications was a sign of the government's

---

[17] Menon, 2016.

responsiveness. They did not see how much hardship the citizens were facing as a result of their ill-thought-through decision.

Soon after the PM's address to the nation, the ministry of finance issued Gazette Notification Extraordinary, Part II - Section 3 - Sub-section (ii), announcing the withdrawal of the 'Specified Bank Notes', that is, the scheme of demonetization. It contained more or less what the PM had announced. The government soon realized that citizens may not be able to carry out many essential activities, so another Gazette Notification was issued announcing where one could transact with the old notes for the next seventy-two hours. Yet another Gazette Notification followed shortly afterwards, making the Rs 2000 note valid.

On 9 November, three more Gazette Notifications were issued. The first specified more places where the old notes could be used. The other two were corrigenda, which means they were corrections to the notification of 8 November. All this indicated lack of preparation for demonetization.

Soon it was realized that truck movement was becoming difficult, so toll payment was suspended at the toll plazas on the country's highways. Next to be tackled were the difficulties faced by foreign tourists at airports in the country. After that it was payment of taxes to Central, state and local bodies that was exempted. Soon it was realized that a crisis was brewing in agriculture, with farmers not having the cash to buy seeds and other inputs to plant their next crop. So there was another relaxation. Then the limits on daily and weekly cash withdrawals and exchange of old notes were tweaked.[18] Even though the limits were raised, it was meaningless, since cash was not available at the bank branches or in the ATMs. Anyhow, there were announcements aplenty[19] to tackle the fast-evolving crisis.

---

[18] See Annexure 4.
[19] See Annexure 2, Table 1.

A committee headed by Andhra Pradesh Chief Minister Chandrababu Naidu was set up on 30 November to boost digital payment systems. But it was, more than anything else, a political move to bolster support for the demonetization and soften the criticism coming from all quarters. The committee submitted an interim report on 24 January 2017. On 16 December 2016, the government announced an email ID to which people could send their tip-offs about black money. Initially, it was announced that a lot of emails were coming but nothing seems to have come of it eventually.

Most Cash Returned to Banks, Data Release Stopped

The Jan Dhan[20] accounts saw a sharp rise in deposits. It was feared that the rich were using the accounts of the poor to convert their black hoards held in old notes into new currency. So, limits were set on the amounts moved to Jan Dhan accounts. The rich also used other accounts of the poor in a similar fashion. Reports indicated that the poor got a premium for their 'service'. There were also reports that business owners were getting their workers to join bank queues to convert their (owners') old notes. Another ploy was for the owners to give their workers advance salaries so that they would not have to pay them later when the revenue would be in new currency. The PM was upset at all these moves by the rich, and exhorted the poor not to return the money they had been given to exchange at the banks. This was like an exhortation to a class war. But he did not realize that the poor were firmly

---

[20] The government announced the Pradhan Mantri Jan Dhan Yojana (Jan Dhan in short) scheme in August 2014. It allowed the poor to open bank accounts, as a measure of inclusion, so that they could get access to banking and also so that direct transfers could be made to them under the various welfare schemes.

in the grip of their employers or landlords in the rural areas and could not cheat on them without severe consequences to themselves. For them, to cross their employers would be to kill their golden goose.

Serpentine queues outside bank branches to return the demonetized notes for new notes meant that most of the high-denomination notes were being returned to the banks. This was irrespective of the fact that the banks did not have currency to immediately give the depositors. But the argument in defence of this was that the money deposited in the banks, after all, was going into the account of the individual depositing it. It was not going to be lost even if one could not draw it immediately.

This rapid surrender of the demonetized notes by the public embarrassed the government. It had expected that black money would not come back into the banks because people would be afraid of depositing it lest they should get caught. Figures of Rs 3 lakh crore to Rs 4 lakh crore were floated about as the amount of cash that was not likely to come back. It was also implied that this money could be given to the poor or spent on schemes meant for the poor. It is unclear on what basis the government made its calculations.

Initially, the RBI announced the amounts of old notes being returned and new notes issued.[21] But when, by 10 December 2016, Rs 12.44 lakh crore of the Rs 15.44 lakh crore that had been demonetized had returned to the banks, the RBI stopped supplying the figures. By that date, only Rs 4.61 lakh crore in new notes had been released. In answer to an unstarred question in the Rajya Sabha on 7 February 2017, it was revealed that new notes amounting to Rs 6.78 lakh crore had been released to the public. This amounted to only 44 per cent of the demonetized

---

[21] Annexure 7, Table 7 and Graph 10, and see article by Kumar and Verma, 2017.

notes. So, the shortage of notes did not end in fifty days, when the pain was supposed to abate.

The excuse for not releasing the figures for returned notes was that reconciliation had to be done to ensure there was no double counting. An additional reason given was that the counterfeit notes had to be separated from the rest since they too had been surrendered to the banks. It also came to light that the new notes were already being counterfeited and that these counterfeit notes were in circulation. Another excuse was that the old notes could be returned up to 31 March 2017 by certain categories of citizens, and that some other categories may return them only by 30 June 2017. It was then expected that after 31 March 2017, when most of the notes would have been returned, some announcement would be made. However, this hope was also belied. The only credible explanation is that the government did not want to face the charge of failure of Demonetization 2016, which was supposed to extinguish a few lakh crores of black money.

Using RBI's data on the notes issued and the notes in circulation, Kumar and Verma[22] calculated that by 13 January 2017, 98.8 per cent of the Rs 15.44 lakh crore that had been demonetized had been deposited with the banks.[23] Only about Rs 18,000 crore had not been returned. Of this Rs 8000 crore was with the cooperative banks which were not allowed to return the demonetized notes they held. Most of the remaining amount would be with the old and the infirm who had forgotten where they had kept their savings or held abroad in neighbouring countries, like Nepal.[24] It is likely that the RBI is worried that more than Rs 15.44 lakh crore may be eventually returned because some of the counterfeit currency may also have come back and been counted.

---

[22] Kumar and Verma, 2017.
[23] Annexure 7, Table 8.
[24] Kumar, 2017h.

Demonetization and 'Pain': For How Long?

The prime minister had repeatedly announced that there would be pain for fifty days, and after that all gain. Fifty days was the period up to 30 December 2016 from the date of demonetization, during which the old currency was to be deposited in the banks. In an emotional speech on 13 November 2016,[25] the PM said:

> *I have asked the country for just 50 days. If after December 30, there are shortcomings in my work or there are mistakes or a bad intention found in my work, I will be prepared for the punishment that the country decides for me.*

From being confident that demonetization would work, causing only temporary pain to the citizens, the PM later changed his line. Now, he said, the pain would start to decrease[26] after fifty days.

> *After 50 days (from November 8), the troubles of honest people will start to reduce and the problems of dishonest people will begin to increase . . .*

When GDP growth data for the third quarter of 2016-17 was announced and it showed that the economy had continued to grow at around 7 per cent despite the demonetization, the official line was that demonetization had not led to any pain. Later still, when the fourth quarter data showed a dip in growth, the explanation was that this decline was not due to demonetization. The question then is what was the pain the PM was talking about, even if it was to last for just fifty days?

---

[25] Gandhi, 2016.
[26] Catch News, 2016.

The currency shortage persisted much beyond the fifty days. Even by end-April 2017,[27] only 80 per cent of the currency that was demonetized was replaced by new currency. So, pain continued for the citizens because there was a shortage of small-denomination notes that could be used for day-to-day transactions instead of the demonetized Rs 500 and Rs 1000 notes. The RBI released soiled notes that had been returned to it for destroying, in an attempt to increase the supply of small notes. There were reports of people being given coins worth thousands of rupees because the banks had run out of currency notes. The newly released note of Rs 2000 was not acceptable to the public because it was too large for day-to-day transactions. Shops did not have change to give for these notes. The new Rs 500 notes were in short supply because their printing had started only after 8 November 2016. So the pain lasted for way beyond the fifty days the PM had initially announced.

The RBI announced that its printing presses were working three shifts. But could notes printed over a period of eleven years since 2005 be replaced within fifty days? No firm stocks raw material for eleven years of work. The same was the case with the RBI presses, which faced shortages of paper and ink. These were tendered for in the third week of November and the first week of December.

Further, as the presses started to print notes of smaller denominations, the pace of replacement of the old currency with the new slowed down. This is clear from the data available.[28] After all, if Rs 10 notes are to be printed instead of Rs 1000 notes, then it would call for a lot more paper, ink and also time—if not a hundred times more, then at least fifty times more. As a result of all this, the shortage of cash persisted for a long time. Even

---

[27] Kumar and Verma, 2017.
[28] Kumar and Verma, 2017.

by April 2017, only 80 per cent of the remonetization had been done.

People, naturally, hoarded the small notes. This aggravated the shortage of cash further. The ministry of finance and the RBI repeatedly announced that there was no shortage of cash, but people did not believe them. The large number of announcements from the government led to lack of clarity on the situation and a sense of panic. This was aggravated by announcements abruptly withdrawing certain provisions, such as those related to charging of highway toll, fuel purchase at petrol stations and the deadline for exchange of old notes.

It must be noted that the well-off are also well connected with bankers. They are wooed by banks and have dedicated managers to take care of their accounts. These high-net-worth individuals are taken care of by relationship managers in their banks. Through these special relationships, these individuals managed, often by not even stirring out of their homes, to get the cash they needed. There was also corruption in the banks so that those with large stocks of old notes managed to convert them into new notes. Some RBI functionaries too were caught for their involvement in such transactions.[29] This prolonged the shortage of cash for the public, prolonging their pain too.

People who were well off or had plastic money started to do more electronic transactions, and this mitigated the cash shortage to some extent. However, the unorganized sector, especially those in rural and semi-rural areas, continued to suffer as very few could resort to electronic transactions. These areas are also not so well served by banks, whose infrastructure there is weak. The urban-rural divide was clearly evident for all to see. The cash shortage mitigated in the urban, especially the metro, areas sooner than elsewhere because they were given special treatment. The media too are more active in these areas and their greater

---

[29] Times of India, 2016b.

nuisance value led to some relief in the metros. After January, in fact, these problems persisted in the rural areas, but were not reported by the media.

The net result of the above-mentioned developments meant that the shortage of cash, instead of lasting for fifty days, lasted for more than eight months. This is a long time for an economy to experience pain, and has long-lasting effects. I will discuss this in more detail in Chapter V.

Coping with the 'Pain'

People used their old notes wherever they were allowed.[30] New items were added to what could be purchased with old currency, and deadlines for use of old notes were changed as the government discovered that people were facing hardship and there would be protests. So people filled their petrol tanks, bought groceries, etc., at the *Kendriya Bhandars* and milk booths, bought medicines in bulk, and so on. They also paid advance tax and arrears of taxes so that tax collections increased. It is reported that people also bought train and airlines tickets so that they could later cancel them and get their refunds in new notes. Temples and other religious places too are reported to have received cash donations.

Immediately after the PM's address to the nation, there was panic. People did not know what to do. There were reports of people buying gold and jewellery at night and of people unloading cash on builders to book real estate. In these purchases, the old notes were going at a discount of 20 per cent to 30 per cent. The jewellers and the builders who accepted such payments made a lot of money in the process. According to RBI data, gold imports in November–December 2016 rose sharply.[31]

---

[30] See Annexure 3, Table 3.
[31] RBI, 2017c.

What did the builders and jewellers do with the old cash they accepted? They would have had to get it exchanged. How did they manage to do this? They were confident that they could exchange, legitimately, their old notes for new currency by showing cash in hand. This also tells us how most businesses can convert a substantial amount of their black cash into new cash and why, by 13 January 2017, 98.8 per cent of the demonetized notes had come back into the banks.

The first day, after demonetization was announced, 9 November, was declared a bank holiday. After all, banks needed time to prepare for the demonetization provisions. But they could not open even the next day, since the preparations required were of a colossal magnitude. And, even after they opened, they could hardly cope with the challenges that confronted them. They had to collect old notes, change old notes for new notes, get ATMs functional for the new notes, manage the crowds at their doorstep, and take care of other things. The government did not know how to cope with the situation, and it announced quixotic steps, such as marking with indelible ink the fingers of those who were coming to the banks to exchange notes (as during elections). People were required to fill lengthy forms, submit documents, etc. Banks were to report daily the amount of money they were dispensing and collecting, and they were to have two officers to receive the money. The banks were badly hit, having no time for their normal operations and having to work overtime to manage their operations.

The banks as well as the RBI did not have the capacity to deal with the magnitude of cash being tendered. There was a shortage of warehouse capacity, and inadequate human resources to document the notes being returned. The help of the military had to be taken for movement of currency and to provide security.

There were long queues at the banks, causing great distress to the citizens, many of whom could not remain standing for such a long period of time. There was the danger of the crowds becoming restive, as there was much tension as to when the cash being dispensed would get over, forcing many to return empty-handed and queue up again the next day. The government made a provision for separate queues for senior citizens, but many Indians will remember the unforgettable picture of a weeping retired military man who had not been able to get cash even after several days of queuing up and had no money left to carry on.

In parts of India where the winter was harsh, people had to endure the cold of November-December as they joined queues early in the morning and sometimes even late in the night so they could get to the bank counter before the cash ran out. Queues would form at ATMs and disperse at discovering there was no cash, only to reform again if there was news that cash had become available. At establishments, often the talk among the staff was about where cash was available. There were reports of people collapsing in the queues and dying. In one case, the callousness of the public came to light when someone in the queue lay dying with no one coming to help him. While there is no doubt that death happens in the normal course of events and that every demonetization queue death cannot be attributed to the event (as some proponents of demonetization have argued), the moot point is that without the tension, stress and exertion induced by demonetization, many of those who died may still have been alive. After all, in normal times, how many people die in queues at banks?

The worst problems were experienced by the unorganized sector of the economy, where 93 per cent of the country's workforce is employed. These people have little bank savings and depend on their daily earnings. They were badly hit. There were reports of mass closures of small and cottage units, and of workers employed in these units returning to their villages. For example, this was the story in the bicycle and hosiery industry in Ludhiana, the brassware industry in Moradabad, the diamond and jewellery industry in Surat and Baroda, in plantations in

Kerala and Bengal, and in small units in Jamshedpur. Newspapers were full of reports of such closures.

These units largely work on cash. They pay their workers in cash and buy raw material in cash. A cash shortage meant they could not buy raw material to carry on production and could not pay their workers. Even if they opened accounts and paid salaries by cheque, the workers could not encash the cheques since banks did not have the money. Businesses, on their part, were constrained too since there was a limit on how much cash they could withdraw. Initially, on 8 November 2016, the limit was Rs 20,000 per week, which was raised to Rs 50,000 on 14 November and to Rs 1 lakh on 16 January 2017. But even getting this amount of cash from the banks was difficult. Further, this absolute limit applied to any business, whether it employed five people or fifty. So even the larger businesses which paid salaries in cash were disrupted.

Due to lack of cash, working capital was short, and many workers were fired and had to return to their villages. These people used to send money to their families back in the villages. This source of money not only dried up, but these jobless workers now added to the burden on their families in the villages. There was little work in the rural areas too, and this led to a sharp spike in demand for work under the Mahatma Gandhi National Rural Employment Guarantee Scheme (MGNREGS). MGNREGS is demand driven; a person can ask for work in rural areas under the scheme, which offers up to 100 days of work.

The lower-middle and middle classes also suffered because of the cash shortage. Even if they had money in their bank accounts, they could not withdraw it or had to stand in multiple queues to get enough to carry on their daily activities. Many of them had plastic money, and in some cases they could use cheques. In spite of this, they faced problems and cut their consumption to the bare minimum. There were reports of a sharp drop in footfalls in the malls and markets.

Wholesale markets in India also work on cash, and with its shortage they came to a standstill. The media carried pictures of empty grain markets. Farmers were not bringing their produce to the market since they were not getting paid. This meant that they did not have money to sow the Rabi crop in time. They had to take loans from shopkeepers at high interest rates, which raised their cost of production. Prices of many perishables crashed so that many farmers dumped their harvest of potato and tomato on the roads or fed them to cattle. In Raipur, farmers distributed vegetables free to customers since it would cost them more to take back the produce to their villages where they would rot, in any case. In Madurai, cattle were sent into the fields to feed on the cabbage crop because it was unprofitable for the farmers to harvest it and take it to the market. Lentil prices, which had been ruling at high levels just six months back, also crashed because of a fall in demand at the same time as there was a bumper crop. All in all, both markets and agriculture suffered.

Social tragedy visited those who had planned a wedding in their family post 8 November 2016. In India, it is considered inauspicious to cancel a wedding. A wedding is a social occasion when considerable expense, especially in cash, takes place. Families were short of cash and had a hard time conducting their weddings as they would have liked to, and had to go to great lengths and endless trouble to rustle up some funds to have a halfway decent ceremony. The rules were repeatedly tweaked to enable families in such situations to withdraw cash, but the procedures were cumbersome, and anyway the banks did not have cash to dispense. All this led to a decline in the businesses associated with weddings: caterers, hoteliers, tent-house providers, jewellers, clothiers, decorators and event managers . . . However, some high-profile weddings took place with the usual pomp; somehow, they got the necessary money.

Soon after demonetization was initiated, reports of people getting caught with large quantities of new notes appeared.

Some RBI officials and bankers were questioned, and arrested too.[32] Apparently, they made a lot of money by accepting old notes at a huge discount.

As will be discussed later,[33] various surveys conducted from November to January showed the huge impact of demonetization on industry and trade. The All India Manufacturers' Organization (AIMO), the Punjab Haryana Delhi Chamber of Commerce and Industry (PHDCCI), State Bank of India (SBI), Nomura PMI and some other entities conducted such surveys. Many of these organizations were afraid to come out openly for fear that they might attract the government's displeasure. The government repeatedly announced that there was no adverse impact arising from demonetization, citing increased payment of taxes to support its claim.

There were many conspiracy theories doing the rounds. The most prominent among them was that demonetization was done to defeat the Opposition in the UP elections in March 2017. The argument was that the entire war chest of the opposition parties was decimated in one blow. The other prominent theory was that this step was taken under pressure from the US, which was acting on behalf of the digital companies. On 9 November there was a big advertisement by one of the prominent digital companies. Was it purely an accident that they had already ordered the advertisement? This company went on to do well after demonetization was announced.

The government hoped that people would lose their black money but when it kept coming back into the banks, it thought that it could offer a chance to such people to come clean by declaring their black funds. So, the government also offered an IDS on 16 December 2016, for cash or bank deposits that were not formerly declared. A tax of 30 per cent had to be paid on the

---

[32] Times of India, 2016b.
[33] Chapter V, Annexure 20.

undisclosed amount, and additionally there was a 33 per cent surcharge tax and a 10 per cent penalty. This made for a total of 50 per cent in levies. On top of that, 25 per cent of the disclosed amount had to be put into the Pradhan Mantri Garib Kalyan Yojana (PMGKY) for four years. On this amount, no interest would be paid. This scheme was supposed to be the carrot, since if anyone was caught with black money after this scheme closed, then they would have to pay 60 per cent tax, a 25 per cent surcharge and a 10 per cent penalty so that the total levies would amount to 85 per cent of the undisclosed income. But people did not bite. And in spite of many extensions, only about Rs 3000 crore, as on 7 February 2017, was declared under this scheme. Those with black money did not fear discovery since they had already worked out ways of hiding their black incomes.

How did investors respond to demonetization? The scheme induced a lot of uncertainty, and that led to a decline in investment, with its long-term implications. However, the stock markets, which are the barometer of investor confidence in the economy, did not respond so negatively. The reasons are both internal and external. Foreign investors did not have many avenues to invest in other countries and they still bought the government line that the Indian economy was the fastest growing in the world. The public-sector financial institutions, like LIC, invested heavily in the stock markets to boost it. Indian retail investors, having deposited their cash in their banks, invested it in a big way in mutual funds, which in turn invested in the stock markets. Real estate faced uncertainty, so the funds which would have otherwise gone into this business also got diverted into the stock markets. Thus, while the economy did poorly, the stock markets did well on the whole. This is another bubble which has the potential to damage the public and the economy.

In conclusion, one can say that Demonetization 2016 became one of the biggest economic events in independent India because of the lack of preparation that preceded it. The only lesson offered by the earlier demonetizations, in 1946 and in 1978, is that there should not have been any cash shortage if pain to the citizens was to be avoided. The 2016 demonetization led to tremendous hardship for the citizens, and especially the poor, because of the cash shortage that resulted. The pain is not yet over, even though it was argued by the government in the beginning that it would only last for fifty days.

Some felt the decision wasn't even legally valid. It has also been pointed out that even if the decision was legal, technically speaking, given clause 26(2) of the RBI Act, it was not so in spirit. Again, the role played by the RBI governor in the decision may have been formally correct, but not in the spirit of the autonomy of the institution.

II

The Role of Money

Demonetization is about money being withdrawn from circulation; as the PM put it—it turns the demonetized currency into worthless paper. This was illustrated by pictures posted on social media showing people eating peanuts out of paper cones made out of Rs 1000 notes. To understand demonetization and its consequences, we need to understand what is money and what happened to economic activity once it was suddenly withdrawn.

Money in the Economy

In a modern economy, everyone needs money to lead their daily lives. We are most familiar with money as the currency we carry in our pocket or wallet. It can be in the form of coins or paper money, or in the form of the credit or debit card in our wallet. When it is in the form of a coin there is some metal in it of some value, but when it comes in the form of paper currency or a debit card, then where does the value come from?

The cost of the material in a coin may not be the value the coin represents. But what about the paper currency? The government has told us that it costs around Rs 3 to print a Rs 500 note and around Rs 3.60 to print a Rs 2000 note. One may add to that the costs of distribution, handling etc., but all this would still amount to far less than the value these currency notes represent. The mystery is resolved when we understand the role of money and how it has evolved in society.

As economies have changed, so have the form and role of money. In a simple barter economy, there was little need for money. The village economy was simple, with the division of labour such that almost everything the villagers needed could be obtained from each other through barter. I produced the grain which I could exchange for cloth, shoes or other necessities. Money was needed only to get something from outside the village. Often what was needed from outside could also be exchanged with traders coming with their wares from different parts of the country.

But barter becomes cumbersome in a more complex urban economy where I need to find someone who needs exactly what I have to offer in exchange for exactly what I want. If I make iron implements and need shoes, I have to hunt for a cobbler who also needs the implements I have to offer. The cobbler may need grain and not my implements. The person who has extra grain may not need either the implements or the shoes, so all of us can go around in circles till we each find the right person with whom we can exchange our goods.

If money is introduced in such an economy, then everyone exchanges what they have in excess for money, and the right kind of coincidence that allows for a satisfactory exchange of goods or services is no longer necessary. Now the cobbler sells his extra shoes to someone for money and goes to someone else who has grain and buys that with his money; the one who has surplus food exchanges it for money and goes to the weaver to get cloth with that money, etc. So, money is the universal token which is acceptable to all in exchange for what they have to offer in the market. This removes the need for the double coincidence of my meeting someone who has exactly what I want and who needs exactly what I have to offer. Money is therefore a medium of exchange of goods and services.

But why would someone accept the token called money that I have to offer? For money to work, everyone would have to accept the same token; that is, there has to be a social sanction to the token. In earlier times, a token could be grain, cattle or 'cowries',[1] since these were seen as having value and were acceptable to all. But these items were inconvenient to carry around, especially if required in large quantities; also, different people may value them differently. Tokens, on the other hand, should be easy to carry and acceptable to all.

If the token itself carried the value of the metal contained in it, then it would become more acceptable to all. Gold, silver and copper could be used as tokens—a certain weight of each was accepted as having a certain value in society. Also, given that gold and silver were rare, a small amount of either had high value and was easier for people to carry around. These tokens became socially sanctioned money.

Money is a social device. The state minted the coins, giving them social sanction. The state guaranteed that there was as much metal in the coin as stated on it. However, the history of money and its evolution across time is not that simple. Many forms of money have come into existence depending on the structure of the economy and the cultural specificities.

As economies became more complex and transactions too became more complex and larger in size, carrying a lot of coins (or other instruments) became a problem, so traders started to give promissory notes to each other on pieces of paper. Credibility mattered for these pieces of paper to be acceptable. This led to the emergence of banks—the organizations that issued these notes, then called 'banknotes'. These banks were owned by the rich and the powerful, who had credibility and whose writ ran in their territories.

---

[1] Cowries were the shells of sea snails used as money in India and also in China.

This system was replaced by the modern system of central banks as the sole authority for issuing banknotes. The state guaranteed that the banknotes had a certain value. And, while earlier they could be converted to gold or silver, now there is no such backing to currency.

'Banknotes', or cash, have value because of the law which backs them. So, they are fiat money—that is, declared by law to have the value stated on their face. As we have seen, the cost of printing money may not even amount to 1 per cent of the value the money is supposed to represent. We accept this value since the state is guaranteeing it and everyone else accepts it too.

Money Creation and Different Forms of Money

Cash—coins or notes—is not consumed. It is used to carry out transactions in the market, or if it is held, becomes wealth, which can be used later on. It is held because a value is attributed to it. So, it is primarily a *means of circulation* of transactions, but is also a *store of value* and can be used for *precautionary purposes*, for a rainy day. Transactions lead to income generation in the economy. Much as blood circulates oxygen in the body, which is needed to keep the body alive, cash is used to carry on activities in the economy so that people can earn incomes which they use for consumption or for saving. Cash is not the only way to make transactions, since I can also use my bank account to write cheques or use my credit card, debit card or electronic money to make payments. All this constitutes money, broadly speaking, cash being just a component of it. So even if cash is short, one can use other forms of money to make payments, and the economy need not suffer.

The need for cash keeps changing. As other forms of money evolve, the need for cash declines. In India, as agriculture has shifted from barter to cash, more cash is needed. But if payments go straight to banks, less cash is required. Similarly, if salaries are paid straight into banks rather than given in cash on the first of the month, then less cash is needed in the economy.

The RBI releases money into the economy on the basis of the government securities and the foreign exchange reserves it has. The money it prints says, *'I promise to pay the bearer . . .'* On the face of the hundred rupee note is written, *'I promise to pay the bearer Rs 100.'* So, it is a liability of the RBI. But it is not that if I go to the RBI and ask to be paid Rs 100 the bank will give me some commodity of equal value. It will give me another Rs 100 note or, say, two Rs 50 notes. This liability is balanced by the assets the RBI has—government securities[2] and foreign exchange reserves. When government securities are picked up by the RBI, the corresponding amount of rupees is released into the economy. The securities become the assets of RBI. When I, as an exporter, bring back the foreign exchange I earn by exporting my goods, I give it to the RBI, which gives me rupees for it. The foreign exchange is then an asset held by the RBI. When importers need foreign exchange to buy something abroad, then they pay rupees to the RBI and get the foreign exchange needed. This reduces the assets and the liabilities of the RBI and so on.

Money Is a Multiple of Cash Released by the Central Bank

When money is released by the RBI into the economy, it goes into circulation through transactions. The government may pay the people it employs, buy goods and services, give subsidies, and so on. Part of this money is kept by the recipients and the rest goes back into bank accounts. A government servant who receives a salary keeps a fraction of it at home and puts the rest in his bank account to earn some interest. The businessmen who sell their goods or services to the government and get money

---

[2] Government securities are financial papers of various kinds with which the government raises funds for its use.

in their bank accounts use only a part of that to carry on their business, while the rest stays in the bank. One can see that most of the money released into the economy keeps going in and out of the commercial banking system where businesses and households maintain their accounts.

The banks have to pay the depositors some interest for keeping their money with them. They too now need to earn some income to pay this interest. They do so by lending the money they get to those who need it for various purposes. I may be setting up a plant to produce some item and may need long-term capital. I may need to set up an office to provide services. I may need capital to pay wages to my workers and also to buy raw material. A part of the profit earned by my business is paid to the banks as interest for the loan I have taken.

What this means is that a bank does not have the money that its depositors deposited with it. If all the depositors come to a bank and want to withdraw their deposits, the bank would not be able to pay them. This is called a 'run' on a bank, and such a bank fails.

This is where the RBI plays the role of a banker to the banks, giving money to the banks. Each bank is required to deposit a certain amount of its deposits with the RBI. This is called the cash reserve ratio (CRR). If a bank gets Rs 100 in deposits and the CRR is 10 per cent, then it has to deposit Rs 10 with the RBI. It now has Rs 90 to lend. This Rs 90 is then given to a borrower, who pays it to someone else who puts it in their bank. That bank then has to deposit Rs 9 with the RBI and can now lend Rs 81. This amount may be lent and may make its way to a third bank, which then has to deposit Rs 8.1 with the RBI. This chain can continue, now looping in another bank which has to pay the RBI Rs 7.29. The banks get Rs 100+90+81+72.9 . . . and the RBI gets Rs 10+9+8.1+7.29+ . . . What the banks are getting is also going out to the public and is being used as money. As the chain of deposits and withdrawals is completed over time, the Rs 100 deposit leads to the system getting Rs 1000 and the RBI Rs 100.

You can see that the banking system, along with the RBI, has created ten times the money that the RBI released to begin with. This is called the *money multiplier*, the amount of money generated by the banking system for every unit of money put in. From the cash released by the RBI, a multiple amount of bank money is created. The smaller the CRR, the larger the multiplier because the banks can lend more of the deposits they get from the public.

However, here one assumes that all the money created by the system comes back to the bank. This does not happen. People who get paid also hold back a part of their earnings for their personal use. This constitutes a leakage in money creation. The larger the leakage, the smaller the multiplier. If the banking habit is strong in society, most of the money will be back in the banks. If people are used to keeping a lot of money with them, then there will be less money going into the banks and the multiplier too will be smaller.

The RBI, the Lender of Last Resort

The advantage of this system is that if a bank is in trouble and does not have the funds to return to its depositors, it can borrow from the RBI. So, the RBI is a guarantor of the banking system. For performing this role, the RBI is also a regulator of the banks and tries to make sure that no bank goes too much out of line with the prudential norms.

When would a bank be in trouble? When it has lent out money to insolvent borrowers who are not paying back the interest on the loans they have taken and are not in a position to return the capital they have borrowed. This becomes a bad debt for the bank. If this debt is large in relation to the total lending of the bank, then the bank is in trouble since it does not have the money to pay interest to its depositors or return their deposits. In India, this problem has manifested itself recently as the problem of NPAs in banks. The RBI has been trying to deal with this situation.

Different Forms of Money, Liquidity

What has been said above also illustrates that it is not just the cash that the RBI releases into the system that constitutes money, but also the bank deposits that are used as a means of carrying on transactions. In the simplified example above, there was only one form of bank deposit, but there are many kinds of bank deposits, with varying functions.

There are current accounts, largely maintained by businesses, which can be used to make payments. There are savings accounts with households, whose members can write cheques to make payments. Then there are the fixed deposits, which cannot be used to make immediate payments but can be used with some delay to make payments. In India, there are also post office accounts that can be used to make payments. All these instruments constitute different forms of money.

This brings in the concept of liquidity. Cash is the most liquid form of money, followed by the current account. The least liquid is the fixed deposit. Correspondingly, there are different forms of money that the experts talk of—cash, M^0, M^3, and so on. Each of these measures of money has different significance for different sections of society. If people have no access to banks, then cash is relevant, and not M^1 (see explanation below).

There is another complication. The cash issued by the RBI is called 'base money' or 'reserve money' (M^0). A part of this comes back to the RBI as CRR. Therefore the entire amount of cash released by the RBI is not available outside.

That portion of the cash which is outside the RBI is the 'currency in circulation'.

The banks themselves hold some money in their ATMs and vaults for their daily requirements, and this money is not with the public. So, the 'currency with the public' is the currency in circulation minus the currency that is held by the banks.

The public can also use its savings accounts and current accounts to make payments, and this is another measure of money available to the public, called M^1. This is the sum of the currency with the public and the deposits of the public in banks.

The public also has deposits with the post offices, and if that is added to M^1, one gets M^2.

If to M^1 the time deposits (fixed deposits of tenure longer than one year) with the banks are added, we get M^3.

And if to M^3 the total post office deposits (fixed deposits) are added, then we get M^4.

To sum it up:

1. Currency with public = currency in circulation - cash on hand with banks
2. M^0 (reserve money) = currency with public + cash on hand with banks + 'other' deposits with RBI + bankers' deposits with RBI
3. M^1 (high-powered money) = currency with public + deposit money of public;
   where, deposit money of public = demand deposits with banks + 'other' deposits with Reserve Bank
4. $M^2 = M^1$ + post office savings deposits
5. $M^3 = M^1$ + time deposits with banks
6. $M^4 = M^3$ + total post office deposits

Money Supply during Demonetization 2016

Annexure 8, Table 9 and Graphs 11, 12, 13 and 14 show the magnitudes of the different measures of money for the post-demonetization period. They show the demand deposits at about a tenth of the time deposits. That is why M^3 is much larger than M^0 (or M^1)—about six times larger. This is due to the action of the money multiplier.

The data in Annexure 8 also show that after the announcement of demonetization, all the money measures declined because the currency with the public declined as high-denomination currency notes became invalid. But, as the public deposited money into their accounts, the deposits rose. The sharpest fall was in M^0 and then in M^1 and M^2, and least in M^3 and M^4.

As pointed out in Chapter I,[3] the above-mentioned graphs do not reflect the full extent of the decline in money supply after 8 November 2016. The valid notes had dropped sharply to about 14 per cent of their 8 November 2016 count. But the RBI data continued to count them as currency in circulation. If this correction is applied, there would be a sharp fall in M^0 to 10 per cent of the 8 November level. It will be less so for M^1 and M^2, which show a drop of 56 per cent, and even less so for M^3 and M^4, which dropped by 12.5 per cent. This has implications for activities in different sectors of the economy, as will be discussed later in this chapter and in Chapters IV and V.

In the black economy, more cash is held and less deposited back in the banks so that there is a greater leakage from the banking system. That lowers the money multiplier. Similarly, in the large, informal economy/unorganized sector, a lot of cash is held, making for another leakage. That too lowers the money multiplier. These characteristics are what distinguish the Indian economy from those of advanced economies, making a comparison with their monetary base or practices difficult.

The various measures of money supply mentioned above show a sharp peak on 31 March 2017.[4] Deposits increased, and money supply measures also peaked. This is the usual pattern, as

---

[3] Table 7 and Graph 10.
[4] See Graphs 11, 12, 13 and 14.

businesses which have to close their books show higher deposits so that they can show higher income from their operations and show higher profitability too.

An important aspect of the expansion of the monetary base[5] of the Indian economy is the change in the composition of the currency notes, with a rapid increase in the high-denomination notes in the economy after 2000-01. This was discussed in the first chapter. The rate of growth[6] of such notes was much faster than of the overall currency in circulation. It was shown that while the currency in circulation grew mostly in line with the growth of the national income and inflation in the economy, most of this increase was due to the rise in the numbers of high-denomination notes.

In his article, K. Rogoff[7] shows that the percentage of high-denomination notes in total in the US, Japan and Europe was in the same range as the figures for India. While it was 86 per cent in India on 4 November 2016, and 84 per cent in 2014, it was 88 per cent in Europe in 2014, 87 per cent in Japan and 83 per cent in the US that year.

Quantity of Money Needed in the Economy: Transactions and Incomes

The quantum of transactions in an economy depends on the nature of the economy and transactions in its different components. Agriculture is simple and does not need a lot of transactions to generate one unit of income. But in the finance sector, there are large transactions for small incomes generated. For instance, on a sale of shares worth Rs 1 lakh, the income

---

[5] Monetary base is the cash which is the basis of creating the money in the economy.
[6] Graph 7.
[7] Rogoff, 2014.

generated is the brokerage, which is 0.1 per cent, or Rs 100. So the transaction is worth Rs 1 lakh, but the income is Rs 100. Similarly, in the real estate sector, brokerage is 1 per cent, so on a property sale of Rs 1 crore, the income generated is only Rs 1 lakh. In the transport, trade, restaurant and hotel segments too, the incomes generated are small compared with the incomes earned.

In industry too, the ratio of transactions to income is higher than in agriculture because of the many stages of sales. The general rule is, the more the stages through which a product passes before its final sale the more will be the transaction-to-income ratio. Take, for example, the sale of a bar of soap. The company makes the soap by purchasing raw material, pays wages and incurs overheads on travel, advertising, telephone services, and so on. If the company sells the soap to the dealer for Rs 10, the company's expenses may be Rs 5 on raw materials, Re 1 on wages, Re 1 on tax, Rs 2 on overheads, and Re 1 as profit. The total transaction amount is Rs 10, but the incomes are Re 1 in profit and Re 1 in wages. The dealer buys the product at Rs 10 and sells to the retailer at Rs 12, his overhead costs amounting to Re 1, Rs 0.50 in wages and Rs 0.50 as profit. So, on a transaction of Rs 12, the income generated is Re 1. The retailer sells the product to the consumer for Rs 15, with his overheads at Rs 2 and wages and profit at Rs 0.50 each. On his transaction of Rs 15, his income is Re 1. Summing up the logic here, there have been transactions amounting to Rs 10+12+15=37 while the income earned is Rs 2+1+1=4. The transactions amount to nine times the income.

As the Indian economy has moved from being predominantly agricultural to predominantly services-oriented, the volume of transactions in the economy has galloped compared with the incomes earned. The industrial sector's share in the GDP has not changed much. But production has become more concentrated, both in agriculture and in industry, and that has led to the use of more services like transport, storage, finance, etc.[8] More transactions are required now than earlier, even in these sectors.

All these structural changes in the economy and the changes in technology have led to a greater volume of transactions, and it takes more and more money transactions to generate a given income. Consequently, the demand for money has increased, both as incomes have increased and as the economy gets more service sector–intensive. In the Indian economy, the share of services now exceeds 50 per cent of the income, while the share of agriculture has come down to 14 per cent. At the time of Independence, these figures were 30 per cent and 55 per cent,[9] respectively. There has been a drastic change in the composition of the economy between 1947 and 2017. Further, during this period, the form of money used has changed from predominantly cash to others, as there is more banking and greater use of electronic forms of money transfer. This has resulted in an increase in demand for money for transactions, but not so much for cash.

Velocity of Circulation and Money

People can hold on to the cash they have rather than spend it and circulate it. They could get their salaries in cash and keep them at home. Alternatively, they could get their salaries in the bank and withdraw money as and when they need it. So, cash and money can go around faster or slower. This brings in the important concept of *velocity of circulation of money*. It tells us how many times a note or a coin goes around in a year. The RBI releases cash into the economy but the cash can move fast or slow. The faster it moves the more money there is available to society for its various transactions. The velocity of transaction is variable, not

---

[8] Kumar, 1987.
[9] Kumar, 2013.

fixed. It depends on the circumstances in the economy. If there is a shortage of cash, people may hold on to what they have so that the velocity of circulation drops and further aggravates the shortage of money. This can impact people in many ways, as discussed later.

There are two kinds of velocity of circulation of money—one with respect to incomes and the other with respect to transactions. As the number of transactions required to generate a given amount of income has increased in the economy, the velocity of money transacted has increased. Moreover, money in the economy in its different forms—cheques, credit cards and electronic transfer—has increased rapidly so that the income velocity of money has decreased. Thus, the two velocities of circulation have been moving in opposite directions. This point is often missed out in the literature, even though it has serious implications for policy.

How much money should an economy have? That would depend on the sum total of transactions and the velocity of money. It does not depend on incomes alone. As explained in the previous section, if more transactions are needed for generating the same income, then more money would be needed. The amount of money required in an economy is directly linked to the volume of transactions in the economy and indirectly to the incomes generated. But most analysts look at money in relation to incomes and argue that cash is excessive, while that may not be the case.

Further, the requirement for money increases due to the presence of the black economy. The black economy is not counted in the official GDP (income), but transactions have to take place to generate the black incomes. These transactions require money. So the money in the economy has to circulate both the black and the white transactions. This means that for a given amount of money created by the banking system, there are higher levels of transactions and incomes in the economy than recorded. So the velocity of money is higher, both with respect to incomes and transactions, than what the white economy alone will give. Further, the black economy generates a large amount of transfer incomes, which results in more transactions.[10] Finally, the black economy is concentrated in the services sector and is minuscule in agriculture, and that raises the level of transactions as well as the velocity of circulation.[11]

The black economy uses many means for carrying out its transactions, but depends a lot on cash. When it comes to criminal activities, it is mostly cash that is used in transactions. Large notes facilitate the circulation of money in the black economy and in transactions associated with criminal activities. Does this mean that large-denomination currency notes should not exist? The moot point is that large-denomination notes, which enable the economy to function, are not the cause of criminal activities or the black economy. If the large-denomination rupee notes were not available then criminals could use other means of payment, such as gold, dollars or *havala*. Eliminating the large-denomination currency notes may make transactions difficult in the white economy without necessarily checking criminal activities or the black economy.

The unorganized sector carries out its transactions using cash. That raises the demand for cash over other forms of money. The velocity of circulation of cash is likely to be less in this sector, since it does not use banking, which can circulate money faster. This sector consists largely of small and cottage units, which do not need large quantities of high-denomination notes for paying wages but which do need them for their purchase of raw material. Their dependence on high-denomination notes may be less than for the organized sector, but it certainly exists.

Both the black economy and the unorganized sector lead to a higher proportionate demand for cash in the Indian economy. The black economy results in a higher velocity of circulation

---

[10] Kumar, 2017b.
[11] Kumar, 1999.

than the velocity of circulation derived from using only the white economy data because there are additional incomes and transactions that are not recorded in the official data. So, a given amount of money is circulating a larger amount of incomes and transactions. These two sectors also need high-denomination notes, but it is not that elimination of these notes will eliminate the transactions in these sectors of the economy. These differential aspects of functioning of the economy need to be factored in when planning for monetary policy or for demonetization.[12]

The RBI's Role and Its Autonomy

Demonetization and remonetization policies in an economy are all about money, which the central bank creates. Further, these policies are to be implemented by the central bank. For understanding the nature of money and demonetization in India and its impact on the economy, it is important to look into the role and functioning of the RBI.

As already discussed, central banks came into their own only in the last few centuries. India got its central bank, the RBI, rather late in the day. It was set up under the Reserve Bank of India Act, 1935. There were some later legislations too which govern the functioning of the RBI—for instance, one legislation says the RBI has to regulate the commercial banks so that they do not go bankrupt. The RBI also has a role in regulating the foreign exchange markets and in setting monetary policy, which includes the fixing of the benchmark interest rates in the economy which sets other interest rates in the economy.

Its main task is to make available enough money in the economy so that transactions can go on smoothly. The legal-tender character of the notes issued by RBI is based on Section

---

[12] These differentials in relation to money are discussed in detail in Kumar, 2017b.

26(1) of the RBI Act, which also provides for a guarantee by the Central government. It is this authority which is used to issue currency. There is also Section 26(2), which provides for extinguishing the legal-tender nature of the various series of notes issued earlier. As provided in that section, this has to be done by the government on the advice of the RBI board. This is the authority which was used to demonetize the high-denomination notes on 8 November 2016.

For creating money in the economy, as explained earlier, the RBI depends on the commercial banking system in the country. The central bank must ensure the banks' viability, and for that it has to have the power to regulate the banking system. Money supply also depends on regulation of the foreign exchange rates and foreign reserves, and the government borrowings or the public debt. The RBI has to have the powers to intervene in these arenas too. Lately, an important objective of RBI has been the maintenance of price stability by setting a target inflation rate. In India, the central bank has also set up institutions like NABARD for extending agricultural credit for rural development. So the RBI performs multiple tasks.

In the context of demonetization and RBI's multiplicity of roles, the question arises as to how much autonomy does it have to perform these roles?

The RBI's autonomy is relative. The government appoints the RBI governor and has a crucial role in the appointment of the deputy governors and the members on the central bank's policymaking board. Usually, the choice for these roles falls on those who are known to be in line with the thinking of the government. The government, therefore, has a large influence in the policies of the RBI.

The ministry of finance sets the fiscal policy, and the RBI is supposed to set the monetary policy. But the two need to coordinate for effective policymaking. To this end, there is regular interaction between the RBI and the ministry of finance.

However, there has also been some tension between the two in recent times, since the ministry has been suggesting a cut in interest rates to boost growth while the RBI board has not done so at the pace at which the ministry would like that to happen because of its concerns about inflation. Different governors of the RBI have practised different degrees of autonomy.

Would a cut in interest rates in the present situation help boost the economy? It is clear that in the present situation lower interest rates may not lead to an increase in investment, given the shortage of demand and excess capacities.[13] The ministry is clearly barking up the wrong tree. Similarly, the RBI, in the Indian context, is unable to influence inflation much, given that there is lot of stickiness in prices and given the inability of monetary policies to influence it much. If the RBI had exercised its autonomy, it would have used its considerable research capability to come up with independent data on growth and inflation so that it could make better policy.

The RBI has continued to use government statistics that have been questioned by many analysts. The real inflation in the economy is neither reflected in the WPI (wholesale price index) nor in the CPI (consumer price index) since they do not take the full extent of the services sector into account.[14] Similarly, growth data are also suspect, after the big change introduced in 2014-15.[15] Given that these are the two variables on which there are differences between the ministry and the RBI, alternative data could have helped the RBI to bolster its stand. But the RBI has not chosen to use its relative autonomy to generate alternative data.

---

[13] See Chapter IV. I have also explained this in the Introduction and the Conclusion.

[14] Kumar, 2006.

[15] The new methodology introduced in 2015 changed the rate of growth in 2013-14 from 4.7 per cent to 6.9 per cent. The base year for calculation was changed and the method of calculating the income was changed. Many economists have questioned this change for a variety of reasons.

There is also the important issue of how to bring the black economy into the database of the RBI. When it is not accounted for in the data for output, the growth rate of the economy, money supply, velocity of circulation and so on, then these variables do not represent the reality. All these are higher than the official data suggest. When flight of capital associated with the black economy occurs, it affects the money supply, the foreign exchange reserves of the RBI and the balance of payments of the country. The black economy is the missing variable which results in the failure of policies in general, and in particular the policies of RBI because of the black economy's impact on the monetary variables, such as money supply, money multiplier and velocity of circulation.

The role of the governor of RBI in influencing the financial markets has become increasingly important. The financial markets run on expectations, and what the RBI governor says impacts them. That is why the governor is not only supposed to speak little but also very cautiously. No wonder then that the governor of RBI said very little on demonetization or on its impact on the economy. A sentence from him admitting that it had an adverse impact on the economy would have sent the markets tumbling and the flight of capital from India.

Another important aspect which is relevant to demonetization is that the RBI has a balance sheet. It has liabilities and assets. It has an income and expenditure statement. The surplus it generates is given to the government, and that helps the latter in reducing its deficit. This surplus has been dented by demonetization.[16]

Implications of Shortage of Money in an Economy

Demonetization led to a shortage of cash for transactions in the economy. Does that matter?

---

[16] For 2015-16, the RBI board approved the transfer of Rs 65,876 crore. However, for 2016-17, it approved only Rs 30,659 crore.

As discussed earlier, the currency in circulation dropped to 14 per cent of what it was pre-demonetization. This led to a shortage of currency and to its hoarding. Consequently, both money supply and the velocity of circulation dropped. The immediate impact was that transactions could not be made and the income-generation process slowed down. The impact was more on those sectors which use cash than on those which also use banking transactions and electronic money. As a result, the unorganized sector was impacted far more than the organized sector.[17]

In the organized sector, it is possible that more transactions came into the banking system and that velocity of circulation increased. This could have compensated for the decline in the money supply relevant to this sector, namely, M^3. In that case the transactions in this sector in the aggregate may have continued as before and the income-generation process may have been only marginally affected.

In the unorganized sector, due to a sharp drop in the money supply and the velocity of circulation, activity almost came to a halt. Transactions declined sharply and the income-generation process was badly affected. Some in this sector turned to banking transactions and electronic transfers, but they were a minority. The drop in incomes may have been 60 per cent to 80 per cent. That is what the initial reports suggested in November and December 2016.[18] Since money supply recovered slowly[19] the impact of demonetization on the unorganized sector lasted a while. It was short for months.

This hit the economy badly and led to a decline in output and prices as demand decreased.[20] None of this would have happened

---

[17] Kumar, 2017b.
[18] Annexure 20.
[19] As Graph 10 of Annexure 7 shows.
[20] Discussed in detail in Chapter V.

if advance preparations had been made by printing enough new currency notes. Also, there was a need for more notes of smaller denominations since the Rs 2000 notes are difficult to exchange. This slowed down the pace of remonetization as discussed earlier.

All this raised doubts on the autonomy of the RBI. The RBI needed to give proper advice to the government about the pros and cons of the sudden and unplanned demonetization. It is clear that the importance of adequate availability of currency in the economy was not appreciated before the decision was taken. The impact on the economy is that the marginalized have become more marginalized due to demonetization.[21]

---

[21] See Chapter VII.

III

Aspects of the Black Economy Relevant to Demonetization

The main goal of demonetization clearly was the elimination or at least a reduction of the black economy. This was not achieved, in spite of the upheaval caused in the economy, and this needs to be understood. Most people believed, and possibly still do, that demonetization should have substantially undermined the black economy. To fathom this mystery, one needs to understand the working of the black economy. I explain below some of its key features in India. It needs to be kept in mind that in its actual functioning the black economy may differ from country to country, but its theoretical underpinnings are similar across the developing countries.

It also needs to be borne in mind that the black economy is a vast subject.[1] Here, only that part of the black economy that is relevant to demonetization and money is discussed, and that too in brief. Aspects such as the causes of black income generation are not touched here, while the consequences of the black economy are only briefly discussed.

---

[1] It has been dealt with in detail in Kumar, 1999, Kumar, 2017a, NIPFP, 1985 and Ram, 2017.

There are many misconceptions about the black economy in India and these need to be cleared up for a better understanding of the subject. Some of them are:

a) Black is all cash
b) The term 'black money' encompasses the complexity of what is black
c) Black money is the same as black economy or black incomes
d) The black economy is a parallel economy
e) Black money is not too large and can be ignored in policy analysis
f) Black money is held abroad
g) Real estate is the largest generator of black money in India
h) 'Black economy' is just a term, and has no real effect on the economy
i) Corruption is the same thing as black money
j) It is speed money and increases efficiency in the economy
k) Black money can be tackled by using technology
l) Black money can be controlled easily by means of some simple steps

Black Economy and Cash

Black is not synonymous with cash. As I will explain in the next chapter, this was the misconception about the black economy which led to the 2016 decision to demonetize. It was not just the prime minister and the few people around him in the government who confused cash with black; the common people also believe that 'black means cash'. Following from this, it logically followed that if cash was squeezed out of the system, the black economy would collapse, without impacting anything else.

When we go to the market and pay money to buy goods or services, a transaction occurs. This results in the seller earning an income. Incomes are used by the sellers to fulfil their daily requirements by incurring expenditures. So, usually, the more transactions take place, the more incomes are earned. In a nutshell, we do not eat money but use it for transactions that are necessary to carry on with our lives. But money may also be held for precautionary purposes, to take care of contingencies. Someone falls ill and we immediately need to go to the hospital and may need cash. A business may have to buy some items immediately, pay a taxi or pay its workers, etc. Money may also be used as a store of value in the house or by the business. I may keep money since there may be a profitable investment that comes up in the future. The economic literature tells us that money is held for transactions, for precaution and as store of value.[2]

Money may be held in the form of cash or bank balances, or in the form of debit and credit cards or electronic money. Cash is the most immediately usable form of money. While the other forms of money can leave a trail, cash is anonymous and does not do so. Hence, if one has to bribe someone, one would mostly use cash. If one used a cheque to bribe someone there is a fear of being tracked down so one would avoid doing so. This is the common perception, and therefore it is generally believed that black money is all cash.

How much cash would I keep on my person or at home? Since cash does not give any return, I would usually invest the savings to earn a return and not hold it as idle cash. When I earn an income of, say, Rs 1 lakh, do I hold Rs 1 lakh in cash? No. I may keep Rs 10,000 with me for my daily requirements and as a precaution against some contingency. So, out of my annual income of Rs 12 lakh I may have an average balance of cash in hand of Rs 10,000, or less than 1 per cent of my income.

Similarly, in the case of the black income I may earn, I would hold only a small part as cash, and the rest would be invested in assets so that I can get a return on it. Business people would put their black funds into their businesses, to expand

---

[2] Discussed in more detail in Chapter II.

them and earn a return. Families too would invest the black funds in a variety of assets. Cash would thus constitute one small component of my black holdings—not the entire amount. One may hold more cash if one does not have the opportunity to invest, and such people always exist. But, by and large, most people would find some way of investing their black savings in some assets. So squeezing out cash, which is what a sudden demonetization does, affects only a tiny part of the black assets held by businesses and households.

How do I earn my black income? By committing an illegality in an activity. If I, as a doctor, see 100 patients in a day but declare my income from only twenty, and if I charge them a consultation fee of Rs 500 but show only Rs 100, then I show an income of Rs 2000 while I actually earn Rs 50,000 per day. I pay my tax only on Rs 2000 and not on Rs 50,000. The same is true of many professionals and businesses. I may be involved in a completely illegal activity, such as narcotic drugs trafficking, and the entire income from that is illegal and black. I may be a policeman and collect *hafta* on my beat from all kinds of legal and illegal businesses in my locality. I cannot declare this income; this is also black income. All these activities will continue in spite of demonetization. Clearly, black income generation is not affected by demonetization.

All bribes do not have to be in cash. It is not true that if cash is not available then bribes cannot be given. One could gift an asset to someone at lower-than-market-price as a bribe. So, hypothetically, a share whose market value is Rs 350 could be allotted at Rs 25 to someone, and that would be a bribe of Rs 325. If one crore such shares are allotted, that would be a bribe of Rs 325 crore. Similarly, a plot of land could be allotted by a builder at Rs 5 crore to someone rather than at the market value of Rs 50 crore, and that amounts to a bribe of Rs 45 crore. Bribes can also be given in foreign exchange in India or abroad, and not just in rupees. So cash shortage is hardly going to stop people from generating and transferring black incomes.

In brief, while the black wealth may be affected by a tiny percentage (less than 1 per cent), black income generation does not stop. Whatever part of the black cash is eliminated will again get generated through savings from black incomes generated in the coming months.

Nomenclature and Definitional Aspects

What the explanations above point to is that black money is only one aspect of the black wealth and only one component of the black economy, the other being black income generation. So, what *is* black money? It is the cash in the black economy that is held for carrying out transactions and also held as a store of wealth. As already argued, this component is a tiny part of the overall black wealth (accumulated over time) or the black incomes generated (every year).

And what is the black economy? It refers to all the activities in an economy in which black incomes are generated. Further, black incomes are *factor incomes* generated in production, and *not transfer incomes* which are generated in exchange of what is already produced. When I produce a chemical and do not declare 20 per cent of my output, I am not declaring my full production. When I sell this undeclared output in the market I will get revenue which I will not declare in my books; so I make a profit outside my books of accounts and do not declare it for tax purposes. This is a factor income not declared to the tax authorities and is therefore black income. As discussed later,[3] transfer incomes are not linked to production and hence not counted in estimating the black incomes generated in the economy. If they are counted then it would lead to double counting and overestimation of the black incomes generated in the economy.

So, there are two critical elements in defining black incomes. Namely, they should be factor incomes, and they are not

---

[3] In this chapter, section on Real Estate.

reported to the direct tax authorities. This last clause captures the evasion of indirect taxes also. Once some production is not declared, it evades both indirect and direct taxes. Capturing it in the end captures the previous stage too. The implication is that black incomes are over and above the declared incomes in the economy. That is why the black economy is expressed as a per cent of the white income (GDP). So, when we say black economy is 62 per cent of the GDP, it means it is 62 per cent over and above the government-declared GDP.

Black incomes should not be confused with the amount of tax evaded. It is the income on which tax is evaded. If we count all the incomes on which various taxes are evaded, then we will be multiply counting the black incomes and this will yield a high figure for the size of the black economy. For instance, in the example of 20 per cent of the chemical produced not being declared, I am evading excise duty, sales tax, octroi, etc. If the income is counted for each tax evaded, then it is not correct. This *multiple counting* of black incomes should be avoided.

The black economy is mistakenly referred to as the *parallel economy*. The connotation is that the white economy and the black economy do not meet and have their own separate existences. This is not correct, since in India the two are intertwined. Black and white incomes are often generated together in the same activity, as in the above example of under-declaration of production or in the earlier example of the doctor declaring only a part of his income. Also, there are mechanisms for converting black to white and white to black using book-entry methods. Since the two parts of the economy are intertwined, each affects the other; attempts to tackle the black economy have an effect on the white economy, as discussed later in the chapter.

The black economy is also referred to as the *informal economy*. This is also incorrect in the Indian situation. This may be true for most advanced countries, and that is why the black economy is often referred to in this way by Western analysts.

In the advanced economies, most people are employed in the formal sector and earn taxable incomes. When they do a second or a third job (part-time) that income also becomes taxable. In India, as discussed earlier, 93 per cent of the employment is in the unorganized sector, and the incomes of most of these employees are way below the taxable limits, so whether they declare their income or not, their income is not black income. This does not mean that some entities in the unorganized sector do not generate black incomes. There may be *dhaba* owners or small traders doing roaring business, and having taxable incomes that they do not declare. But they are small in number compared with the vast bulk of those operating in the unorganized sectors.

In brief, it is the mistaken belief that the black economy is cash or that it is the informal economy or a parallel economy that led to the wrong notion that demonetization would finish the black economy.

Is Indian Black Money Held Abroad?

A common misconception is that black money flows out of the country and that most of the black wealth is held abroad in Swiss banks. This is not true; only about 10 per cent of the black incomes generated annually go out of the country; 90 per cent of it remains in the country.[4] Out of the funds that make their way abroad, a part is 'round tripped' back to India via investment in the share markets and in financial instruments. Another part is consumed, and yet another portion is invested in assets abroad. Very little of it is in liquid form, which may be in the 'Swiss' banks and which can be theoretically brought back to India.

Unfortunately, in the cut and thrust of the 2014 general elections and due to incorrect advice he must have received, Modi promised that within a month of his coming to power,

---

[4] As shown in Kumar and Chattopadhyay, 2013.

he would bring back all the black money lying abroad and this would be enough to give each Indian family Rs 15 lakh. This was a seductive promise. It reinforced the public perception that most of the black money is lying abroad. Compared with the UPA, which was perceived to be corrupt since there were weekly revelations of big scams during its reign, Modi appeared to be someone who would clean up the system. He seemed to be a doer who was promising '*achhe din*' (good times); the public believed him and gave him a clear mandate.

Since the government had not done any studies on how much and where black money is lying abroad, very little money held abroad has been tracked or brought back since 2014. Amit Shah, the BJP president, was forced to say that Modi's promise of bringing back black money held abroad was a '*chunavi jumla*' (election promise). The implication is that this promise should not be taken seriously.

It is interesting that in spite of successive governments' claims of having signed treaties with many foreign governments[5] since 1990, no one has been caught with their black money abroad. Whatever money has been tracked abroad has been done on the basis of stolen data from LGT bank in Liechtenstein, HSBC bank in Switzerland, the British Virgin Islands and Panama. The government's own efforts have not yielded much, not even a tiny fraction of what has been taken abroad over the years.

Some Not-so-obvious but Common Misconceptions

The list of misconceptions about the black economy is large. Some are not so obvious, but being common need clarification since they can lead to a basic misunderstanding about the black economy and what needs to be done to control it.

---

[5] These are Double Taxation Avoidance Agreement (DTAA) and Tax Information Exchange (TIE) treaties.

Corruption Only a Small Part of the Black Economy

People think that corruption is the same as black economy. Definitionally, corruption involves a quid pro quo, either in cash or in kind for work done. The work may be illegal or legal. Someone may encroach on public land and bribe the police and the municipal authorities to keep quiet. I may construct more than I am allowed to and bribe the inspector to overlook it. These are illegal activities, and to get officialdom and the politicians to overlook them I pay a bribe. I make a gain and share that with the state machinery. Alternatively, I may want my legitimate work to be done, such as payment of property tax or income tax, or get a housing clearance or an electricity connection. Because the work is getting delayed and I have to make many trips to the authorities, I may pay a bribe to get the work done.

Sometimes, this kind of bribe is considered as speed money for legitimate work. However, one must understand that first the work is slowed down so as to extract a bribe and then speeded up. Overall, the work is slowed down by creating impediments. Those unable to pay a bribe have to go through endless troubles. Overall, this results in inefficiency in the system. The above examples are of small bribes for small work. For big contracts, such as defence purchases or allotment of resources like coal or spectrum, large bribes are paid. In these cases, the price is inflated, or the work is substandard to account for the bribe to be paid.

Anyway, the point is not whether the bribes are large or small, but about the quid pro quo. Many activities in the black economy involve no quid pro quo but only an illegality. For instance, in the example of a doctor, given earlier, she sees 100 patients but only declares twenty, she generates a black income but there is no quid pro quo. I could be a teacher and take tuitions but not declare the income I get from them; I generate a black income, but I do not have to bribe anyone to do so. Most of the cases of black incomes are of this sort and do not involve any quid pro quo.

So, corruption is one aspect of the larger phenomenon of black economy where illegality is committed. No doubt, the two are interlinked. As corruption increases, the black economy increases, and as the black economy grows, corruption grows. Data show how scams that have come to light (there may be many others that have not been exposed) in India have grown exponentially since the 1950s.[6] The average amount of money involved in the scams also grew exponentially. This is an indication of the growth of the black economy in India.

Real Estate Is Not the Biggest Generator of Black

It is believed that real estate in India is the largest generator of black money. The government in its 'White Paper on Black Money' in 2012 also reinforced this view.[7]

Let us understand what happens in a real estate transaction. I buy a property from Ms A. She has already constructed it or she is selling a piece of land to me. In the transaction, no production is involved. Whatever property existed is being transferred to me, and in lieu of that I am paying Ms A the price we settled for. I had also saved money from my past incomes and will transfer that to Ms A. In both directions, it is already existing assets that are changing hands; this is a transfer activity. Any capital gain—what I give Ms A minus what she had paid when she bought or constructed the property—that Ms A earns is a paper gain. The price could have dropped too from what she had paid earlier, and she could have made a loss.

If I pay Ms A a part of the money in white and the rest in black, I have to generate the black somewhere and transfer it to Ms A. So, I am transferring the black part also and there is no generation of black income but a transfer of it. I have to count the black income where it was generated. Otherwise I would be double counting the black incomes.

---

[6] Kumar, 1999 and 2013.
[7] GoI, 2012.

This distinction between generation of black income and distribution of black incomes needs to be understood. This is the same distinction as in the white economy, where also the capital gains in real estate or in the share markets are not counted in measuring the size of the national income. That is why in my estimation of the size of the black economy,[8] I do not count capital gains in real estate or in the share market.

In the secondary share market, when a share of BHEL is bought, it is not that BHEL gets the money, so production at BHEL is unaffected. The buyer gets the share and transfers his/her savings to the seller. Another exchange has taken place, and capital gain earned is a transfer income.

For the same reason, bribes are transfers and are not to be counted in the estimation of the size of the black economy. In the case of bribes too, I transfer a part of my savings for some work that I want done. The official doing the work has already been paid by the government for the work to be done. She is extracting another amount from me for not harassing me.

The argument that transfer incomes are not to be counted does not mean that they do not have an impact on the economy. They do affect distribution and consumption. An agriculturist getting a big capital gain on the land she has sold on the city periphery may buy cars and refrigerators. The media have run stories of BMWs parked next to the cows in the yard of a farmer. The sellers of such land may invest their money in opening a *dhaba* or starting a transport company. So transfer incomes do have an economic impact.

Simple Remedies Have Not Worked

There is much talk of remedies for the black economy. Demonetization was thought by the PM to be a remedy. During the Ramdev and Anna Hazare movements in 2011-12 too, people talked about what could be done to control the black economy. A view exists that the problem is economic and can

---

[8] See Kumar, 1999, Kumar, 2016c and Kumar, 2017a.

be solved by making markets work and by the use of technology. The government currently believes that demonetization has not worked, but that going 'cashless' via use of digital technology will help. Many have proposed that black money can be tackled by some simple steps.[9]

I have often argued that we are like the seven blind men and the elephant. Each blind man touches a part of the elephant and thinks of it as something else—a broom, a hosepipe or a pillar of a building. Since an overview is missing, none thinks it is an elephant he has touched. The problem of the elephant remains unresolved. No solution to controlling the black economy, such a complex and all-encompassing social problem, can emerge from taking a partial view of it.

There have been dozens of committees and commissions[10] since 1948 that have analysed aspects of the problem. They have dissected and explained the problem. They have also suggested many remedies, a large number of which have been implemented. But the problem has only grown, since it is not a narrowly technical or an economic problem.

The problem is, above all, political. I have been arguing that underlying the black economy is a 'triad' consisting of corrupt businessmen, politicians and the executive.[11] Unless this is disbanded, the black economy will continue to exist and to grow. This nexus among the corrupt is convenient to the three partners, and since they are the ruling elite they not only do not wish to disrupt it, they do all that they can to protect it. They find ways to circumvent whatever new laws and rules are devised. To plug loopholes, new rules and laws are devised, and then people find ways of circumventing them. The end result is more and more complex laws, which are in fact easier to violate.

---

[9] For instance see NIPFP, 1985.

[10] Kumar, 2013.

[11] Kumar, 1985.

More Laws and Regulations Have Not Helped

A law is a law in letter and spirit. India has wonderful laws of every kind but most of them are violated. The spirit is not willing. The elite find ways of circumventing all the laws. People jump traffic lights, violate environmental laws or building and zoning bye-laws, industrial laws or food safety norms. All these rules and laws are required at a minimum for a society to function.

I have been arguing that there is no perfect law. If the spirit is not willing, ways can be found to circumvent any law. There have been so many changes in the law to prevent defections from parties. The 'aya rams and gaya rams' of the parties were changing loyalties for a consideration. Laws have been promulgated to stop this practice but without much success. Once one has defected in the mind, because one's only desire is to get to power, nothing can stop that person from defecting.

When payment above Rs 20,000 in cash by businesses was disallowed, people started paying Rs 19,900 in cash. It caused inconvenience, but that was acceptable. Now the government has announced that payment above Rs 2000 to political parties has to be listed. Earlier, this threshold was Rs 20,000, and 80 per cent of donations to political parties was in amounts less than this. What stops people from donating in multiples of Rs 1900 now. It is an inconvenience, but so what.

The elite are not only feudal but want to get ahead in the race to accumulate capital by any means. The result is a lack of consensus as to how to run society. It is a case of each for themselves—a kind of jungle *raj*. This missing consensus needs to evolve, and that can only happen politically. Every section of society must be a part of such a consensus in a democracy. In the weak democracy that India has, every section of the population is looking for ways, fair or foul, to get ahead. That is what propels the black economy.

What does the argument for use of technology imply? It is being suggested that computerization will replace the corrupt and reduce the black economy. It is said that the replacement of entitlement to cooking gas cylinders by direct benefit transfers (DBT) to the real beneficiaries has saved the government thousands of crores of rupees. These technological solutions pushed by the ruling elite amount to replacing the human element with technology. So many times in the past, new technology has been introduced hoping that the problem will be solved but it has only led to new problems. Activists worry that when instead of an essential good, cash is given, it adversely affects the family. Money transferred to a poor family may simply be appropriated by the moneylender for some past loan.

Is it not a case of society giving up on its citizens? Taken to its logical extension, the idea would result in computers running everything. But what about the persons who are to operate the computer and technology? If they are corrupt, then they will use the technology to propagate more illegality and generate more black income. The real reform required is to get people to believe in society, end their alienation, curb the feudal tendencies and democratize society so as to build accountability all around and especially in institutions of democracy. All these actions require strengthening political processes, and that is difficult at best. It requires movements which are time-consuming in normal times.[12] But when has reform of society been easy? That is the only way to bring about real social change.

Terrorism and Counterfeiting of Currency

An important aspect of the black economy is the illegal activities going on in the economy. The most disturbing of them are counterfeiting of currency and terrorism. They hit at the core of the Indian state and pose a deep threat to its very existence. These activities are unlike smuggling, land

---

[12] Kumar, 2017a.

encroachment in a city or allocation of mining leases for a consideration.

As discussed in the last chapter, money is fiat money, guaranteed by the state and therefore has a legal sanctity. Counterfeit currency damages this character of currency. Use of currency is based on its credibility, and this is eroded by the presence of fake notes. It brings doubt in the public mind about the legality of the country's currency. This is what damages the credibility of the state. It disrupts trade and production when people stop accepting a certain currency because they doubt its legality. The public often cannot tell a fake note from a genuine one since the copies are very well made. Only experts can distinguish the good fake notes from the genuine ones.

Further, the state gets the benefit of printing notes since the cost of printing them is much less than the value of the notes. The difference accrues to the state as an additional income (seigniorage). When fake currency is printed, the benefit goes to the counterfeiter, so it is a theft from the resources of the state, and the authority of the state is challenged.

The question arises as to how serious the problems of counterfeiting and terrorism in India are. From the published data, it does not appear that there is much by way of counterfeit currency in the system. What the RBI detects annually is only a few notes per million.[13] According to the ministry of finance, counterfeit notes in circulation may number 250 per million.[14] A Rajya Sabha answer to a question, citing a study conducted by ISI, Kolkata, suggested that there may be Rs 400 crores worth of counterfeit currency in circulation.[15] This represents only 0.02 per cent of the currency in circulation on 8 November 2016, of about Rs 18 lakh crore.

---

[13] RBI, Annual Report, 2016.
[14] Chauhan, 2016.
[15] Lok Sabha, 2016.

The problem is a serious one, but not so serious that to eliminate it one should jeopardize the entire economy and subject a large number of people to economic hardship for months together. Further, since foreign state actors are involved in counterfeiting, they can continue this activity, and that is what seems to have happened in a big way since November 2016.

It needs to be borne in mind that published data on counterfeiting is perhaps based on the notes caught. But the problem lies with the notes not caught. How much that amounts to is hard to estimate. If the example of gold is any guide,[16] then illegal activity is thirty-three times what is detected. So, one could say that if a few notes per million are detected then the total of such notes in circulation may be a few hundred per million. The problem is significant, but still not greatly out of line.

It needs to be appreciated that counterfeiting is a worldwide phenomenon. US dollar notes are regularly counterfeited, in spite of all the effort at preventing it. All kinds of security features have been introduced in the dollar bills but to little avail. Since dollars are globally used, it is an important currency, and if it loses credibility it will cause a great deal of trouble. The problem again is that state actors are involved in counterfeiting.

This has been the case historically. The British counterfeited the currency of the fledgling US states during the American War of Independence to discredit the currency. During World War II this was an instrument of war on the enemy. Spy agencies routinely indulged in this activity, especially during the Cold War period. So, counterfeiting has spread as a routine practice globally and is hard to stop. The genie is out of the bottle.

India has faced terrorists and separatists for many years now—in Kashmir, Punjab, in the North East, in the south (LTTE) and the Maoists (earlier Naxalites) in the heartland of India. They have all challenged the Indian state. Most of

---

[16] Kumar, 2002.

them have received support from state actors abroad, from the neighbouring nations and others. The militants have had local support too so they have not needed as much outside support as would have been otherwise necessary.

It is said that counterfeiting helps finance terrorist activity. And that eliminating it will help end terrorist activity. But terrorism is financed in many ways such as smuggling of guns and other goods, narcotic drugs trafficking, use of foreign currency, and the like. These activities will not stop and have not stopped with demonetization.[17] Kashmir and the Maoist-affected areas have continued to seethe with trouble.

It also needs to be appreciated that counterfeit currency can be used only once to finance terrorist activity. When it is printed and put into the market, it gets used and then circulates in the market without giving further funds to the counterfeiter. Then it acts like any currency note until it is discovered and eliminated. Terrorists need to counterfeit currency continuously to get funding; that is what they do. That needs to be stopped, but since terrorism is sponsored largely by state actors, unless that ends, terrorist activity cannot be stopped from within India. The routes for inducting counterfeit currency into India via the porous border with Bangladesh and Nepal cannot be blocked easily. Anyhow, the point is that action is needed elsewhere to deal with these problems and demonetization is not the solution.

Impact of the Black Economy

If the black economy is small, it can be ignored. This is the case in some advanced countries like the Scandinavian nations or New Zealand, where the black economy is estimated to account for about 1 per cent of GDP. Even if it is 3 per cent,

---

[17] Annexure 10, Table 14 gives the data on casualties due to terrorism and these have not slowed down in 2017 compared to the previous years.

as in Germany, or 5 per cent, as in the US or the UK, it may be ignored. However, if it is larger than this, it cannot be ignored in economic analysis.

In India, it was estimated to be 62 per cent of GDP for 2012-13.[18] If it is assumed to be the same in 2016-17, the black economy amounts to Rs 93 lakh crore. Hence it cannot be ignored. In 1955-56, it was estimated by Prof. Kaldor[19] from Cambridge University to be 4-5 per cent of GDP. Its growth has been rapid, and as already stated, it is intertwined with the white economy and results in growing inefficiencies.

It impacts all the macro- and micro-variables.[20] Inflation is higher and the trade deficit larger. The savings rate rises while the investment rate falls. Employment is lower than potentially possible, and the rate of growth below the potential. Educational standards are pulled down and people live in unhygienic conditions.

Black Economy, Inefficiency and Slow Growth

Inefficiencies are a result of a particular aspect of the black economy, characterized as 'digging holes and filling them'. What this implies is that during the day one person is employed to dig a hole and at night another to fill it up. The next morning the output is zero, while two incomes have been earned. This is 'activity without productivity'. Capital is wastefully utilized. It does not yield the output it should yield. Production does not rise, even though work is done.

For instance, the police collect *hafta* from the illegal activities in their beat area, overlooking the illegalities being committed. They collect *hafta* from establishments, encroachers, pickpockets and many others. Illegalities, instead of being controlled, are now

---

[18] Kumar, 2016c.
[19] Kaldor, 1956.
[20] Kumar, 2002.

encouraged. One former home secretary in an interview said every additional police station in Delhi means more crime since the new station has to generate *hafta* for the officials heading the station.[21] The police spend their time on activities other than maintaining law and order so that there appears to be a shortage of police for routine activities. Further, those committing illegalities are emboldened to do more of the same. The result is poor law and order in the city. So, the state's investment in the police system does not give the desired output, and in fact does the opposite.

Take another example. A road is to be made. Due to corruption, the contractor uses less tar than required. He saves money not only for himself but also to pay off the politicians and the engineers overseeing the construction of the road. As a result, the road is poorly made, and when the rains come it gets washed away or potholed. Vehicles tend to break down and need more repairs; their springs get damaged, more fuel is consumed, and so on. The corruption has resulted in more expenditure than is required. Additionally, the roads have to be repeatedly repaired, sucking out funds that could have been spent on making new roads. Thus, the investment is not properly utilized and there is inefficiency. Such examples are all pervasive, when you consider other fields like education, production and the legal system.

Due to the inefficiencies associated with the black economy, the productivity of the economy declines and that lowers the rate of growth of the economy. This is the paradox of the black economy. While the black economy is additional to the white economy so that the total economy is larger than the white economy, it lowers the potential rate of growth of the economy as a whole. Thus, if there was no black economy, the rate of growth of the economy would have been higher. In fact, black economy is not just a question of a term, but has real adverse effects.

---

[21] Kumar, 1999.

In one of my papers[22] I showed that the Indian economy has been on an average losing 5 per cent in its rate of growth since the mid-1970s when the black economy became significant. If 5 per cent is added to the economy's rate of growth since then, today the Indian economy would be eight times larger and roughly the size of the US economy. The per capita income would have been eight times larger too. And instead of being one of the poorest countries in the world, India would be a middle-income country. Those generating black incomes could have also been richer in the same proportion, but their attitude is that of a frog in the well, with its narrow perspective.

How did the South-East Asian countries and China achieve their high standard of living after they achieved independence? We all got independence at roughly the same time and we were all at the same level of development in 1947. But these countries grew at 7 per cent to 8 per cent per annum over decades, while we faltered. If the black economy was not so rampant, India too could have achieved similar growth rates since the 1970s. So the black economy is singularly responsible for the lack of development in India and the poor living conditions prevailing today.

Black Economy, Policy Failure, Poverty and Inequality

The above examples also show that the black economy results in policy failure and poor governance. Macro- and microeconomic policies fail because of the large size of the black economy.[23] Rajiv Gandhi in 1988 had said that when the government sends out Re 1, only 15 paisa reaches the ground. The entire loss is not due to the black economy but also due to administrative costs and failures. If this is the case, targets for health and education are not achieved, law and order deteriorates, people are harassed,

---

[22] Kumar, 2005.
[23] Kumar, 1999.

and justice is delayed (or miscarried). People live in uncivilized conditions since civic amenities are not available or are of a poor standard. So, 'expenditures do not lead to outcomes'.

Due to corruption, the environment is adversely impacted and pollution levels are higher than they need be. Forests and green areas are encroached on, leading to a loss of green cover. In the cities, not only is the number of vehicles rising but they are also poorly maintained. All kinds of production units spew out pollutants into the air and water. In the rural areas, there is massive burning of stalk after harvest to clear the fields for the next crop. Most people flout environmental pollution laws, building bye-laws and zoning laws, and this results in high levels of pollution at a low level of per capita consumption.[24]

Poverty is aggravated as a result of this environmental pollution, and policy failure results in poor sanitation and health facilities. This has led to a higher level of health expenditure for the poor, who are the worst affected by the increased pollution of air and water. So, even when their incomes rise, they end up having less for their daily requirements and remain poor. They are also trapped in poverty across generations because their children do not have access to proper education and nutrition. This stunts their growth and they lack the skills to move up the income ladder. As the minister of finance said in his 2005 Budget speech, 'expenditures do not lead to outcomes'. This phrase captures the policy failure witnessed in the country.

Not only is there more poverty, inequality has also increased. The white economy has been showing a skewed pattern of growth, with the rich getting richer much faster while the incomes of the poor lag way behind. But the real reason for inequality in India is the black economy, which is concentrated in the hands of the few who make up around 3 per cent of the population.[25]

---

[24] Kumar, 2013.
[25] Kumar, 1999.

The inequality, therefore, is much higher than what the official data suggest, and poverty is rising rather than declining, in spite of the growth in the economy.

Black Economy and Shortage of Resources for Development

By definition, black incomes escape the tax net. Neither direct or indirect taxes are paid on them. If the current black economy of 62 per cent of GDP[26] could be brought into the tax net, then an additional 24 per cent of GDP could be collected as taxes (both direct and indirect). The current tax/GDP ratio is about 16 per cent. This is one of the lowest in the world. If the black economy had been brought into the tax net, India's tax/GDP ratio would have stood at about 40 per cent, among the highest in the world. The twin problem for our budgets is this: First there are inadequate resources to spend, and second, whatever is spent does not give the result it should because a large part of the expenditure is misappropriated.

The nation should spend at least 6 per cent of its GDP on public education, but it usually spends only around 3.5 per cent to 4 per cent of GDP on it annually. Public schools, colleges and universities are in bad shape (with some exceptions). This has led to the rise of the private sector in education, which has resulted in high levels of malpractice in this field, aggravating the problem instead of solving it. Public health should get at least 3 per cent of GDP but barely gets 1 per cent. Public hospitals are mostly on the verge of breakdown. The poor are left at the mercy of the private sector, which by and large is highly rapacious and corrupt. Roads, ports, railways, power and other physical infrastructure are also of poor quality and wholly inadequate. Urban areas are mostly unplanned and have poor infrastructure,

---

[26] Kumar, 2016c.

with a few exceptions like New Delhi. They are like vast slums which lack water, sanitation and public transport.

The Union budgets year after year face a debt crisis as a result of the black economy. Due to shortage of resources and rising demands for development, the budgets have had to depend on borrowings. This has led to a rising burden of interest payment. In fact, it is the largest single item in our budgets. So the government borrows with one hand and gives it back with the other.

This has resulted in the problem of high fiscal deficits (excessive expenditure over the resources of the government) in our budgets. If the black economy could be tapped, then the deficit would turn into a surplus and the interest burden would be negligible, freeing vast resources for development. The implication is that the nation has the resources, but they cannot be properly mobilized for its development because of the presence of a large black economy.

Steps to Curb the Black Economy

If the black economy creates such problems for the economy and is the key to India's various problems, something needs to be done to tackle it and reduce its size. That is what the PM was trying to do by ordering demonetization. He did it without understanding either the black economy or demonetization and its impact. But it must be said that the NDA government has indeed been making attempts to tackle the black economy.

The PM, in his speech,[27] listed the steps that had been taken. He said:

We began our battle against corruption by setting up an SIT headed by a retired Supreme Court judge, immediately upon

---

[27] See Annexure 1.

*taking office. Since then a law was passed in 2015 for disclosure of
foreign black money;*

- *agreements with many countries, including the USA, have been
  made to add provisions for sharing banking information;*
- *a strict law has come into force from August 2016 to curb
  benami transactions, which are used to deploy black money
  earned through corruption;*
- *a scheme was introduced for declaring black money after paying
  a stiff penalty.*

So, it is not that Demonetization 2016 is the first time that an
attempt has been made to control the black economy. In the
last seventy years, dozens of committees and commissions have
gone into the problem and made thousands of suggestions.[28]
Hundreds have been implemented in the past. So it is not true
that demonetization is the first attempt to deal with the problem.

The problem is that if the correct cause is not identified, any
action would be futile. As mentioned earlier, we are like the seven
blind men and the elephant. Without an overview of the problem,
each one looking at the problem partially has a different solution to
offer, but none is correct since the overall problem is different from
what the partial frameworks suggests. An NGO may look at it from
a social point of view, while a lawyer may suggest a legal remedy
or a taxman may look at it from the point of view of taxes, and a
technology expert from the viewpoint of a technological solution.

In the past, thinking that high taxes are the cause of existence
of the black economy, the tax rates have been drastically cut, but
the size of the black economy has only grown. Believing that
controls and regulations are the cause of the black economy, they
have been drastically reduced, but that has not helped either.
Other steps have been tried, like acquisition of undervalued

---

[28] Kumar, 2013.

property, in the belief that real estate is the generator of black incomes. Voluntary disclosure schemes have been tried too. The Government of India in a White Paper on black money[29] lists the steps undertaken by the UPA II regime.

The root of the problem can only be understood if one asks how can there be illegality in 62 per cent of the economic activity in the country. If it is so widespread, it is not anecdotal or accidental. It is *systematic and systemic*, and that is only possible if the state apparatus is a party to the illegality. So, the policymaker, the politician and the executive of the state have to be a party to the generation of black incomes.[30] This is the *triad* consisting of corrupt businessmen, corrupt politicians and a corrupt executive. If even one of these arms were not a party to the illegality, the black economy would collapse.

In order to check the black economy, there is a need to dismantle this triad, and that is a political and not an economic matter. It is not merely a technical matter. Of course, use of technology may change the nature of the problem, as already discussed. Today there is a need for political change in the country, which requires new parties and political reform.[31] The existing parties are a part of the triad and cannot be expected to take the tough steps needed to tackle the problem.

After the failure of demonetization to tackle the black economy, the NDA government has continued to take steps to tackle it. In the Union Budget 2017-18, it announced some steps. For instance, one step was to facilitate corporate donations to parties via bonds so that anonymity can be maintained. The government has also suggested that all donations above Rs 2000 have to be reported. But these measures cannot dismantle the triad; even the Election Commission has termed these steps inadequate and possibly

---

[29] GoI, 2012.
[30] Kumar, 1985.
[31] Kumar, 2017a.

counterproductive because of the anonymity they provide to the donors. It may allow bribes to be given in white.

One final point that may be considered in this matter is whether demonetization will produce a 'psychological shock' and make people more compliant. The issue is, how big a shock has it given that it has failed to unearth black incomes? Also, have there not been other shocks in the past which have had little impact? Unfortunately, the matter is confused with formalization of the informal and digitization. These steps have little to do with demonetization and can be taken separately.[32] Indeed, these steps require a lot of preparation and should be implemented independently. The present confusion resulting from mixing these steps with demonetization may eventually come in the way of their implementation.

Conclusion

The PM, in his speech on 8 November 2016, correctly pointed to the black economy as the key reason for the continuing problems facing the people of India. His intention in tackling it to improve the lot of the common person is spot on. But the method he chose was not the correct one. Demonetization tackles neither black wealth nor black income generation.

Tackling the black economy is an urgent task if the country is to become a civilized one. It would also make the country strong. That would really bring India on to the world stage, as the PM has been wanting to do. It would make the country respected in the comity of nations. Since the black economy implies a negative-sum game in which the elite benefits at the expense of the non-elite, curbing it would be a positive-sum game where all gain, including the elite who generate black incomes.[33]

---

[32] See Chapter VI for more discussion on this.
[33] See Kumar, 2017a.

IV

Some Sectoral Aspects of Demonetization 2016

Earlier in the book, I discussed the implementation of Demonetization 2016. I showed that there was a lack of preparation resulting in crisis for a large number of people. A variety of problems were encountered by people. In this chapter, I discuss the impact of the move on some key sectors of the economy, like agriculture and banking.

As mentioned earlier, the important premise underlying the 2016 scheme was that 'black means cash'. People have the visual impression of sacks full of cash lying with the black money generators. It is generally believed that those who deal in the black economy hold large sums of cash. If this is true then it must follow that for ease of holding, most of this money would be in large-denomination notes. Think of holding crores in notes of Rs 100 denomination; it would occupy ten times more space than if one held it in Rs 1000 currency. One is reminded of the time when, in the early 1990s, Harshad Mehta[1] claimed that he gave a bribe of Rs 1 crore in cash in a suitcase. At that time, the largest denomination available was Rs 100. People doubted that Rs 1 crore could fit into one suitcase, even a large one.

---

[1] Harshad Mehta was supposed to be responsible for the big 1992 stock market scam.

Mehta tried to demonstrate that live on television. Now, it is perfectly possible for Rs 1 crore to fit in a suitcase if the Rs 500 or the Rs 2000 notes are used.

If black means cash, it would follow that by squeezing out the big-denomination currency notes, the black hoards of the corrupt would be destroyed and the black economy would collapse. Simple! That is what the PM thought, on the basis of advice from some quarters.[2] I shall explain why that has not happened and should not have been expected to happen.

The general impact of demonetization on the economy has been negative, and this has been discussed in the previous chapters. However, the government announced that there would be some specific benefits from demonetization, such as for the banking system which received a large amount of funds from the public. It was felt that this would be beneficial for the economy. The government also argued that the public finances would improve because of demonetization and the check on the black economy, and that could help in the development of the country and especially the uplift of the poor. These claims need to be analysed to see what positive benefit, if any, would follow. One crucial sector of the economy is agriculture, which still employs roughly 50 per cent of the workforce even though its contribution to the national income has come down to only 14 per cent. The impact of Demonetization 2016 on agriculture is discussed here.

Who Holds the Cash?

How the black economy links with people holding cash needs to be understood. In this context, there are two important questions:

First, how many people hold a lot of cash in the country, and why? Say, can 1 lakh people hold an average of Rs 20 crore?

---

[2] See Chapter I.

Indeed not, since that would amount to Rs 20 lakh crore and that would be more than Rs 17.9 lakh crore of currency held by the public on 8 November 2016.

Second, is cash holding only linked to the black economy?

The economy is divided between households and businesses. Currency is held by households for their day-to-day requirements. They also hold some amount of cash for an emergency, such as a health situation. Finally, they also hold cash as a part of their wealth. Businesses need a lot of money to carry forward their daily work. This is called working capital, and a part of that is held in cash. Businesses pay wages, buy raw material and pay for transport and other overheads. While those in the organized sector of the economy can use cheques and banks for these expenditures, the small and cottage sector does not have that facility and operates using cash. Further, most businessmen do not trust each other and prefer cash payments over payments by cheque. In India, the practice of bouncing cheques is rampant. This forces businesses to hold more cash than they would have, if there was less fraud. So most of the currency held by the public is with businesses and with households for their legitimate expenses.

If the total currency in circulation on 8 November 2016 is divided among the approximately 26 crore households in the country, every household would have an average of Rs 69,000. Of course, the poor hold very little, so most of this amount would be with the rich and middle-class households. But the numbers will not be staggering (Rs 6.9 lakh) even if we assume that only 10 per cent of the households hold all this cash. Per person, the amount would be Rs 1.4 lakh for these well-off households.

The amount held by the households would be drastically lower if we took into account the cash that businesses hold. Go to a petrol pump and you find that it gets lakhs of rupees of cash daily. It deposits that in the bank the next morning when it starts collecting cash again. The same would be true of travel agents, airlines, telephone companies, gas and utilities, wholesale dealers, shopkeepers and so on.

Those in the unorganized sector and in farming typically work with cash and hold much more than their daily need in cash. There are millions of such businesses and 138.35 million farm operational holdings. Together they produced 45 per cent of the GDP, or Rs 70 lakh crore of output in 2016-17. This output goes through the stages of purchase of inputs, sale of output, transportation, wholesale and retail trade . . . the likely transactions on an average would be four times the incomes—about Rs 280 lakh crore. If these businesses on an average keep ten days of their requirement in cash, then the amount of cash needed by them would be Rs 7.7 lakh crore.

The organized sectors produce Rs 80 lakh crore of output and they have many more and larger transactions due to the long line of distribution, so their average transactions are likely to be six to eight times the income, or about Rs 560 lakh crore. If their cash holding requirement is only two days' worth of transactions, they would hold about Rs 3 lakh crore. So, the total requirement of cash for businesses would be about Rs 10.7 lakh crore. The balance from the Rs 17.9 lakh crore of currency in circulation on 8 November 2016 would be Rs 7.2 lakh crore, which would be with the households. For the 26 crore households in the country, this works out to Rs 28,000 per household. If only 10 per cent of the households keep this cash, then the amount would be Rs 2.8 lakh held by each such household.

How much cash does a household need? If I earn an income of Rs 1 lakh a month, how much cash would I hold? Not Rs 1 lakh, but a fraction of it, say Rs 20,000 for my day-to-day needs and say, another Rs 20,000 for precautionary reasons. Hence, out of my annual income of Rs 12 lakh I may hold cash of Rs 40,000 during the year, which is 3.5 per cent of my income. Since cash does not give a return, it is better for me to hold it in a bank and withdraw cash when I need it. If people hold 3.5 per cent of their annual income as cash at home, that amounts to Rs 4.5 lakh crore.

The balance of Rs 3 lakh crore may then be thought of as being held as balances from black incomes. This is indeed small compared with the size of the black economy and the total black wealth held by people.

Consider, from one's black savings, why would one keep the funds in cash which does not give a return? Just as it is in the white economy, here too there is the option of investing in assets which give returns. Most businesses would put the black savings in their businesses to expand them. Only if I do not have the opportunity to invest my black savings will I hold them in cash. Even then I would divide it between gold and other such assets that can be acquired. So cash is only a tiny component of the black wealth that I may possess. Only a few people who may not have links with businessmen may hold more cash since their opportunity to invest may be limited.

In brief, in the example presented above, it emerges that most of the cash with the public is required for running the economy—for running the businesses and the households. The example is realistic, but if the ratios are changed around a bit, slightly different numbers can be obtained. However, even then it would be the case that only a small part of the cash with the public can be said to be part of the black hoards.

Black Not Affected by Demonetization

The impact demonetization had on the black economy needs to be understood. For this, one needs to understand the difference between a flow and a stock. This is standard macroeconomics and is taught in the very initial lecture in an economics course. The water in the overhead tank in my house has a stock of water which flows down into my taps. I may have a lot of water in the tank, but I use a small amount of it so that the flow is small.

It may also be the case that my stock of water is little but it is flowing in fast and going out to the taps fast so that the flow is high even though my stock of water is low. So, from the stock, I cannot tell what the flow is, and vice versa. In the economy too, this holds true.

I work to earn an income, and that is the flow. Out of the income, I consume a portion and save the rest. What I save I invest to earn a return. Annually, what I save and invest adds to my stock of wealth. The wealth grows. The wealth is in the form of various assets, so it is called a portfolio of assets.[3] It could consist of real estate, gold and jewellery, shares, fixed deposits and so on. I also keep a little bit of cash for precautionary purposes (as discussed above). In the above example, such cash amounted to 3.5 per cent of the annual income. As my savings accumulate, my wealth becomes a multiple of my annual income so that my cash holding will amount to less than 1 per cent of my wealth.

If similar numbers apply to the black economy, cash as a proportion of the black wealth may be only 1 per cent or less, and will amount to about 3.5 per cent of the black income generated annually.

Thus, if the entire stock of black cash had been neutralized because it did not come back into the banks, still only 1 per cent of the black wealth would have been destroyed. But, as argued earlier, by 13 January 2017, 98.8 per cent of the denotified currency had come back into the banks;[4] only Rs 18,000 crore had not, and most of that too would have come back[5] by now. There was a window of time up to 30 June 2017 to deposit much of the remaining money, which would also have come back. So, not even 0.1 per cent of the black cash got nullified, or less than 0.01 per cent of the black wealth.

---

[3] See Annexure 11, Table 15 and Graph 17.

[4] Kumar and Verma, 2017.

[5] See Chapter I.

While the black wealth was hardly impacted, black income generation was not impacted at all. If a doctor was getting a cut from laboratories for recommending tests, that continued. If a businessman was under-invoicing sales, that continued. The mechanisms of generating black income did not get impacted. Further, if there was a decline in output due to cash shortage, it impacted both the black and the white economies.

As clarified in Chapter III, most of the black incomes are generated in the organized sectors and not in the unorganized sectors, so the black economy was relatively less effected than the white economy. Further, as pointed out earlier, black economy can be transacted using non-cash means. So, it was again less impacted than the white economy. In brief, the ratio of black to white is likely to have risen. Since this is how the black economy is expressed, one can say that it increased even though in absolute amount it contracted for a temporary period.

Activity in the black economy was temporarily disrupted just as the white economy was disrupted, but the processes did not get disrupted. It is the process of black income generation that needs to be dislocated to stop it. Demonetization does not do that. Further, cash continued to be available to carry on black income generation. Even if cash was not available, payments could be made in alternative forms, via gold coins, dollars and undervalued assets.

It has been argued that real estate prices fell after demonetization and that amounted to a decline in black wealth. Gold prices initially rose and then fell. That would have also lowered the value of gold and jewellery holdings. Does this fall in prices mean that demonetization impacted black wealth? If that is so, the impact of demonetization on black wealth cannot be captured by the amount of currency that did not return to the banks. Reports suggested that sale of real estate, especially high-end real estate, declined sharply as a result of the uncertainty in the market. There were few buyers and sellers in the market for such properties.

The decline in asset prices does not amount to an impact on the black economy, because black income generation continues. A fall or a rise in price of assets only leads to paper gains and losses. This happens in the white economy too. Trends can reverse, leading to a revaluation of the assets over time. It is the real assets that count as wealth.

Shortage of Money, Output and Emergence of Near-money Forms

When the government announced demonetization, it made the notes of high denomination invalid. Since these constituted 86 per cent of the currency in circulation, this meant that cash and money supply in the economy reduced immediately. Unfortunately, the RBI did not show this sharp drop in cash with the public.[6] It only counted what was returned to its chests. That was incorrect because even though the public still held the old notes till the time they returned them to the banks, these notes had become worthless paper, as the PM had said in his speech.

The public deposited the old notes and they went into their bank deposits. They could have used these deposits, but since there was a shortage of cash, the banks did not return the deposits to the public in the form of new notes, so the deposits in the banks could not be used. In effect, even though people had money which they should have been able to use, they could not. Even bank deposits could not be put to use for day-to-day transactions. Anyway, most people, and especially the businesses, do not trust cheques, since unscrupulous elements bounce them. Thus, the public could not use cheques to a much greater extent than earlier even though they had funds in the bank. The problem was compounded because many workers who were given wages

---

[6] See, Annexure 7, Graph 10.

and salaries via cheques could not encash them because of the shortage of cash. So they were loath to accept cheques.

Given the shortage of cash, people held on to the notes they could collect rather than spending and circulating them. This lowered the velocity of circulation of money and aggravated the shortage of money in the economy. Shortage of money for circulation prevents transactions from taking place, and that results in a fall in activity and incomes. All this impacted the common people adversely.

The public could deposit the old notes in their bank accounts up to 30 December 2016. This led to a rise in public deposits in the banks. The result was that valid currency in circulation (M^0) immediately contracted sharply, while the deposits with the banks increased only slowly as the public deposited its old notes.[7] The former dominated over the latter so that the money supply (M^3) in the economy contracted. The new deposits by the public with the banks were to be relinquished to the central bank and eventually returned to the public in the form of new notes with which they could meet their transactions and other needs. The new notes were not available to the banks to give back to the public immediately. Further, due to low demand for credit, banks could not lend the additional deposits. All this reduced the velocity of circulation further. The banks were also so busy dealing with old and new notes that they had little time to lend the large sums of money they got. In times of shortage of cash, even those who had money in their accounts postponed their discretionary expenditures, further reducing the velocity of circulation.

The sectoral implications are important.[8] The unorganized sector which is dependent on M^0 faced an immediate and sharp decline in output. Since this sector produces 45 per cent of the output, it impacted demand in the entire economy, with the

---

[7] See Annexure 8, Graphs 11 to 14.
[8] See Kumar, 2017b for detailed analysis.

spillover affecting the organized sectors, even though they are less affected by cash shortage. The reduction in discretionary spending led to a further decline in demand for both sectors. Thus, the rate of growth of the economy as a whole came down sharply.

As discussed in Chapter III, the unorganized sector is not the same as the black economy, as is the case in the advanced economies. In India, most incomes in the unorganized sectors are below the taxable limit, so whether reported or not they are not necessarily black incomes.[9] Thus, a contraction of output and incomes in the unorganized sector is not the same as a decline of the black economy.

Shortage of currency typically results in the emergence of substitutes called, 'near-money forms'. For instance, gold and foreign exchange may be used for high-value transactions. The newly minted gold coins of high value under the gold monetization schemes are now available for use to serve as money. Further, the sudden demonetization and the consequent trouble the public has faced has led to an erosion of trust in the system, and over time this would also result in people shifting to other forms of money.

Impact on the RBI and Its Operations

As discussed in Chapter II, the RBI plays multiple roles in the economy. Many of these roles were impacted by demonetization. Of course, its first task was to collect the old notes and issue new currency to replace them. Due to the suddenness of the decision, new notes had not been printed in advance so that the central bank had to deal with a shortage of cash with the public. This created a law and order situation in the country.

---

[9] Kumar, 1999.

The RBI and Currency Printing

Adequacy of currency after demonetization depends on several factors. First, how much currency the public needs. Second, how quickly the new notes needed can be printed. And finally, to what extent the public will switch to alternative forms of transaction like cheques, plastic and electronic money.

If the government does not print adequate amounts of currency, then it is likely that the shortage mentality will continue. The net impact could lead to demand for cash exceeding the amount of currency that was demonetized. There is also a lurking fear that the newly issued Rs 2000 notes may be demonetized at some point in the future. In fact, initially there were reports to this effect. People may now prefer to hold more of the lower-denomination currency notes, and those take longer to print, and this may lead to a continuing shortage of currency.

The shortage of cash would disappear slowly as more notes were printed, but the question was, how quickly could the government print the notes? Clearly, what had been printed at least since 2005 could not be printed overnight or in fifty days.

In 2015-16, the increase in high-denomination notes in circulation was 3.3 billion pieces.[10] The total of such notes in existence (which were demonetized) in March 2016 was around 22 billion pieces, and these had to be replaced. If it is assumed that the capacity of the presses was 3.3 billion pieces annually, then to print 22 billion pieces would take about six and a half years. Even if three shifts are run and there is no shortage of ink and paper, it would take more than two years. If the Rs 2000 notes are assumed to replace the earlier Rs 1000 notes (in value), then the number of notes to be printed would come down by about 3 billion pieces. Even then the time required to print the required quantity of new notes would be two years. Remonetization was

---

[10] See Annexure 9, Table 10.

80 per cent complete by April end, that is, in six months.[11] One can infer that the printing capacity was greater than 3.3 billion pieces. But even at this rate, full remonetization would take not less than eight months from 8 November 2016.

The government was required to print small-denomination notes too, since they were in great demand. This slowed down the printing process. So it is likely that the shortage of cash could continue for up to twelve months after 8 November 2016.

Another possibility that was discussed to achieve faster remonetization was to import currency notes. Critics argued that the government could have made advance preparations for it so that there would have been no currency shortage. The counterargument was that secrecy might have been compromised if it had done so. It was also suggested that notes could be imported soon after the announcement. But this was also not possible since outside printers cannot ramp up production immediately. There has to be a process of tendering, and then capacity must be available, and both take time.

To sum it up, secrecy about the decision meant that a shortage of currency had to be endured by the country, no matter what the cost.

Impact on the RBI's Balance Sheet

The old notes with the public were no longer legal tender, but when deposited they led to a rise in deposits with the banks. To deal with the situation, in case it led to inflation, the RBI raised the CRR to 100 per cent for a while; that is, it impounded the entire amount of new deposits. So the banks deposited the entire amount of new deposits with the RBI. The central bank need not have insisted on this because the banks had no time to lend

---

[11] See Annexure 7, Table 7.

the new deposits. Banks earned a low return on these deposits, and this impacted their margins.

The RBI soon realized that the banks were not able to lend the money and would anyway have deposited their money with it, so it withdrew the 100 per cent requirement. Further, given the pace at which the new notes were going back into the market, the RBI realized that the deposits were temporary and the public would withdraw the money they had deposited. So, no long-term lending was possible anyway.

There has been pressure from the government for the RBI and the banks to lower interest rates to spur investment and growth in the economy. This pressure increased after demonetization was announced. The argument was that with their excess liquidity, the banks could now afford to lower their interest rates. Indeed, the banks lowered the interest rates marginally, but as will be discussed in Chapter V, there was little impact on investment and output.

The real impact of demonetization on RBI was that it had to make policy under increased uncertainty. RBI policy has been to control inflation. It has been of the view that keeping interest rates high will help meet this target. However, demonetization made prediction of inflation and output difficult, and upset the framework used by the RBI. RBI had no experience of what happens to prices and output when a severe cash shortage is induced in the economy.

RBI had to bear the cost of demonetization. Collecting old notes and destroying them called for accounting, transportation, shredding and other activities. There was the cost of printing new notes and distributing them all over the country. All this called for a high degree of security. A lot of paperwork and record-keeping was involved in the collection of the old notes. Dealing with excess liquidity had its own costs for the RBI.

RBI's balance sheet and income and expenditure are given in Tables 17, 18 and 19 in Annexure 13. The annual cost of printing and distribution of the notes is 4.5 per cent of the total income of the RBI.[12] Further, all costs of operations of the RBI amount to about 20 per cent of the income. Thus, RBI generates a large surplus every year. This is passed on to the government as the surplus of the RBI and provides support to the government's finances.

A large chunk of the liability of the RBI is the currency in circulation and the deposits that it holds for its various operations.[13] Currency is like a promissory note issued by the RBI. The liabilities are matched on the asset side by the foreign exchange reserves, gold and rupee securities. Demonetization impacted the liability side of the balance sheet, as the notes in circulation dropped sharply. The asset side remained mostly unaffected. This is what gave some people the idea that there may be a windfall gain for the RBI, which may translate into extra funds for the government.

Windfall Gain for the RBI Unlikely

It was expected by the government that people would not deposit their black money hoards, held in the form of the old high-denomination notes, at the banks. Out of the Rs 15.44 lakh crore of the demonetized currency, it was thought that an amount in the region of Rs 3–4 lakh crore may not be returned to banks and that would be a windfall gain for the RBI. Since a currency note is a liability of the RBI, then if some notes do not return as a result of demonetization, then the RBI's liability goes down by the corresponding amount. Its balance sheet would then show a surplus.

---

[12] See Annexure 13, Table 18.
[13] See Annexure 13, Table 19.

It was thought that this surplus could be given to the government as a dividend. The budget of the Central government would have a windfall gain, which could then be used to give to the poor via various schemes. It could also be distributed purely through cash transfer to, say, 10 crore poor families. This would amount to roughly Rs 30,000 per family. True, the promise of giving Rs 15 lakh per family could not be fulfilled, but the amount that could be given, if Rs 3 lakh crore of surplus accrued to the government, would make an impression on the poor and they would become a permanent vote bank for the ruling dispensation. A kind of Robin Hood image for the government would follow.

The money deposited in the banks belongs to the depositors and the banks are obliged to return it to them when asked for it. Remonetization meant that the RBI printed new notes and released them to the public since the demand existed. People are restocking currency in their homes and businesses, which they had earlier maintained in old notes. So, 98.8 per cent of the old currency had come back by 13 January 2017,[14] and by the end of April 80 per cent remonetization had already taken place and the level of remonetization was continuing to rise as RBI released more new notes.[15]

Digitization may mean a reduced demand for currency, but hoarding may add to the demand. It is also possible that people, losing faith in Indian currency, in the long run may go for more gold and foreign currency holdings. That would have balance of payment implications. Since both gold and foreign currency are bought with foreign exchange, the foreign exchange reserves would fall. That would reduce the assets of RBI and the surplus in its balance sheet

---

[14] See Kumar and Verma, 2017 and Annexure 7, Table 7 and Graph 10.

[15] Earlier it was mentioned that it would take eight to twelve months for full remonetization. By April end, it was six months after demonetization, so 80 per cent remonetization by that time is not out of line. Especially, since old and torn notes meant to be destroyed were also reissued.

would tend to decline. Thus, it is not clear what the long-term (net) effect on the surplus in the RBI's balance sheet would be.

It is clear that since most of the old notes have come back and the RBI is obliged to issue that much currency, RBI's liabilities did not decline with the return of the old notes. Also, since remonetization is continuing apace, in the short run there is no possibility of a surplus resulting from printing less currency notes than existed prior to demonetization. So it may be premature to think of a windfall gain for RBI and the Central government.

Impact on Banks

Banks were the front for the demonetization and remonetization of notes. They bore the brunt of the immediate burden of demonetization. They performed admirably, in spite of their lack of preparedness. They had to deal with the constant changes in rules which led to much public ire. They had to do extra paperwork and work overtime to deal with the situation. Since currency was in short supply, they had to bear the brunt of public anger. If people died in queues and the senior citizens complained of harassment, they were at the receiving end.

However, as it is always, there were the bad pennies who fouled up the system by giving new notes to favoured clients. According to news reports, old notes were changed for new notes at a 30 per cent discount by some corrupt bank employees. So some in the system made a lot of money in the process. This aggravated the shortage of notes for the general public and justified the public feeling that the bankers were deliberately not giving them the new notes they should have got.

Deposits in Jan Dhan Accounts

There was massive misuse of the Jan Dhan accounts opened two years earlier for the poor. There was a large number of zero-balance accounts. One RTI found that bankers had deposited a few rupees into these accounts so as to lower the number of zero-balance accounts. There was a spurt in deposits in these accounts after 9 November 2016.[16] It is not that a large number of accounts were opened. Rather, a lot of deposits came into the existing accounts from which simultaneous withdrawals took place. In the beginning, the pace of deposits was high, but withdrawals took place only slowly. After 30 November 2016, the pace of withdrawals increased. The total deposits in these accounts reached a peak on 7 December 2016. By 20 January 2017, almost Rs 50,000 crore had been deposited in Jan Dhan accounts and Rs 28,000 crore withdrawn. What happened with Jan Dhan accounts also occurred with the other accounts that the poorer classes had opened earlier. They became the money 'mules' for the well-off.

The PM's exhortation that the poor should not return the money of the rich who were using their accounts to recycle their old notes went unheeded. This should have been expected, since the poor are under the thumb of their employers, whether they are the farmers in rural areas or the employees in urban areas. They cannot back-stab their bosses without inviting serious consequences.

The other possibility is that the Jan Dhan accounts were not opened only by the poor but also by the lower-middle class people and petty businessmen. It stands to reason that people who are poor and in debt to private moneylenders at a high rate of interest would not open accounts to keep savings at negligible interest rates. Or, those who are poor and do not have enough to eat are not going to keep savings in the banks. If there are 26 crore Jan Dhan accounts and there are 26 crore families in the country, it is very likely that many of the accounts are fictitious or opened in the name of the poor by those who are really not poor, and who must have used these accounts to deposit their cash.

---

[16] Annexure 12, Table 16 and Graph 18.

Lower Interest Rates Did Not Help

The interest charged by banks on loans that they give is important for them to pay their depositors a return, to cover their cost of operations and make a profit for their shareholders. On the other side, the interest rate is important for economic activity, since all else being the same, if the interest rate is higher, the cost of economic activity rises and less business is done. If I wish to borrow to buy a flat and if the interest rate is higher, I have to pay a higher equated monthly instalment and my affordability declines given my salary. So I would tend to invest less. The same goes for a business which, given its profitability, would invest less at a higher interest rate.

With demonetization, a large sum of money came back to the banks as deposits, and they were flush with funds. It was expected that they could lend this money to businesses at a lower interest rate and that would spur economic activity. Indeed, the banks lowered the interest rate they were charging on loans. It was especially argued by government officials that the small-scale sector could benefit from this. But the small-scale sector was closing down because of demonetization and had no need for more credit even if the bankers had had the time to give them loans.

Businesses borrow more only when they want to expand their activity. That is when they want to increase their production capacity or produce more with the capacity they have. Unfortunately, businesses faced a decline in demand and did not need more money. Many people who wanted to buy real estate property also held back their purchase since the times seemed uncertain and they did not want to commit to a losing proposition.

The uncertainty was a result of the fact that housing prices were expected to fall, with the expected decline in the black component of the price. It was also felt that the interest rate could come down further and it would be better to wait.

Businesses faced uncertainty since the industrial sector had hardly grown in the preceding two years and there was a lot of unused capacity. Because of a decline in demand after demonetization, capacity utilization fell further. Therefore it was no use investing more.

As a result, credit off-take from the banks in October 2016 (just before demonetization), which was at a historic low for the last fifty years, fell further and became a historic low for the last sixty years. It is clear that in an economic downturn, even when interest rates drop, demand for credit does not pick up and the economy does not improve.

Banks were already suffering from high NPAs, and because of a stagnation and decline in business, the probability of a further increase in NPAs became higher. This created further uncertainty and made it difficult for the banks to lend. As discussed below, many farmers found their profitability hit and they too found it difficult to take further loans or repay what they had borrowed.

All this imposed extra costs on the banking system in the country. They had to bear the additional costs of taking back currency and reissuing currency, managing queues, counting currency, depositing it in chests, recalibrating ATMs, getting additional paperwork done for returned notes, providing additional security at the banks and stocking up the returned currency. They also had to pay interest on the old notes deposited in the bank accounts. They did deposit the extra funds they thus obtained with the RBI and got a return on that. But that was small compared with what they could have got from commercial lending. This hit their profitability.

In brief, the banking sector suffered from an overload of work, increase in deposits without a corresponding increase in lending, additional costs of ATM recalibration and so on. Costs increased without additional income, impacting the health of the already stressed banking system. It is also clear how unprepared the entire banking system, including the RBI, was to undertake the stupendous task of demonetization and remonetization.

Impact on Government Finances

By curbing the black economy, it was expected that the government's finances would improve greatly. As discussed in Chapter III, checking the black economy would lead to a sharp rise in the tax-to-GDP ratio. Even if half the black economy could be curtailed with demonetization, additional tax resources that could be collected would amount to 12 per cent of GDP, which would be twice the direct taxes collected currently. Thus, the shortage of resources for essential development would be over. This would be in addition to any windfall gain that was expected, as mentioned above. Further, if the black economy was checked, the funds spent would not get eaten away or wasted as at present. Governance would improve and the economy, and especially the poor, would benefit enormously from it. These were the crucial benefits expected of demonetization.

Increased Tax Collection Unlikely

Since the black economy has not been impacted by demonetization, any gain in tax collection is unlikely to materialize. However, it is argued that people who have made large deposits of cash can be investigated and their black incomes unearthed. Based on this, the Income Tax Department has sent out 18 lakh notices. Most of those sent notices have responded to say their income source was legitimate. The government also announced an IDS (in December 2016) to enable those with large amounts of black funds to come clean. However, this has not yielded much, and little has been declared. Clearly, the government has not been able to scare people into declaring their black incomes.

An IDS was in operation between June and September 2016. That too had not yielded much by way of declaration of black incomes.[17] The IDS during demonetization, coming so soon after the previous scheme, was not expected to do well, and that was what happened.

In his Budget speech in 2017, the finance minister said: 'Deposits of more than Rs 80 lakh crore were made in 1.48 lakh accounts, with average deposit size of Rs 3.31 crore . . . deposits between Rs 2 lakh and Rs 80 lakh were made in about 1.09 crore accounts, with an average deposit size of Rs 5.03 lakh.' These two categories of deposits added up to about Rs 10 lakh crore. Thus, two-thirds of the total of Rs 15.44 lakh crore of old notes returned to the banks were accounted for by 1.1 crore accounts. Even if 1 or 2 lakh crores of this sum proves to be black (after years of litigation, etc.), this would hardly dent the black economy, which generated as much as Rs 93 lakh crore in 2016.[18]

Simply having data that people deposited high amounts of cash does not mean that it was black money or ill-gotten money that was deposited. As already argued, many businesses collect large amounts of cash daily, and they legitimately deposit these sums into their bank accounts. The Income Tax Department can question them about the source of the funds they deposited, but cannot declare these sums to be black without investigation. And investigation takes time and effort.

The government barely audited 5 lakh income tax assessees in 2012-13. So how would it audit either the 18 lakh persons who have been sent notices, or the 1.1 crore accounts in each of which more than Rs 2 lakh in cash was deposited? In July 2016, the chairperson of the Central Board of Direct Taxes had announced that the income tax department has data on 90 lakh

---

[17] Kumar, 2016a.
[18] Kumar, 2017e.

high-value transactions carried out between 2009 and 2016. But these could not be analysed to pin down those that were illegitimate and hence linked to black income generation.

Now it is being said that the data is being computerized and big data analytics would be deployed for a 360-degree approach so the illegal deposits can be tracked. It is also claimed that with digitization, more complete information would be available and people would be caught. It is also argued that with the coming into force of GST, there would be a trail that can be tracked and the black economy checked. But the point is that big data analytics, digitization and GST have little to do with demonetization and could have been implemented independently of it. In fact, each of these policies would require a lot of preparation, and demonetization actually comes in the way of their proper implementation. We are already witness to the chaos around GST implementation because the policy was not properly planned or implemented.

Difficulty in Budget Making

A budget is drafted on the basis of likely revenue and expenditure to be incurred in the coming year. That is why the budget consists of 'estimates'. These are not final figures since these figures keep changing as the year passes and actual revenue collection and expenditure figures become available, which are then used in the government accounts. So, the budget numbers keep on changing during the year and also in subsequent years. The final budget figures become available with a time lag of several years.

The amount of revenue that can be collected depends on the growth in the economy. The expenditures depend on the continuing government schemes and what new plans are in the offing for the coming year. The government tries to match revenue increase with expenditure increase so that a deficit does not occur. In short, both revenue and expenditure have to be estimated, based on projections from the past and the plans for the future.

Planning for the future becomes difficult during a period of uncertainty since one cannot accurately plan for what is likely to happen. In such times, budgets often go wrong by big margins. Demonetization has introduced a big uncertainty in the economy. We do not know with any degree of certainty the rate of growth in 2016-17. Since that is the basis for projection of various economic measures for 2017-18, we cannot tell what will be the rate of growth in 2017-18 either. Therefore, we cannot accurately calculate the amount of revenue that can be expected. Revenue projections can go wrong because of the slowdown in business activity in the organized sector. This is the sector which pays the bulk of the taxes.

Similarly, the expenditures that need to be planned cannot be accurately calculated. For instance, when there is distress, higher allocations are required for schemes to alleviate the distress. MGNREGS, which provides employment to those in rural areas who need work, may have to be expanded since many in the unorganized sector lost work and went back to their homes in the villages. Already, in 2016-17 the expenditure on this scheme went up from the allotted Rs 38,500 crore to Rs 47,000 crore. It is said that the demand for work was even more but the funds were not available. Similarly, rural areas may need greater funds, since vegetable and fruit prices crashed and led to distress among farmers. The small-scale sector may need greater assistance since it was hit badly by demonetization.

If revenues fall short and expenditures rise, the fiscal deficit will tend to rise. Since the government is committed to lowering the deficit, it would have to cut back on expenditures. If it does not do so, the credit rating agencies may downgrade India, since for them the fiscal deficit is a key number to watch out for. Such a downgrade will send wrong signals to foreign investors. It may also lead to a rise in the rate of interest at which Indian investors borrow funds abroad.

If the government cuts back expenditures it will have to do so on the capital account items and new projects, since funds will be committed for continuing schemes and the revenue account items. This will imply lower investments and less money for expanding infrastructure and that will only aggravate the economic slowdown. The government is caught in a pincer.

Impact on Agriculture

Agriculture is a major part of the unorganized sector. It was immediately hit by the cash shortage induced by demonetization. Farmers found that cash shortage meant the Kharif crop, which had been harvested in October, could not be sold immediately. There were reports of empty '*mandis*'[19] and of traders whiling away their time since farmers were not coming to the market as they could not get cash for their produce.

However, there was a difference in what happened in north India and south India. The crop in south India is harvested earlier and also gets sold earlier. It was the north Indian farmers who were the worst affected.

The farmers who cultivate two crops a year had to sow their Rabi crop soon after harvesting the Kharif. There is moisture in the fields, which helps the new crop. Delay meant that the crop required more inputs. Delay also meant loss of productivity over time. Cash shortage also meant that the application of inputs for the Rabi crops was delayed.

Rural and semi-rural areas have fewer bank branches, and these branches also carried less cash than their city counterparts did. There were pictures of farmers queuing up overnight to withdraw money, and reports of banks running out of cash within hours of their branches' opening. The rural areas had to bear a lot of distress. However, rural areas also work on informal credit from the traders. This came in handy for many for buying their inputs, but at a high cost in terms of interest to be paid or maybe

---

[19] See Bhattacharya and Varma, 2017 and Philipose, 2016.

in terms of the premium on the price of the input. Anyhow, the cost of cultivation would have certainly gone up. Due to the protests from farmers' groups, during the demonetization period, the farmers were allowed to buy seeds and inputs using old notes after mid-November.

Due to the good monsoon after two years of drought, the area sown during the Rabi season was expected to be higher than in the previous two years. The acreage did go up,[20] but perhaps not as much as it should have. The good news is that all over north India, the weather was conducive to agriculture, and production during Rabi is expected to be a record high. The question really is, what might the productivity have been (that is, without demonetization), and how much did the farmer lose? No one has the answer to that. It also remains to be seen how much productivity suffered as a result of the delay in sowing and the delay in providing the crop inputs at the correct time. Another question to ask is, how much did the cost of production rise because of the delays in sowing and the more costly inputs?

While delay in the sale of foodgrain is not much of a problem (except for the liquidity aspect), inability to sell perishables like fruits and vegetables poses a problem. They cannot be stocked without cold storage facilities, which are limited. Potatoes, tomatoes and peas are routinely stored in the cold storage, but there is a limit to that and farmers need liquidity to carry on operations. So when the produce came to the market while demand was down, their prices collapsed.[21] In the case of pulses, there was a bumper harvest and their prices too fell sharply.

---

[20] Annexure 15, Table 21 and Graph 19, show that in spite of a good monsoon, the acreage is just about normal in 2016-17. It is less in cereals and oilseeds but higher in pulses. If the shock of demonetization was not there, perhaps it would have been higher overall.

[21] Annexure 15, Table 22 shows the fall in prices of some key agricultural commodities.

While output went up, demand flagged because of the liquidity shortage among consumers and loss of incomes in the unorganized sectors. There were reports of dumping of potatoes and tomatoes on the roads by angry farmers. In Ranchi, farmers distributed vegetables free to the consumers since it was more expensive to take the produce back. In some places, cattle were allowed to eat the crop.

The wholesale trade in foodgrains suffered, to begin with, because of the shortage of new notes. Newspapers carried picture of empty *mandis*. Farmers were not willing to take the old notes. However, there were reports of a kind of credit system evolving, with the farmer pledging his crop to a dealer for getting inputs for the next crop. Here too the farmers who had lesser capacity to hold on to their crops sold their harvest under distress at lower prices.

All these losses to farmers due to a decline in prices, their inability to sell their produce and the rise in the cost of farm inputs, have limited their ability to repay their loans in time, and this has led to an increase in NPAs. The distress to the farmers has led the new UP government to waive loans made to them. This demand is being made elsewhere in the country too. In Maharashtra, the farmers went on strike by dumping vegetables and milk on the roads and not supplying them to the urban markets.

In brief, the difficulties faced by the farming community have increased because of demonetization and could lead to an increase in problems for banking and for farming operations in the coming times. With farm loan waivers being promised by the various state governments, the fiscal crisis of the states is set to intensify.

Conclusion

This chapter looks at the possible cash holding of households and businesses, and argues that large amounts of cash cannot be held by a large number of individuals/households. So the idea that black means cash is not valid, and that is why demonetization cannot curb the black economy. It is argued that what demonetization did was to create a shortage of currency for transactions. It is argued that this has impacted production.

The impact of demonetization on the RBI and banks was most severe, since they are the entities directly involved in demonetization and remonetization of currency. The balance sheet of RBI was impacted, and there was no windfall gain. The banks had to bear extra costs. Jan Dhan accounts were misused. And, even though banks lowered interest rates consequent to increased deposits and excess liquidity, they were in no position to lend more. Businesses too did not want more credit because they were adversely affected. That is why credit off-take fell further.

Demonetization was expected to boost the government's resources, both because of its supposed impact on the black economy and declaration of higher incomes, and also because of a possible windfall gain for the RBI. This has not happened. Further, given the uncertainty about production and prices, planning for Budget 2017-18 became difficult and the figures contained therein may turn out to be erroneous, upsetting policy goals.

Finally, the impact on the all-important agriculture sector employing 47 per cent of the country's workforce was discussed, and it was pointed out that while prices of perishables and some other items collapsed, costs of production increased. This has impacted the incomes of a large number of farmers and has led to a crisis in the rural areas, which in turn has resulted in large-scale agitations and demands for farm loan waivers. This will lead to fiscal problems for the state governments.

The difficulties set into motion by demonetization leading to cash shortage will dissipate slowly. However, as will be discussed in the next chapter, its long-term impact set in, with the cash shortage giving way to the setting in of recessionary conditions arising from a fall in output, employment and investment. These conditions will take quite a while to go away because of the change in expectations.

V

Demonetization: The Macroeconomic Cost

The prime minister had said that there would be pain in the economy. But, post-January 2017, the government has said that the demonetization has not imposed any cost but instead has been beneficial. The minister of finance categorically stated, after the third quarter data for 2016-17 showed the economy grew at 7 per cent, that there was no adverse impact of the 2016 demonetization on the economy. The implication is that nothing happened to the economy and that all the hundreds of press reports on the state of affairs in the country from November 2016 to January 2017 were simply someone's imagination. More concretely, the finance minister was combative when the data in December 2016 showed that the economy was doing well. This needs analysis, to see what was actually going on in the economy.

Demonetization: A Shock to the Economy

Demonetization gave a sharp jolt to the economy by all accounts. This, in technical jargon, is called a shock. A drought leading to a fall in agricultural output is a shock. The global financial collapse in 2007 was a shock to the world economy. So, in simple terms, an economic shock is when the normal flow of the economy is severely disturbed. Many things can change the flow of an economy, such as a policy of privatization or the announcement of loan waivers. These are important, but not severe enough to disturb the entire flow of the economy. They have a sectoral impact at best, while a shock impacts the entire economy and large numbers of people.

It is in this sense that Demonetization 2016 was a shock to large parts of the economy (as discussed in the previous chapter). The unorganized sectors collapsed, and each of the three main sectors of the economy—agriculture, industry and services—was impacted. Some entities benefited though. During the global crisis that began in 2007, people suffered from depression and psychiatrists did well. Sales of antidepressants shot up and the demand for security services soared, but that did not mean the global economy did well. During demonetization, new black incomes were generated, or the digital platforms did well, but that does not mean the economy as a whole did well.

As discussed earlier, production in agriculture went up because of good rains and ideal weather conditions, but that did not mean the sector did not receive a shock in November 2016. Its output could have been even higher if the disturbance in November had not taken place. Its price realizations could have been higher if demand had not collapsed, sending the incomes of a large number of farmers plunging instead of rising. This was evident from farmers' strong agitation demanding loan waivers.

An economic shock imposes costs on the economy, of which there are a variety. The Centre for Monitoring Indian Economy (CMIE) first came out with a conservative figure of the costs to the economy of Rs 1.28 lakh crore over the fifty days from 8 November 2016 up to the end of December[1] that year. These costs consisted of the following:

1. Loss of wages due to people standing in queues
2. Costs to banks on account of the extra work and from not being able to do their normal work

---

[1] CMIE, 2016.

3. Costs to the RBI and the government
4. Costs due to postponement of discretionary demand and loss of production

These items do not cover the full impact of demonetization. The list should consist of additional items, such as the impact on the unorganized sector, which is where the main impact took place. The impact was not just the discomfort of standing in queues but loss of employment. Demand fell not only due to discretionary demand being postponed but due to the fall in employment and the shutting down of unorganized-sector units. The impact on trade, transport, real estate, finance and other industries also needs to be taken into account. The cost of new ways of generating black incomes also needs to be factored in. Finally, the impact continued for much longer than the fifty days up to the end of December.

Not only were the costs economic, to which some numbers can be attached, but also political and social. I will discuss them in more detail in Chapter VII. To these costs no numbers can be attached. People who could not feed their families two square meals due to unemployment, those whose family members did not get timely attention at hospitals, those who faced difficulties in conducting a wedding in the family, or those who had to postpone their important travel plans had to bear costs that cannot be factored in.

There was the impact on some crucial institutions of democracy—the functioning of the Parliament or of the RBI, the reliability of the budget numbers and of the statistical division of the government which puts out data on growth of the economy. The accountability of the system was eroded (more on this later in the book). The tax departments had to work overtime and tried to unsuccessfully trace those with black money. What would this do to the morale of the departments, which are grossly understaffed? People were forced to use electronic means of transactions when they were not comfortable with them. The impact on the credibility of the banking system and of currency also needs to be factored in. The rise in NPAs leading to loss of profitability for the banks, and also the pressure on them to waive loans are other costs to factor in.

While the social and political costs, and costs due to damage to important democratic institutions cannot be calculated, the cost in terms of lost output can be calculated. This is the biggest cost and also the long-term one because it is associated with the decline in investment.

The shock of demonetization lowered the rate of growth of the economy in comparison to what it might have been if the shock had not been administered. How much was this impact? The government has been arguing that ever since it came to power in 2014-15, the economy has experienced a rising trend of growth. The data on quarterly growth rates[2] contradict this. They show that over the last year and a half there is a declining trend of growth. If the annual trend of growth is taken from 2012-13 and projected to 2016-17, then it would indeed come to 8.5 per cent.[3] The Economic Survey 2017 projects this, and the Union budgets 2016-17 and 2017-18 are formulated on this assumption.

So, by a crude estimate, assuming that the government-announced rate of growth for the last quarter of 2016-17, at 6.1 per cent, is correct, there is a drop in rate of growth for one quarter of about 2.4 per cent. The third quarter rate of growth has been estimated at 7 per cent, and that is a drop of 1.5 per cent. This implies that there was a drop in output of Rs 1.5 lakh crore compared with the potential. However, this is an underestimate because the actual rate of growth of the economy for the two quarters under reference was much lower than the government

---

[2] See Graph 3 in Annexure 5.
[3] See date in Graph 2 in Annexure 5.

data suggests. It needs to be remembered that these government figures are not firm figures but guesses, and that is why they are called provisional, advance and revised estimates.

Government Data on the Impact of Demonetization

The finance minister, arguing that demonetization has not had any negative impact, quoted data from the Index of Industrial Production, Rabi sowing,[4] tax collection[5] and so on, to show how robust the government growth numbers were. Let us analyse these one at a time.

Higher Tax Collections in November

The mystery of higher growth in industrial production can be resolved by simply looking at the methodology of estimating India's GDP (more on it later in this chapter). As discussed earlier, the real impact of cash shortage was felt in the unorganized sectors of the economy. These sectors are not captured in the data on the industrial sector. Hence the data on the industrial sector's growth is incomplete, and it is so precisely where the sharp fall in production occurred. The fall in production in the industrial sector could not be captured.

Data show that production in the unorganized sectors of the economy accounts for 45 per cent of the total output.[6] Employment in this sector is 93 per cent of the total employment. So, demonetization impacted 45 per cent of the output and 93 per cent of the workforce in the country. Even if agriculture is separated from the unorganized sector, since it was affected differently from the rest, the unorganized non-agriculture sector

---

[4] The Indian Express, 2017.
[5] Ray, 2017.
[6] See Table 24 and Graph 21 in Annexure 16.

accounts for 31 per cent of GDP or almost a third of it. If this is severely hit then it will certainly lead to a lower rate of growth in the economy.[7]

Even the organized sector got hit, as the data on corporation tax seems to suggest.[8] Corporation tax is paid by companies on their profits and they may be taken to represent the organized sector of the economy. The data show that even before demonetization, corporation tax collection was not growing, and in fact was negative for many of the months preceding demonetization. October and November data show a sharp upsurge in this tax payment, 31 per cent and 164 per cent. As stated earlier in Chapter I, because the companies were allowed to use old notes to pay their taxes there was an upsurge in tax payments. Also, there was a rush to claim cash in hand and also for payment of tax arrears. That is why in December and January, growth became negative. For the year as a whole, the increase in corporation tax payment was only 6.7 per cent, which was barely above the rate of inflation and indicated very tepid growth in this sector.

Further, from 2016-17, advance income tax had to be paid in June so that more tax was collected in the initial nine months of the fiscal year. Since old currency could be used to pay the taxes, many paid their taxes in advance to get rid of their demonetized currency. Again, after spiking in November 2016, the rate of growth in corporation tax fell. But, while the unorganized sector suffered a decline in demand, some of the demand shifted to the organized sector and prevented its demand from falling off sharply. So the organized sector was not as badly affected as it could have been.

Union excise duties and service tax payments showed a consistent high growth during the year. This possibly reflects the

---

[7] For a rough estimate, see Annexure 19.
[8] See Table 27 and Graph 24 in Annexure 17.

rise in their tax rates in the Budget 2016-17. Also, the government took advantage of the fall in prices of crude petroleum to raise the duties on petroleum products. Both these taxes also showed a spike in November and then a drop. Again, there was a rush to pay these taxes and the arrears using old notes.

It must be noted that some commodities were allowed to be bought with the old notes, and these saw a spike in demand. Of these, petro goods saw a spike as people got their vehicles' tanks filled. Medicines could be bought, which people stocked up in bulk. As mentioned earlier, people booked tickets on airlines and railways only to cancel them later. In a sense, the indirect tax data do not suggest a spike in production. The corporation tax data are a better indicator of the health of the organized sector and that does not support the finance minister's argument of a booming economy.

There was a very sharp spike of 500 per cent in payment of other taxes. It was also reported that property tax collections rose sharply, and again many paid their arrears using their old notes. None of this suggests a sharp rise in output. It only represents a response to a crisis for the organized-sector businesses.

Another argument in defence of demonetization was that many firms may have declared their actual production, including their earlier undeclared production, to legitimize the cash they held. Thus, even though their total production may have dropped, their declared production may have continued to rise at the old rate of growth. The implication would be that black income generation declined as a result of demonetization. However, this would not explain the sharp rise in tax payments in November and then a sharp fall in their rate of growth. This, then, is an unlikely explanation.

The government has claimed that tax buoyancy was high in 2016-17, and it argued that this supported the contention that production did not suffer and continued to grow as before. But this does not factor in changes in policy, like the introduction of IDS1 and IDS2. Be that as it may, since most of the tax is paid by the corporate sector and the organized sector, this could be true. But this does not capture what happened to the unorganized sectors of the economy, and that is where demonetization really hurt.

Increase in Acreage under Rabi Sowing

The agriculture minister claimed that Rabi sowing up to 31 December 2016 was 7 per cent higher than last year.[9] The implication was that demonetization did not impact agriculture. The critics, however, had argued that there was a crisis in agriculture and that was why sowing was affected.

An increase in Rabi sowing was expected, because after two drought years in 2014-15 and 2015-16, the monsoon was good and planting in Kharif had shown an increase. Since moisture levels in the ground were good, a higher sowing of the Rabi crop was natural. The question is, how much should the sowing have increased by? As data show, planting was less than in the earlier good-crop years, like 2013-14.[10] It was also not much above the normal for Rabi crops in the past.

It is also likely that productivity in agriculture was higher than earlier because of the better weather this year, but the issue again is, if timely inputs had been available, productivity in agriculture could have been even higher. The real issue is, how much was the impact of the increase in output on farm incomes?

As argued earlier in the book, there was the twin impact of a rise in output and fall in demand because of the squeezing of incomes so that the prices of many agricultural products, like vegetables and lentils, declined. Simultaneously, the costs of cultivation rose because of the higher cost of both credit and inputs (purchased using old notes). This squeezed the incomes of a large number of farmers even more, dragging down their contribution to the national income.

---

[9] The Indian Express, 2017.
[10] See Table 21, Annexure 15.

In brief, the government's argument based on some sketchy data that demonetization did not affect the economy is not convincing. It does not capture demonetization's real impact on the economy.

New Black Incomes

Demonetization 2016 also threw up opportunities for the generation of some new black incomes. These had not been generated prior to demonetization.

For instance, people sold their old currency for a discount of 30 per cent to 40 per cent. Those who took these notes made a profit.

The rich used the poor and the workers as 'money mules'. They provided the poor with a certain sum of money to deposit in their bank accounts, withdraw it, return 70 per cent to 80 per cent of it and keep the rest for themselves. While this was not black income in the hands of the poor or the workers, it helped legitimize money which was black. Jan Dhan accounts were used in this way and the deposits in these accounts rose sharply.[11] Some businessmen were reported to have paid advance salary to their workers. The old notes got used and when their company's sales materialized later, their revenue was all in new notes so that their black cash got converted into new currency.

Companies also used shell companies and *havala* to transfer funds and/or legitimize them. While this may have resulted in increased tax payments to a certain extent for a month, as discussed in the previous section, it strengthened the black economy further.[12]

---

[11] See Annexure 12.

[12] Of late, the government has taken action against shell companies but it is not clear what the impact of this step would be.

As discussed earlier, the credibility of currency and of banks has been dented. Over time, this will result in a shift towards the holding of more gold and foreign currency, which will be used to circulate black money. Many may demand payment abroad for the assets they sell. This would accelerate the flight of capital from India. As mentioned earlier, this would impact foreign trade, demand for gold, real estate markets and foreign exchange reserves.

In effect, while the benefits of demonetization in curbing the black economy were few, it led to some new ways of generating and converting old black notes to new notes. Would there be a long-term psychological impact on black income generators, and would they now be more afraid to generate black incomes? At this point of time it is hard to tell. Given the way people have recycled their black hoards and the poor response to the PMGKY and IDS, it does not seem likely that the black money generators have turned over a new leaf. Any psychological makeover will take time.

Transactions Difficult: Demand Hit

It is clear that a one-shot demobilization does not help in controlling the black economy, even if surprise is achieved. So the question is whether the cost of demonetization is justified in any way. If the real purpose was only to eliminate counterfeit currency, that could have been achieved by a gradual withdrawal of currency, as was done with high-denomination notes printed before 2005. That was done over three years. However, it is clear that that did not help eliminate counterfeit currency. The government, by raising this issue as one of the reasons for Demonetization 2016, has admitted that fake currency notes of the new variety have reappeared.

If demonetization had been planned and an adequate amount of new currency was made available as the old notes were withdrawn, then the impact on the economy would have been minimal. As argued earlier in Chapter II, cash exists only to enable transactions to take place, especially in the unorganized sector, which has little or no access to banks and electronic modes of transactions.[13]

With the withdrawal of Rs 15.44 lakh crore out of the Rs 17.9 lakh crore of currency in circulation with the public, there was a massive shortage of the medium of exchange. This made transactions difficult. It is true that cash can be substituted with plastic money or cheques, but the poor and small businesses hardly use them. The habit of using plastic money picks up slowly. That is why, as remonetization has increased, people who had switched to using electronic means of transactions have been switching back to using cash. At petrol stations, one can again see a lot of cash being used.

Even those who had cash in smaller denominations did not use it out of abundant caution. There was a sharp rise in the holding of currency for precautionary purposes, and a part of the available cash with the public was immobilized, thus aggravating shortages. As discussed earlier, several such reasons aggravated the shortage of cash for the ordinary public.

Banks complained that the money they were issuing was not coming back to them. Usually, people spend the money they withdraw from their bank account and that comes back to the banks via expenditures. It is then recycled to the public again. This determines how quickly money circulates in the economy. This is referred to as the 'velocity of circulation'.[14] If it increases, it can mitigate shortage of cash with the public. But the opposite happened, aggravating the shortage of cash with the public.

The net result of all this was that the shortage of cash with the public lasted longer than the government expected. This

---

[13] Kumar, 2017b.
[14] See Chapter II.

made transactions more difficult. Also, people reduced their transactions by postponing their discretionary purchases. Those in the organized sectors reduced their demand for consumer durables and semi-durables or curbed their visits to restaurants or their travel plans. For those in the unorganized sector who lost jobs and incomes, the decline in demand from them was much more drastic.

Impact on Economic Growth

The government's argument that demonetization has had no impact on the economy because growth has been robust belies its own earlier exhortations to the public to bear the pain for long-term gains. As discussed above, there was pain for major sectors of the economy, primarily in the unorganized sectors. The government is quoting the quarterly rates of growth to prove its point. There are problems with this. No data are available for the non-agriculture component of the unorganized sector on a quarterly basis. The numbers for the various parts of this component are based on data which comes from benchmark surveys conducted once every few years. In the meanwhile, some indices from the organized sector are used to project the data for these sectors.

Measuring the Quarterly Rate of Growth of the Economy

How is GDP growth calculated? It is based on data from the various sectors and sub-sectors of the economy. Data are needed from the sub-sectors, and because of the specificity of each of them a different method is used for calculating the growth rate for these sub-sectors. The methodology is changed from time to time as lacunae are found and fixed after consultation, and this practice is usually not questioned by analysts. However, the actual data are not usually available immediately so that some indicative data are used. Thus, immediately, only 'estimates' of growth can be made. These are revised from time to time and therefore they are called provisional, advance and revised estimates.

One must ask whether the methodology devised for normal times can be applied when the economy has experienced a big shock. Surveys by manufacturers, business associations and other entities in December 2016 and January 2017 show that after 8 November 2016, employment, production and investment were hit hard in a whole range of sectors. Was this taken into account in the estimation of GDP growth?

The government document,[15] 'Methodology For Estimating Quarterly GDP', says, 'The production approach used for compiling the QGVA [Quarterly Gross Value Added] estimates is broadly on the benchmark-indicator method.' The document adds, 'A key indicator or a set of key indicators for which data in volume or quantity terms is available on quarterly basis are used to extrapolate the value of output/value added estimates of the previous year.' It also says, 'In general terms, quarterly estimates of Gross Value Added [GVA] are extrapolations of annual series of GVA.' All these statements point to the use of the 'benchmark-indicator' and extrapolation of the 'value of output/value added estimates of the previous year'.

What the quotation from the government document means is that for the unorganized sectors for which data are not immediately available, some indicators are used—for instance, the ratio of production in organized industry to that in the unorganized sector, along with how much employment is being generated. But when the economy is severely impacted, can the same benchmark indicators be used as in earlier years? Indeed not, because the ratio of the organized to unorganized sectors changed on 9 November 2016. So, how can the projection from pre-8 November 2016 be valid for the period immediately

---

[15] GoI, 2013.

following? Projection from the previous year (2015-16) would be even less valid.

As already argued, the impact of shortage of cash was different for the organized and unorganized sectors, and therefore the impact on their output was also different. That is why the ratio changed. The government's press note giving the growth figures for GVA says, 'GVA from quasi corporate and unorganised segment has been estimated using IIP [Index of Industrial Production] of manufacturing.'[16] But, as argued above, the IIP reflects the growth of the organized sector. So, in the changed circumstances after 9 November 2016, it cannot be used to estimate the unorganized-sector production. The incorrect assumption is that a sub-sector that is declining is taken to be growing at the same rate as the organized sector.

The government's press note adds, 'IIP from manufacturing sector registered a growth rate of (-) 0.5 per cent during April-December 2016-17.' But the data show that the manufacturing sector grew at 7.7 per cent. Is this an overstatement of the organized-sector growth? If so, it is doubly wrong to use it to estimate the unorganized-sector growth. It is due to this series of mistakes in the methodology that the official data showed a 7 per cent rate of growth. Should a note of caution not have been inserted? The head of the government's statistical department had argued that at present the impact of demonetization on the economy cannot be estimated. A lot more data are needed. If that is so, the official estimates are premature. As such, instead of relying on official data, one should go by the reports of what is happening on the ground.

The Likely Rate of Growth

To estimate the real rate of growth in the economy, one would have to create alternative scenarios. This can be done in two ways.

---

[16] GoI, 2017g.

Overall, let us assume that for the first seven months till October 2016, the economy grew at the rate given by the government statistics, namely, 7.7 per cent.

In Scenario 1 in Annexure 19, it is assumed that there was some impact of demonetization on the organized sectors, but not too drastic. So, in the period November to January when there was a cash crunch, this sector did not grow. As the cash crunch declined, this sector is assumed to have grown at 2 per cent in February-March 2017. Agriculture is assumed to have grown at the rate given by the government, namely, 4 per cent.[17] The final assumption is that the unorganized non-agriculture sectors collapsed at -60 per cent in the November-to-January period and then at -30 per cent in the February-March period.

When all this is factored in, the table shows that post-November 2016, the economy declined by 14 per cent, and for the year as a whole it declined at 1.2 per cent.

In Scenario 2, all the sectors were taken to be affected less than in Scenario 1. The organized sector was taken to grow at 2 per cent in the November-to-January period, and by 5 per cent in February-March. Agriculture was assumed to grow at the same rate as given by the government.[18] The unorganized non-agriculture sector was taken to grow at -50 per cent in the November-to-January period and at -20 per cent in February-March.

So, in this milder scenario, in the post-demonetization period, the economy declined at -9 per cent, and for the year as a whole grew by 0.55 per cent.

These growth figures are far from the government-announced 7 per cent rate of growth for 2016-17. The government takes refuge in the corroboration received from international agencies like, the IMF, the World Bank and the ADB, supporting its contention that the economy grew at around 7 per cent in

---

[17] GoI, 2017c.
[18] GoI, 2017c.

2016-17. But, this is of little use since these agencies do not collect independent data and rely on what the government provides them. There is also an understanding that these agencies consult the government before releasing their results. So what they put out cannot be considered as independent corroboration of the government's position.

In brief, the shock to the economy was that up to October 2016, the economy grew at 7.7 per cent, and after that, under the 'better' scenario, it declined at 9 per cent. The overall rate of growth for the year fell by 7.1 per cent. With a GDP of Rs 135 lakh crore in 2015-16, this amounts to a reduction of GDP of Rs 9.4 lakh crore. This is the real cost of demonetization. And this does not include the decline in the production in the agriculture sector due to the shock.

Recessionary Conditions Taking Hold

The previous section showed that the cost to the economy was primarily the decline of the growth rate of the economy. The other costs estimated are small compared with this.[19] However, this is a short-run cost. There are bigger long-term costs as well.

There was unemployment in the unorganized sector as business and trade suffered. Workers and owners lost incomes and that also led to a decline in demand from the organized sectors. As already mentioned, discretionary demand was also hit as even those belonging to the organized sectors experienced shortage of cash. This also impacted demand from the organized sectors. A wide variety of companies in the organized sectors reported a drop in sales.[20] This affected capacity utilization in industry. Initially, sales in malls and fancy shops also declined, but this picked up since customers could use other forms of payment.

---

[19] For instance the cost given in CMIE, 2016.
[20] See Annexure 20.

Demand from e-commerce platforms increased because of the possibility of use of plastic money. There was a shift in demand from the informal to the formal markets. But, in the net, there was a dislocation of trade and commerce.

The FMCG and the two-wheeler industries are examples of the slowdown in the organized sector. Even sales of luxury cars fell, for the first time in twenty-five years. Hotels and restaurants reported lower footfalls. Transporters and wholesale markets reported a decline in volumes.[21]

If the decline was only for a short period of time, say fifteen or twenty days, the economy could have recovered quickly. Since a substantial shortage of cash lasted for more than five months, the economy as a whole, and more specifically the unorganized sector, remained stressed for at least this period and even after that their recovery has been uncertain. This has resulted in increased uncertainty in the economy and has affected investment.

As discussed earlier, industry's rate of growth had been sluggish since 2014-15. Its capacity utilization was already down to 75 per cent before demonetization was announced.[22] When capacity utilization is down, industry reduces investment. If it does not do so, it will be saddled with even more excess capital which lies idle, and that lowers its profitability. So, investments typically decline when there is excess capacity in an industry, and that is what happened in India after 8 November 2016. In the December quarter, 2016, according to CMIE, investment proposals were down to Rs 1.25 lakh crore, which was the worst for this quarter compared to the preceding nine quarters.[23] The average for the nine preceding quarters of the Modi government

---

[21] Annexure 20 gives a list of sectors and industries reporting a negative impact in the months immediately following the announcement of 8 November 2016.

[22] See Annexure 21 and RBI, 2017d.

[23] ET Bureau, 2017.

was Rs 2.36 lakh crore in investment proposals. It had reduced to almost 55 per cent of what it had been on an average in the preceding nine quarters.

In brief, for at least five months till the end of 2016-17, the economy saw a fall in output, employment, profits, capacity utilization, bank profitability and investment. Various surveys conducted in December 2016 and January 2017 showed the adverse impact of demonetization. This could have been a short-run phenomenon, so long as investment was not hit. But once investment is hit, then it becomes a longer-term impact, referred to as recessionary conditions in the economy.

Uncertainty, NPAs and Credit Off-take

The problem was aggravated by what was happening to the banking system in India. Banks were already saddled with NPAs.[24] These are loans where the borrower is unable to pay the interest due, much less the principal amount borrowed. NPAs lead to balance sheet problems for the banks and reduce their capacity to lend more. Demonetization, leading to a fall in profits in many industries and increasing the possibility of loan default in agriculture, increased the chances of a further rise in NPAs of banks.

The largest amount of NPAs was on account of the large-infrastructure companies. India is woefully lacking in infrastructure and this is where additional investments can be made to revive the economy. But given the large NPAs with banks, they were not in a position to lend more and given that the companies could not repay their loans, they were not in a position to borrow more to increase their investments. This reduced the prospect of a revival of demand in the economy. As a result, private-sector investment has declined to rather low levels

---

[24] Its historical evolution in the last decade is given in Annexure 22.

(mentioned above) and cannot rise in the near future unless the balance sheets of the banks and the companies are cleaned up.[25]

The NPA problem is partly the reason for the low off-take of credit from the banks. However, there is another reason for this. Prior to demonetization, demand for credit was low because industry had found other avenues of borrowing, such as private parties or mutual funds. However, this does not explain the sharp decline in credit off-take from the banking system, which had fallen to a historic, fifty-year low. After demonetization it fell to a sixty-year low. Only a slowdown can explain this.

A key driver of investment in an economy is the level of uncertainty. Uncertainty implies that the expected return on investment may not materialize. So, at a given level of expected profits from an investment, if uncertainty rises, that investment may not take place. While each investment carries a specific level of risk or uncertainty, there is a general level of uncertainty associated with an economy or an industry. When the general climate turns adverse, the specific industry-level climate too usually deteriorates.

Due to demonetization, there was a decline in profits and an increase in uncertainty since it was not clear when a turnaround may take place. These factors raised the level of uncertainty in the economy, which is bad for investment. The problem is compounded by the uncertainty emanating from external factors. There is the changing global environment, with Mr Trump increasingly protecting the US markets, BREXIT leading to complications for Indian companies doing business in the EU, and sentiment against immigration in many countries. Thus, there is uncertainty about exports as a source of additional demand in India. The rising sentiment against import of workers in many advanced countries will lead to fewer remittances and rise in unemployment in India.

The implementation of GST has brought about a huge uncertainty in the economy. This tax is so complex that no

---

[25] It is referred to as the twin balance sheet problem in GOI, 2017c.

one understands what is going on.[26] Companies and banks are grappling with the fact that they would have to register in each of the states and union territories they operate in. Since there are going to be three taxes, SGST, CGST and IGST, and there are thirty-one states and union territories, there will be ninety-three registrations required. Other paperwork or computer work has increased, making the task of compliance difficult.

Finally, if the economy is adversely affected by all the above-mentioned factors, tax collection would rise much less than planned and the fiscal deficit would expand. The government is sensitive to the credit rating agencies, and they frown on any rise in the fiscal deficit. That could lead the government to cut back its expenditures, which would in turn aggravate the demand shortage in the private sector.

In brief, the problem would convert from a short-run problem of a few months of demand decline to a long-term problem of recessionary conditions taking hold of the economy.

V-shaped Recovery Not in Sight

The government propagated the idea that there would be a V-shaped recovery in the economy: There would be a temporary fall in demand and a decline in output because of the cash shortage, but as the shortage declined there would be a sharp recovery in the economy. Businesses and most financial analysts bought this line. This has not happened, and the economy continues to slow down. Even at the end of April 2017, only 80 per cent of the remonetization had taken place, and shortage of cash continues in the rural and semi-urban areas. The experts did not factor in the other changes that take place when there is a shortage of currency notes. Once investment and employment decline, there are long-term effects which delay recovery.

---

[26] See Kumar, 2017k for an exposition of the difficulties faced by businesses.

An argument justifying the higher-than-expected rate of growth during the months November to January is that businesses declared their true production to legitimize their cash holdings—that, even though production actually declined, some of the formerly undeclared production was now declared so as to justify the black money being deposited in the banks. How far is this correct? It is possible—maybe that is why the collection of excise and direct taxes rose during the period—but unlikely.

Doubts emerge about this line of argument as businesses have not declared much under the new IDS announced and had only deposited Rs 4900 crore. The PMGKY was a kind of amnesty for declaration of black incomes. Be that as it may, even if businesses declared their black incomes, that still implies a decline in production and a fall in their capacity utilization.

If the black economy could have been checked, then that could have given a boost to the economy via better tax collection and a boost to the pro-poor expenditures.[27] This is not going to happen since the black economy has been hardly affected by demonetization. If banks flush with funds could have lent more to businesses, especially to the small ones, then could that have helped? Indeed, but as already argued a little earlier, with a decline in demand, investment is declining and not rising. So, in spite of a cut in interest rates, demand for credit has not increased and investment has not risen. The experience of the global financial downturn in 2007 suggests that in the advanced countries, demand and investment did not revive even after interest rates were cut to almost zero. A prolonged cash shortage has meant that more permanent changes have emerged via decline in output, employment and investment, and that has led to the setting in of recessionary conditions in the economy.

---

[27] As discussed in Chapter III.

Conclusion

All in all, a move that was expected to be a historic high for the government has led to a crisis where none existed before the announcement of demonetization. A shock was dealt to the entire economy; it did not mean a decline in just some sectors. The government produced data to show that there was no negative impact of demonetization but the data do not support that. There was a spurt in tax growth in November for special reasons, which then fell sharply in most cases.

There was a fall in incomes and employment, which the government data does not capture because it does not separately factor in the unorganized sector's decline. If this is factored in, then under alternative scenarios, the rate of growth of the economy for 2016-17 turns out to be negative or close to zero rather than 7.7 per cent. So the monetary cost of the demonetization to the economy is roughly Rs 10 lakh crore. The intangible costs to the political and social fabric of the country cannot even be calculated. Finally, it is pointed out that the already low capacity utilization in industry fell further, and that impacted their profitability and led to an increase in the NPAs of banks. These in turn led to a further decline in investment in the economy. The end result has been that a short-run problem became a long-term problem, with recessionary conditions setting in. A V-shaped recovery was nowhere evident.

VI

Shifting Goalposts

Moving Towards a Cashless Economy

The government quickly realized that demonetization was not going to impact the black economy or counterfeiting or terrorism. To get out of this embarrassing situation, suddenly, within two weeks of its initial announcement, it started saying that the move would make the economy 'cashless'. It argued that this would have tremendous advantages for the economy. The large informal sector would become formalized and come into the tax net. It was argued that there would be greater efficiency in the economy because use of cash is costly for the economy. People would not have to carry currency and would not have to visit banks.

However, it was also realized that most advanced economies in the world also use a lot of currency, so India was not going to be cashless any time soon. In the top ten most cashless countries, the percentage of non-bank use of cash is still substantial.[1] In South Korea, the use of cash is still to the extent of 30 per cent. Soon the realization dawned on the government that a cashless economy was not going to happen soon. The official line then changed and it was said that the objective was for the country to become a 'less cash' economy. But India has been moving

---

[1] See Table 32 in Annexure 23.

in that direction for some time now, with the increasing use of credit, debit and electronic means of transferring money.[2] The use of cheques was never widespread because of the enormous fraud that goes on in business. People deliberately bounce their cheques. Even though this is a criminal offence under Section 138, of the Negotiable Instruments Act, 1881, cheque-bouncing cases, which should be solved in a few months, go on for years so that there is little fear of prosecution. This situation is not going to change any time soon given the amount of fraud in the system.

There is another reason for greater use of cash in India, and that is, the well-off have black incomes which they wish to spend and they do that in cash. So it is not just the poor who spend cash, it is also the very rich who do so. Unless the black economy is curtailed, the widespread use of cash will continue and slow down India's path to a 'less cash' economy.

However, one has to be clear that use of cash in India is not unduly large. The measure for this is the ratio of cash to GDP. It is said that this is about 12 per cent for the Indian economy. However, that is for the white economy. There is also a 62 per cent black economy which circulates cash. For the white and black economies together, the ratio of cash to GDP in India would come down to about 7.2 per cent of the actual GDP (black plus white). This is not a large number. In fact, the ratio for an advanced economy like Japan is 18.6 per cent.[3] Economies like Nigeria with considerable corruption, have a ratio of 1.5 per cent, which is similar to the ratio in some of the least corrupt countries like the Scandinavian nations. So, cash and corruption are not necessarily related.

The government is not going about its task of promoting a 'less cash' economy in a systematic manner. It has allowed

---

[2] Table 34 in Annexure 23 shows the extent of infrastructure for electronic transfers in India.
[3] See Annexure 23, Graph 36.

banks to impose levies on withdrawal of money and use of ATMs, forcing people to hold on to larger amounts of cash. Additionally, given that the credibility of banks has been dented because people could not withdraw their own cash, people are likely to hold more cash than earlier. It is another matter that the credibility of currency has also been dented and people would now tend to hold more gold and foreign exchange than earlier. This would dent the balance of payment (BOP) for India, which is not doing all that well even though it is currently under control.

'Less Cash' Economy, a Difficult Objective

However, a 'less cash' economy also needs two critical requirements that are missing at present. First, a huge infrastructure of banks, point of sale (PoS) machines for reading debit and credit cards, and good Internet connectivity for the use of mobile wallets. India is way behind other countries in this respect.[4] Above all, without assured electricity and an adequate number of towers so that call drops do not occur routinely, none of this would work smoothly. Creating such an infrastructure needs time and advance preparations. None of this was immediately possible after Demonetization 2016, given that the entire attention of the government was focused on handling the cash shortage and its fallout, both economic and social.

So, in just the same way that demonetization was announced without preparation, the country was unprepared even for a 'less cash' situation. Once the cash crunch came, people started switching to more digital forms of transactions.[5] The data and graphs show that in November there was a decline in cashless transactions because overall transactions dipped. In December there was a spurt, but again there followed a dip. Another spurt

---

[4] See Annexure 23, Table 33.
[5] See Annexure 24, Tables 35 and 36, and Graphs 37 to 40.

came in March 2017 which was tax related, to be again followed by a dip. So, as remonetization proceeded apace, people started to switch to using more cash.

There is also the issue of financial literacy among the population. Any time a new technology is introduced, it takes time for people to switch to it because individuals are not automatons. They do not understand the technology and often resist change in their habits. They need to be trained for use of the new technology. Given the vast amount of illiteracy and poor training among the bulk of the population, financial literacy will take time. This would be especially true of the elderly, who are loath to use new technologies and are comfortable doing things the old way. Many worry that a wrong button pressed could mean a loss of money without trace. They know about hard cash and that it can be stolen, but it is still something in their control. What happens in the cloud is not clear to them.

Two more issues come up in this context: Cybersecurity, and regulation of banks and companies providing digital platforms for digital transactions. Those using the Internet have often been victims of phishing and hacking. If financial-sector accounts get hacked in spite of increased security, people would lose money. Credit card companies are constantly improving their security measures since so much hacking is going on and card theft taking place. To begin with, there was only a signature required at the establishment where the card was used, afterwards a chip was placed in the card, and now one has to key in a PIN or, in the case of Internet transactions, use a one-time password or an SMS when a credit or debit card is used.

The increase in cybercrime in India is depicted in Annexure 25. The rise in cybercrime in the period 2013-15 has been rapid.[6] Among the motives for these crimes, greed was the

---

[6] See Table 37.

dominant one.[7] Many websites, including the supposedly more secure government sites, were hacked and many cybersecurity breaches took place.[8] Finally, it is important to note that some big cybersecurity breaches have taken place globally in 2016.[9]

SBI had data of millions of cards stolen in 2016, and had to reissue 3.2 million cards.[10] The WannaCry ransomware virus attack in May 2017 stopped a large number of companies from doing business electronically, and this included Indian banks which shut down their ATMs and other machines, and had to work manually. If Edward Snowden could steal the data of NSA, one of the most secret US agencies in the world, the data of any entity can be stolen. The Indian government has not prepared itself with a plan for cybersecurity, which is crucial for digitization. If a big theft takes place or data is stolen, people will revert to use of cash, and digitization would be discredited.

There has been data leakage in India from the supposedly foolproof Aadhaar Card system. In the US a marketing company working for the Republican National Committee accidentally left sensitive personal details of almost 62 per cent of the US population exposed.[11] Thus, by mistake or by the design of interested parties, huge amounts of data are getting leaked all the time and this has the potential of discrediting digitalization.

The issue of regulation of the companies and banks going in for digitization is crucial so that the consumer does not get cheated. Transaction charges are constantly being raised to take advantage of the helpless public. If digitization makes services cheaper than use of cash, then the public should not be charged for using these services. Use of ATMs was free till recently, and

---

[7] See Table 38.
[8] See Annexure 25, Table 39.
[9] See Annexure 25, Table 40.
[10] See Shukla and Bhakta, 2016.
[11] Wilts, 2017.

now, suddenly, substantial charges are being levied. There is an oligopolistic element in all this. Banks, having lost a lot of money due to NPAs, are trying to recoup their losses from the hapless public, which now has less choice. Electronic transfer charges by banks are also becoming costly. These steps dissuade people from voluntarily going digital. If digitization leads to increase in efficiency, then the charges should be reduced. Regulation is necessary so that the public does not lose out.

In brief, going 'less cash' or cashless was an afterthought, to cover up the government's lack of success in dealing with the black economy. In the initial announcement, this was not mentioned as a goal of demonetization. In fact, these two have no link with each other and they could have been done independent of each other. Going 'less cash' is also not easy in the Indian context, what with the country's poor infrastructure. There exists a digital divide in the country, and the benefit of any shift to 'less cash' will go to the well-off and not to the poor.

Other Steps—Raids and *Benami* Property

The government realized soon enough, in December 2016, that even the 'less cash' economy was not realizable any time soon. This would be a slow process, so it again shifted ground by announcing that it was catching people with unaccounted wealth via raids. It also announced that it was sending notices to people, asking them to show where they had got their money from. The government also announced another IDS. This came close on the heels of the previous one, which had ended in September 2016.

To show that demonetization was working and that black money was being caught, the government had to show some success in catching the wrongdoers. There were images in the media of people from all over the country, caught with crores of new currency notes. What did the government get—a few thousand crore rupees of black money revealed? Compared with the size of the black economy of Rs 93 lakh crore, this is a negligible amount and makes but a small dent in the black economy.

However, the embarrassment was that the banking system and the regulatory mechanism of the government were so weak that people were exchanging their old notes for new ones beyond the limits allowed. There was possible connivance of the corrupt in the banking system, with the politicians, administration and police. The embarrassment was compounded when fake new currency notes started surfacing. These were getting into the banking system too and not just into trade.

It needs to be remembered that raids are a normal part of the Income Tax Department's functioning. They are nothing new. They are also not linked to demonetization. Raids are made based on data that the department collects on individuals. They are fruitful only if the department does its homework properly. It has been seen that raids have been mostly unsuccessful in catching the people generating black incomes. In most income tax cases, the department loses its case because of connivance by the evader with officials, or for other reasons. There is hardly any final prosecution. This will not change with demonetization, and any raid conducted in a hurry is even less likely to yield results.

The spokespersons of the government also began announcing that demonetization was only the first step and that more arrows will be fired. It was said that implementation of the Benami Property Act would be speeded up. A limitation was put on holdings of gold. However, businessmen are made of sterner stuff and do not get frightened by such pronouncements.

As discussed earlier, the government sent out 18 lakh notices to people who had deposited large sums of money in the banks. The government announced it would use data mining to catch people henceforth. But, as pointed out earlier, the Central Board of Direct Taxes chairperson had announced that the government had data on 90 lakh large transactions made from 2009 onwards and that it would use the data to catch offenders, but nothing has come of that and the government went in for demonetization instead.

One senior economist in NITI Aayog wrote[12] that more than 8 lakh people had declared more than Rs 80 crore of income in 2012-13. This amounts to 6.7 times the GDP that year. The black economy would thus be more than 570 per cent. In that case, why has the department not investigated these 8 lakh people and caught their black incomes. Clearly, it is almost impossible for 8 lakh persons to earn Rs 80 crore from agriculture. It must be the black incomes that are being recycled. Obviously, nothing has been caught from these people in the last few years. Thus, having data does not mean that one can catch the offenders.

If data are available in some form, notices have to be issued and replies sought. One cannot automatically assume that if a notice is issued, this would end up in prosecution for black income generation. The replies need scrutiny, and only then may prosecution take place, that too if something is found remiss. All this takes years in our system. So, even if a few lakh crore rupees of black income is discovered in the process of giving notices, no tax will be collected from these disclosures for a few years.

Similarly, catching *benami* property is not an easy matter in our corrupt and leaky system. The government also referred to the Real Estate Bill, which seeks to regulate the builders who hoodwink the public by taking money for property which they do not deliver. It is unclear how that would impact black income generation. Anyhow, little has come of these announcements or from other announcements made in quick succession in December and January.

---

[12] Debroy, 2017.

Conclusion

The goalposts were shifted repeatedly by a government that found itself cornered. It announced steps that had little to do with demonetization. These steps could have been taken independent of demonetization, and that would have been better because the government's attention would not have been divided. Each of these steps required the full attention of the establishment, which none of them got.

VII

Wider Social Impact

Increasing Marginalization of the Marginalized

The social and economic impacts of demonetization are intertwined. In society, the social and the economic always work together and should not be put into isolated compartments. As pointed out earlier, the country is divided between the organized and the unorganized sectors. There is great inequality between them. It was also pointed out that the latter has been disproportionately hit by the demonetization-induced cash shortage.

The unorganized sectors consist of the small and cottage units in the urban slums and rural areas, and they have little access to banking. They often depend on the informal money markets for their credit needs to carry on their production and consumption. Since these sectors also cater to the demand of the poor, they suffered a decline in demand and lost incomes. A vast majority of the farmers belong to the unorganized sector. They suffered as prices of lentils and vegetables collapsed because of increase in production as well as a fall in demand. This hit their incomes. The unorganized sector suffered a loss of incomes and employment.

For the organized sectors, the cash crunch mattered less since they had alternative means of carrying out their transactions. They are well banked and have access to the digital modes of transaction. Many of them are fixed-income earners so that they did not suffer a loss of incomes. They did not suffer loss of employment either. Thus, the existing divide between the two sectors widened as a result of Demonetization 2016.

The push for digitization and for a 'less cash' economy, which was discussed in the previous chapter, is further adversely impacting the unorganized sectors of the economy. The cost of banking is also being raised with digitization, so that banking will now be more costly and less affordable for the unorganized sectors. So, in every sense the trend of growing marginalization of the already marginalized in society has only accelerated.

Many weddings, a crucial social event for families, were impacted by the shortage of cash. There were heart-rending stories about how families that had already planned a wedding coped with the situation. People had to run from pillar to post, since in India postponement of a wedding is considered inauspicious, especially for the bride. Of course, the rich remained unaffected since they could get the new cash. This illustrated another divide between the rich and the poor.

Only the poor and the lower classes stood in long lines at the banks. The well-off sections often have dedicated bank managers (called client managers) to help them, and in the aftermath of demonetization they got a lot of help. The well-off not only give the banks large deposits but also invest through the bank managers, and this is highly profitable for the banks. Such clients are willing to pay the extra charges for the convenience of the special services they get. The poor and the lower classes have no such facilities.

Of course, as mentioned earlier, some of the poor who had Jan Dhan accounts or other bank accounts acted as 'money mules' for the well-off and made some money. They took some cash from the well-off and deposited it in their accounts. Later, they withdrew the money and returned it to those who had given them the cash to be recycled. In the process, it is reported, they made 20 to 30 per cent of the amount of money they were given to recycle. Even if about a fourth of the Jan Dhan accounts were so used to recycle about Rs 50,000 crore, then that would mean an extra income of Rs 10,000 crore or about Rs 2000 per Jan Dhan account. In the overall scale of things, this was small, hardly enough to overcome the negative impact of demonetization.

There were reports of the poor running from pillar to post to get cash for medical treatment. While government hospitals were allowed to accept the old currency, this was not the case elsewhere. So, hospitalization and treatment, especially for the poor, became difficult because of the cash shortage.

Impact on Institutions

The RBI and the Banks

The prime minister stated on 8 November 2016 that other departments of the government were finding out about demonetization only as he was speaking.[1] It is reported that the Cabinet did not know of the decision and heard of it as the broadcast to the nation went live. It is unclear whether the finance minister was consulted on this. He has not categorically said anything on this, as can be expected. From the RBI governor's note[2] to the Rajya Sabha Committee, it appears that the government asked the RBI board to consider the matter only a day earlier. The RBI board met at a single day's notice, and it is not clear what discussion it had, but it approved the move and sent its advice to the government, and demonetization was implemented that evening.

The chain of events described above suggests that such a momentous move was not thoroughly discussed, either by the RBI board or the Cabinet before the decision was implemented.

---

[1] See Annexure 1.
[2] Mishra, 2017.

The banks were expected to implement the collection of old notes and issue of new currency. Yet, there was no consultation and advance preparation on this. The RBI was not ready with enough new notes, and the shortage of currency continued into July 2016—eight months after the decision was announced. ATMs had to be recalibrated in a hurry, etc. Procedures were not clear and had to be repeatedly changed as new problems were discovered.[3]

The new notes that were printed were of a different size from the old notes, and that required ATMs to be recalibrated. The logistics of getting the old notes into the money chests and distributing the new currency evenly across the country had not been worked out. In fact, the help of the armed forces had to be summoned for this. The law-and-order problems were not anticipated.

The credibility of the RBI seems to have been damaged. If it was indeed consulted and had not prepared for the problems in advance, it speaks ill of this hallowed institution. If it was consulted only at the last minute and it gave its concurrence without thoroughly considering the matter, again it does not speak well of the institution. Its relative autonomy is in question.

The proponents of demonetization argue that consultation was not possible because secrecy was crucial, otherwise the move would have failed. People with black money would have got wind of it and all the black money would have gone. But gone where? It could only have passed from one to the other or been given to the poor. One wonders if the RBI board bought this line given by the proponents. Acceptance of such an argument clearly shows a poor understanding of the phenomenon of the black economy. It is in line with the arguments given by this author that the government agencies have ignored the

---

[3] See Annexures 2, 3 and 4.

phenomenon of the black economy and that is why they have not learnt enough about it.

The black economy impacts every aspect of what the RBI deals with—money supply, foreign exchange, balance of payments . . . If the RBI continues to ignore the black economy then it will continue to trip, as it has in the context of demonetization. As discussed earlier in the book, banks were hit badly, and in spite of their best efforts during a very difficult time, their credibility was dented in the public eye. There were bad pennies in the banks, but that has been well known for a long time now, but what happened during demonetization went way beyond what was known. If decision-making in RBI is under a cloud, it will also impact the working of the banks.

Parliament and Politics

For the survival of a democracy, with all its weaknesses, the institutions of democracy are crucial. When these weaken, democracy weakens, since checks and balances are eroded, and then those with vested interests are able to effectively manipulate democracy to their end. As pointed out earlier, there was no debate on this crucial policy step in Parliament and that weakened this institution. Debate is the bedrock of accountability of the government. And, accountability of the government is the only check on the enormous power it wields.

When the government and its head, the prime minister, do not answer questions in Parliament, it undermines the accountability of the highest office of democracy. This is in sharp contrast to the earlier Parliaments, when the prime minister not only attended most important debates but also actively answered questions. When this does not happen, the Opposition also stalls the functioning of Parliament. It is democracy that suffers as a result.

The PM not only did not answer questions in Parliament or in an open press conference, but only addressed rallies to brand the opponents as people with black money.

On the extremely important question of demonetization, which was affecting the lives of hundreds of millions of citizens, the lack of debate in Parliament damaged democracy. The PM sat in the Parliament but did not answer the questions raised by the Opposition. Parliamentary committees were stalled because their members took a partisan stand. All this bodes ill for the nation, as debate did not take place in Parliament and the public did not get enlightened about the issues involved. One can draw the conclusion that the ruling party thinks it has the majority in the Lok Sabha, and if it does not wish to answer questions, it need not. It follows that even on lesser issues where the government is cornered, it can stall discussion with its unresponsiveness.

The government had to be more responsive in the Rajya Sabha, since it does not have a majority there. To counter this, the government started passing legislation via the route of Money Bills, which do not require approval in the upper house. The suggestions made in the Rajya Sabha need not be accepted. The Speaker of the Lok Sabha can certify a Bill as a Money Bill, and that suffices. The plea given by the ruling party is that if a Bill has financial implications, it has to be designated as a Money Bill. If this is the definition to be followed, then all Bills can be so designated since almost every action of a government will have some financial implications.

It is clear that the role of the Rajya Sabha is being downgraded in our parliamentary system. In India, elections to the Rajya Sabha are staggered, with one-third of the members retiring every two years. So the composition of the upper house changes slowly over a period of time. This is a check on any authoritarian tendencies of a brute majority in the lower house. The role of the Opposition in a parliamentary democracy is crucial because the majority may turn out to be wrong, especially in the long run.

The Opposition may point out the shortcomings in what the majority may wish to implement. No one has monopoly over truth. So the responsiveness of the ruling dispensation to the Opposition and to opposing views is crucial for the functioning of democracy, and above all, for the nation.

If the debate had taken place in Parliament and the Opposition had been able to show that the decision would not achieve its stated goals (which has happened) but will damage the economy (as is the case) perhaps the PM would have agreed to reverse the decision. If this had been done within the first fifteen days of the announcement, the ill effects of demonetization would not have become long term, as they now have. This will deepen the social crisis.

Political Aspects

Politics is about power to serve certain ends. In a democracy, political parties seek to come to power through the ballot to serve the interest of their groups. They effectively serve the limited interests of their backers when in power, even though to get the vote they profess to stand for the interests of all sections of the population. When in power they effectively serve the limited interests of their backers. It is no wonder that Gandhi said parliamentary democracy cannot serve the interest of the nation.[4]

Opposition Means Black and Anti-national

Political leaders who criticized demonetization were branded as justifying the holding of black money and worse, branded as holders of black money. Those leaders, such as the TMC leader who criticized the decision and took it up politically, were

---

[4] Gandhi, 1909.

browbeaten. Three MPs from the TMC party were arrested on charges of corruption. Another leader from UP who opened her mouth found her brother under investigation, and a chief minister from south India had to pipe down due to investigations opened against those close to him.

Since all political parties deal with black money, all felt threatened. It is no wonder then that none took up the challenge of mobilizing the people who were suffering. They did not dare face the public, which believes that all politicians are corrupt and that they are only interested in protecting their ill-gotten wealth. This is leading to the further decline of Indian democratic politics. It is not that the ruling party is clean and it is trying to clean up the system. In fact, it should clean up its own stables first to have the credibility to embark on a clean-up. By threatening the Opposition selectively, its role in educating the public is being undermined, and that is damaging democracy.

It is not only the political Opposition, but also the intellectual class that is under attack. Opposition to government policies is characterized as being anti-national. Centres of intellectual resistance to the ruling dispensation (of any hue) are systematically being branded as anti-national and are sought to be dismantled. There have been cases where the leadership of these institutions has been changed, and replaced by those belonging to the ideology of the ruling dispensation irrespective of their intellectual potential.

This is not to condone the practice of the earlier regimes, which put up their own favourites as leaders of the institutions. But earlier, the calibre of the candidates selected did matter, and they had some idea of how these institutions should run.

The chief economic adviser (CEA) to the government was constrained to say that most experts advising the government are sycophantic.[5] While this was true even before the NDA

---

[5] Kumar, 2017f.

government came to power in 2014, this tendency has only increased in recent times. The CEA in his argument has ignored that there have always been critics external to the system and they have been ignored in policy circles. He seems to be referring to the critics who are within the system and this government has gone a step further in ignoring them too. The CEA also said, quite correctly, that without proper critique, good policymaking is not possible.

One can classify experts into four categories—the insider-inside, the insider-outside, the outsider-inside and the outsider-outside. The first is the believer who is within the policy circle. The second is in the policy circle, believes in the basic thrust of policy, but can also be a critic from within the system. They know their limits and stay within those bounds. The third is outside the policy circle but supports the system and agrees with the policymaker. These are the sycophants. They change their opinion when they see the wind changing direction. The last category consists of the true critics, and they are kept outside the circles of discussion in policymaking, even though their role is the most crucial for the long-term interest of society.

This argument applies with even greater force in the political and social spheres, where certainties are even fewer and the potential for things to go wrong even greater. As the most diverse country in the world, India cannot go for simplistic solutions regarding what its people should eat or drink or how they should dress, or on issues of gender, minority and language. The ruling dispensation is pushing hard with its agenda and forcing its thinking without adequate discussion.

There is also the recent phenomenon of trolls harassing free voices of dissent systematically. Critical comments are met with mindless messages in the hundreds and thousands. Debating ideas is not the objective of the trolls. At one level, it is easy to ignore them, but at another level one cannot help but assume that the ruling dispensation is linked to this phenomenon. Trolls do not critique ideas but try to bully the critics into silence. This has affected the media, which sees the writing on the wall.

In brief, the dangerous tendency of going for simplistic solutions when the situation is complex has increased, and that is why a decision like demonetization was implemented. As its economic failure becomes more manifest, more autocratic and authoritarian behaviour will follow.

Politics by Slogans: Creating a Robin Hood Image

If democracy weakens because of the nature of politics being practised, it can only add further to the burden of the poor. India's policy framework since Independence has been based on a top-down approach, and that is at the root of the marginalization of the weak and the poor.[6] For them, an accountable democracy is the only check on the power of those with vested interests.

The government has been announcing various schemes under catchy names—Swachh Bharat, Good Governance, Digital Cities and Beti Bachao, Beti Padhao. Demonetization and control of black money has become another one. These schemes sound great and no one can disagree with what they are supposedly meant for, but the problem has been delivery, because neither has the road map for these schemes been worked out nor is there a dedicated machinery to deliver them. This has also been seen in the context of demonetization. Governance cannot be by sloganeering. One can create an initial euphoria, but unless there is delivery, the system loses credibility in the eyes of the citizens, as has happened in the last many years.

If delivery is weak, slowly cynicism spreads and dents democracy. Faith in the system and institutions gets eroded. Since black does not mean cash, and as demonstrated earlier, none of the stated goals of demonetization have been achieved,

---

[6] See Kumar, 2013.

the government is in danger of further losing its credibility over time.

The purpose of demonetization seems to be to create a Robin Hood image for the prime minister. He thought the scheme would help him create an image for himself, similar to what Indira Gandhi achieved in 1971 with the 'Garibi Hatao' slogan. He may have felt he would be able to convince the people that he was going after the money of the 'bad' guys which he would give to the poor. The opening of Jan Dhan accounts, allotment of gas cylinders, the electoral promise of giving each family Rs 15 lakh, and now the various announcements of farm loan waivers, are all with a view to creating a pro-poor image for the government. However, these are temporary steps to ameliorate some of the immediate distress, but the more important long-term steps of creating jobs and incomes for the poor and the youth are nowhere in sight. So, just as 'Garibi Hatao' got discredited so could the Robin Hood image.

If political accountability is dented and politics is to be done via sloganeering, then democracy and the marginalized sections would be the biggest losers.

Opposition Confused: Unable to Mobilize

Politics is about perception. Through slogans one can create a positive perception of a doer—someone who means business. The prime minister has been successful in this endeavour. The public has accepted the image of the PM as a doer. Demonetization was positively received. Even those standing in queues at the banks after demonetization accepted their misfortune stoically since they thought the black money holders would get caught and that would benefit them. Journalists who visited the farms came back with similar stories told to them by the poor. The poor were hurt, they reported, but they were willing to give the prime minister a chance since he had taken on the rich and the corrupt. It shows how desperate the marginalized are to see some action that would improve their lives. Modi has successfully changed the image that stuck to the previous PM of someone who did not speak and remained '*maun*', which loosely means quiet, even during a crisis.

The PM reaped the electoral dividend in the polls held after the demonetization phase. The big win was the UP election. The Opposition was not only divided, but lacked an effective strategy to change the public perception. It did not challenge the BJP narrative. The reality is that hardly any black money was caught and the rich did not stand in the bank lines along with the poor. The Opposition could not point out any corruption in the ruling dispensation. The PM got away by saying '*na khaoonga na khane doonga*' (neither will I make money nor will I let others make money). Congress (I) was so demoralized that it could not hold on to Goa and Manipur, where it actually did better than the BJP. So the latter formed the government in those states too.

The poor can live with distress for long periods of time—they have been doing so. They do not get mobilized on their own. They have to be mobilized. The Opposition did not ask where the BJP was getting its funds for the massive election campaigns it mounted in 2014, or in the UP election. It did not challenge the lifestyle of some of the BJP leaders and the build-up of their wealth over the years.

The politics of catching the Opposition for corruption while condoning the ruling party functionaries for the same offences is cynical in the extreme. Of course, corruption everywhere should be dealt with, but it is more important in a democracy that the ruling dispensation starts by cleaning its own stables. Cleaning out corruption should not become a means to mow down the Opposition whose role in strengthening democracy remains crucial. The public is all too familiar with the corruption and scandals that happened during the UPA regime. It is well known that many political leaders have resorted to black money not only for their parties but for building their personal wealth. That is why the public punished these parties in the 2014 general elections, and after that in many of the state elections.

Would a Benevolent Dictator Deliver?

What has come out the Vyapam and DMAT scams, and the mining scams in Goa and Karnataka? There have been other cases where action was needed on the part of the government but has not been forthcoming.

What is emerging is an autocracy, which is riding roughshod over the Opposition and the institutions of democracy. Fear is being instilled among important sections of the people and the media. As L.K. Advani said in 2014, there is an 'undeclared emergency'. Arun Shourie too said the same thing in 2015. Privately, businessmen and the media concur with this view.

The media is being manipulated via advertising revenue and access to official information. Demonetization made the situation worse, since private-sector advertising has declined as corporations try to protect their profits. The media are now more dependent on government advertising, and this has affected their independence. Many journalists have been fired. For instance, the *Hindustan Times* closed down seven bureaus and four editions quickly.[7] According to reports, many other TV media houses and print houses have also been impacted. Advani had famously said during the Emergency in 1975 that when the media was asked to bend, it crawled. This seems to apply now with greater force because many owners of media houses have other business interests which depend on being on the right side of the government.

---

[7] Samrat, 2017.

The question arises as to whether a well-intentioned autocracy or a benevolent dictatorship is good for the country. The world over, dictatorships have led to the worst forms of suppression and corruption. There may be exceptions, such as Lee Kuan Yew in Singapore, but the conditions in Singapore are absent in most countries, especially in India. Hence this dictatorship experiment, good or bad, is not replicable in other countries. The examples of dictators in Pakistan, the monarchy in Nepal, Marcos in the Philippines, Sani Abacha in Nigeria, Hosni Mobarak in Egypt and Suharto in Indonesia, to mention a few, all ran undemocratic and corrupt regimes which ran down their countries.

Let us be clear, the black economy is propelled by the 'triad' consisting of corrupt politicians, corrupt businessmen and the corrupt executive.[8] It is the lack of accountability of these three arms of the ruling elite of our society that leads to the systematic flouting of the laws of the land. To correct this, political change is crucial. In effect, the existence of a substantial black economy represents a weakness of our democracy. We have had rulers come to power on the promise of controlling corruption (like Rajiv Gandhi) who themselves got embroiled in corruption cases.

The party in power in the Centre currently, which seems to be crusading against black money, won after spending thousands of crores of rupees in its campaigns. Its high-powered campaigns for the subsequent state elections were also heavily funded. This is an indication that the black economy is continuing to flourish. In brief, the fight against the black economy is political, but cannot be partisan since all political parties are implicated. Authoritarian or dictatorial regimes are no guarantee that the system will be cleaned up, in fact it will very likely be easier to corrupt.

---

[8] See Chapter III and Kumar, 1985.

Inclusiveness Undermined: Unorganized Sector Hit

In India, the unorganized sectors have increasingly become marginalized over time since the organized sectors are politically powerful and are able to corner resources. The financial sectors are a conduit to collect the savings of the bulk of the people and channel them to those who are seen to be more profitable—the corporations.[9] They have the technology and the capital, and the state intervenes in their favour in the name of globalization and the country's global competitiveness. Naturally, the share of the organized sector in the national income has been rising, even though the percentage of the workforce employed in it has not changed.[10]

As argued earlier in the book, demonetization has hit the unorganized sectors the most so that even in the brief period since 8 November 2016, production has further shifted in favour of the organized sectors. There is a likelihood of a permanent loss for the unorganized sectors. For instance, the well-off, with their access to banking, went to the malls or e-commerce channels more than they did earlier since they could use credit and debit cards. Similarly, the current push for digitization is shifting the balance in favour of the organized sectors which have the financial literacy and the infrastructure required to more quickly adopt new technologies and practices.

The push for digitization indicates a preference for technology over people's needs—another undemocratic tendency in the current dispensation. This is continuing from before, but it is being pushed more strongly now. The belief is that we can push people into doing something because we think it is good for them. It is not even being considered necessary that they be given the time and the chance to adjust to the new situation.

---

[9] Kumar, 2013.
[10] Kumar, 2013.

So, Aadhaar is being made compulsory for all kinds of activities in society. It is even being linked to PAN and tax filing. When it is claimed that digitization is being done to tackle the black economy, it is again an indication of more faith in technology than in the reform of society.

The idea that there needs to be a formalization of the informal sectors is being pushed hard in the belief that this would help tackle the black economy. But again, there is an error of judgement. It is not the informal sector that generates the bulk of the black incomes, since most of the incomes in this sector are way below the taxable limit. It is the organized or the formal sector that generates a bulk of the black incomes.

As discussed earlier, if the government is not able to tackle the already large number of tax returns filed, how is it going to be able to deal with the returns filed by millions more entities if they are brought into the tax net? The system is likely to be overwhelmed. It must be borne in mind that since the late 1990s, while the number of tax filers has increased manyfold, the number of entities effectively paying taxes has only doubled. As a percentage of the population, the numbers have hardly changed, in spite of all the efforts to get more people into the tax net.

So, it is unclear that greater formalization of the economy by forcing a change of technology on those who are ill-equipped to deal with it would fetch more tax collections. What it would certainly achieve is a further marginalization of the unorganized sectors, but that has been a continuing trend since Independence.

Push for Technology and Rising Unemployment

Access to technology is not easy and its adoption costs money. Modern technology usually requires heavy investments, which the unorganized sectors usually cannot afford. So, emphasis on greater use of technology can only strengthen the organized sector and undermine the unorganized sectors further. Technology is being propagated in the name of modernization and is seductive for the young and the middle classes.

However, it has become amply clear that modern technology is displacing large numbers of the less skilled. The organized sectors in India are generating few direct jobs but they are getting most of the investment. Per Rs 1 crore of investment, the cottage and small sectors generate far more jobs than the organized sectors do. But the former is getting less and less investments so they are generating fewer jobs. There is a problem at both ends. The sectors that can generate jobs are getting very little investment and where investment is going there is job loss due to automation.[11]

In agriculture, greater use of tractors, combine harvesters, threshers and so on has not only ensured little job creation, but has led to the displacement of a large number of landless workers. Since these people do not have the skills to service the new machines entering the rural areas, they cannot even get non-farm jobs.

In the construction sector, which has grown faster than most other sectors, again because of mechanization, very few jobs are generated compared to earlier, when work was manually done. In the retail sector, which is a big employer, the rapid rise of e-commerce has impacted both the organized and the unorganized businesses. While the former have the resources to face the challenge, the real struggle is being faced by the latter.

In recent decades, to produce more output, India is using less and less labour, and this is leading to jobless growth. Both youth unemployment and massive underemployment are rising, and this is triggering a revolt among the youth. The push for modernization using more technology may be seductive, but it is adding to the difficulties for our youth. The situation is similar in the advanced countries, even though the technology

---

[11] Kumar, 2013.

mismatch there between the advanced and backward sectors is not as severe as in India. This trend towards jobless growth due to the adoption of more automation is leading to a right-wing upsurge in many advanced countries. The rise of Trump in the US, the vote for Brexit in the UK, the rise of Le Pen in France and other right-of-centre leaders in the world represent these tendencies. The common people are upset with the loss of jobs and they blame it on globalization and not on technology, which has been the big disrupter in modern times.

The future offers no new hope for additional employment for the informal sectors of the economy, given the rise of artificial intelligence (AI), which has the potential to displace millions of jobs, (perhaps not as quickly in India as in the advanced countries). While these cutting-edge technologies may take time to penetrate into India, the indirect effect will be fewer Indians going abroad to get jobs and that will add to the pressure on jobs in India. We have the example of driverless cars and trucks, which may become a reality in less than a decade and could displace the jobs of millions of drivers all over the world. There is also the likelihood of fewer people owning private cars so that the automobile industry could see lay-offs. With AI, outsourcing of jobs to the developing world in the form of call centres and BPOs is likely to decline rapidly. A move against these services is in any case being pushed in the US as Trump is putting pressure on businesses to bring back the jobs to the US for its own citizens.

In brief, the income gap between the organized and the unorganized sectors has been growing because of the cornering of investments by the former. Demonetization disproportionately hit the latter, increasing this gap. The push for digitization will increase the gap even further since the unorganized sectors are less capable of switching to new technologies. New technologies mean fewer jobs so that there has been jobless growth around the world. This forces the young into the unorganized sector, thereby creating a huge reserve army of labour, which weakens the position of labour and adversely impacts the unorganized sectors.

Demonetization has aggravated the differential between the organized and unorganized sectors thus denting inclusiveness in the economy and society. In a democratic set-up, people should take precedence over all else. The government, rather than bringing about change in society, is trying to replace people with the use of technology. The need was to strengthen the struggle for democracy rather than to cause a crisis in the lives of the vast majority.

Social Aspects

The social aspects are linked to the economic and political impacts of demonetization. The social aspects result from: a) marginalization of the marginalized, b) inability to tackle the black economy through a change in wider consciousness in the public and especially in the minds of the ruling elite in the country, and c) the autocratic tendencies following the failure of the demonetization programme and the shifting of goalposts.

Impact on the Marginalized Sections

The discussion earlier points out that demonetization has aggravated the existing trend of marginalization of the already marginalized. It is a policy that, in the name of modernization, is benefiting the organized sectors while the unorganized sectors are unable to cope with the new situation and hence they are getting marginalized further. As the poor face further marginalization in society, there will be social consequences.

For instance, women will have to carry the extra load of earning higher incomes by doing more work. This will impact their health adversely and also come in the way of child-rearing. Children's education will get disturbed since they would be expected to contribute to the family income. These children would not be able to acquire the modern skills needed for modern jobs and they would be stuck for life in menial, unskilled jobs that pay poorly. All this would adversely impact the long-term prospects of the family.

The poor would face higher health costs. Due to a deterioration in their situation, they would tend to overexploit the environment, and that would further damage their health. Finally, due to poverty, they would be unable to pay for the civic amenities needed for a civilized existence and would be condemned to live in poor conditions. These trends can be reversed only if the state steps in with subsidies for public services and provides competent health and education facilities. In India, this has not happened because the government has often complained of lack of resources. This approach will continue, and in fact it may get aggravated, because the government has often argued that subsidies are wasteful. The government had stated that demonetization would help reduce the black economy and that would release resources for the development of the poor. This goal is unlikely to be fulfilled, leaving the poor to their own devices as before.

Farmers are an important marginalized section of society. Their share in the workforce is the largest.[12] It is not just the farmers, but the rural areas have also been marginalized, since the bulk of investments go to the urban areas. It is not that the farmers or the rural areas are a homogenous whole. There is a great deal of differentiation among them too. For instance, there are rich farmers and casual labourers.

For the farmers, as mentioned earlier, the collapse of prices of perishable and even other commodities, like dal, has meant that a large number of them have lost substantial incomes. Coming after two droughts in which the farmers suffered loss of

---

[12] See Annexure 16.

incomes, this was unexpected and a terrible blow. Their crop was good but demand collapsed (due to demonetization) and led to a sharp downturn in prices. This led to agitations in various parts of the country—in Tamil Nadu, UP, MP and Maharashtra—for price support and farm loan waivers. The agitation is likely to spread to other parts of the country over time. The implication for banks and for the budgets of the Centre and the states will be serious. There are reports of farmer suicides increasing since their costs increased while their incomes collapsed, leaving them unable to repay their loans. All this has deepened the crisis situation in the rural areas in India.

Agitating Youth

The youth are agitating all over the country for jobs. A large number of them do not want to stay in agriculture, which they consider unprofitable and which cannot sustain the lifestyle they now aspire to. With high-decibel advertising beaming images of the good life, the young wish to live that life. Movies and TV serials beam similar images. But the majority of the youth, trapped in low-paying, unorganized-sector jobs, or jobless, cannot acquire such a lifestyle, even if they work hard.

The growing black economy based on illegalities shows the youth an easy path through the world of crime. Those high up in the system making easy money set the wrong example for the youth to emulate. The choice before the youth is to survive in a low-income trap in the unorganized sectors of the economy or to move into crime with high incomes but a life of uncertainty. No wonder the youth is dissatisfied and crime is on the rise all around.

The young in some of the most prosperous communities in their respective regions are agitating for reservation in jobs. The Marathas in Maharashtra, the Patels in Gujarat, the Jats in north India and others are agitating for reservation. They know that reserved-category jobs are few and that reservation is not a solution to their bigger problem, but something is better than nothing. Above all, this has given a focus to their demands which they are unable to articulate otherwise. They know that the market is producing jobless growth and they cannot go against the market, so the only thing left to do is to demand reservation from the government. How desperate the situation is can be gauged from the fact that in 2015 the UP government advertised for 368 jobs and got 2.3 million applications.[13] Where the requirement was fifth grade pass, there were 255 Ph.D., 2.22 lakh engineers, and M.Com and B.Com degree holders who applied. This is an indication of the frustration facing the youth.

Demonetization, by marginalizing the unorganized sectors, led to a further decline of any reasonable prospect for any kind of work—even the poorest paying. No wonder the demand for work under MGNREGS increased substantially in December 2016.[14]

The frustration of the youth is boiling over and resulting in not only the farmers' agitation or the fight for reservation, but also taking the shape of lumpenization. It is expressing itself along regional, communal and caste lines, accentuating the pre-existing divide. Matters flare up rather quickly, as in the case of *jallikattu* in Tamil Nadu. In that case, even the orders of the Supreme Court could not be implemented because of overwhelming public opposition to them. There has been unprecedented vigilantism about food, clothing, transportation of animals and so on in north India. Parties with vested interests are using these issues to divide and polarize communities for electoral gains. Demonetization is not the cause of all this, but it is accentuating the social divides and making the situation worse.

---

[13] Ali, 2015.
[14] See Table 23 in Annexure 15.

In fact, if demonetization had been able to tackle the black economy, it could have freed the resources needed to take care of the poor, as discussed earlier. It would also have led to better delivery. Both, more resources and their better utilization, could change the shape of the country. As argued before, there would be more employment generation and less leakage of resources abroad via flight of capital. This could help improve the living conditions of the marginalized who would have more employment, higher incomes and better civic amenities, but this is not on the anvil, with demonetization and the consequences following it.

Conclusion

Demonetization has adversely impacted some crucial institutions and affected the nature of our democracy. There was an attempt to browbeat opposition to it and brand opponents as those with black money. The intellectual climate is sought to be changed and criticism is not tolerated. The weakening of democracy leads to a further marginalization of the marginalized in society.

Demonetization was a technical device that does not impact the causes of generation of black economy, namely, the political or the social aspects. It would do nothing to change the ethics of the elite who generate black incomes. They would continue to do so. It does not address the issue of accountability of the rulers, which is so crucial to check the growth of the black economy. It reposes faith in technology rather than in people and their transformation to a more democratic ethos. It is also leading to growing cynicism among the people and to their increased alienation, which is the opposite of what is needed.

The poor got fooled into believing that the dramatic step taken would tackle the black economy. As they discover that this did not really happen, they will become even more cynical. The media played a role in praising the demonetization decision. The manner in which the decision was taken and then implemented goes against the grain of democracy and weakens its institutions. The public has come to such a stage that it believes an authoritarian decision like this was the only way the problem of the black economy could be tackled and that it was the best for the country. They have been led to believe that authoritarianism is required and can be a substitute for bringing accountability into the entire system.

The media has also been impacted by demonetization. As already argued, many journalists have been retrenched, and those remaining in employment are scared of losing their jobs. This is coming in the way of the independence of the press. The ruling dispensation is able to use a substantial section of the media to further its ends. This is widening the various divides in society rather than bridging them. Television, which thrives on TRP ratings, is busy creating a spectacle rather than conducting a proper and informed debate. Programmes based on crime and superstition abound, trouncing rationality.

In brief, the social divides always existed in society and were already getting worse before demonetization was announced. But the social and economic crisis in the lives of the ordinary people that demonetization has triggered is leading to a deepening of the divisions. The end result can only be growing social and political instability in the country.

Conclusion

Demonetization is one of the most important economic events in the country, not only of 2016-17, but possibly of the last two decades, even though other momentous events have taken place, such as India joining the World Trade Organization in 1985. Its implications are playing themselves out even now and will continue to impact the economy for some time. Its legal validity has been questioned by some, but what is not in doubt is that it was a big shock to the economy and it hit every section of society and every sector of the economy. While a few benefited from it, the vast majority lost out due to this step. The PM exhorted the nation repeatedly to bear the 'pain' for long-term gains. This book analyses the long-term impact of this step and points out that most of the impact would be adverse.

Regarding the legal status of the move, even if technically all the formalities may have been fulfilled, in spirit, the move did not follow the norms and procedures that should have been followed. Consequently, the advance preparation that should have been made was nowhere in evidence, and that is why there was chaos. In justification, the government has said that secrecy was required for the step to succeed in unearthing the black money in the economy. How erroneous this understanding was has been brought out in this book.

The Principal Argument

The book points out that theoretically it was clear that demonetization by itself could not help tackle the black economy. It has been clear that this move does not stop the process of generation of black incomes,[1] while it may have at best extinguished 1 per cent of the black wealth which is held as cash. In reality, not even 0.1 per cent of the black wealth has been extinguished by the 2016 demonetization, given the cleverness of the black wealth holders in recycling their hoards of black cash. It was shown that by 13 January 2017, 98.8 per cent of the demonetized currency was back in the banks. Only Rs 18,000 crore of the money had not come back, and most of that would have come back over time.[2] The expectation that Rs 3-4 lakh crore would not come back into the system was not realized.

It is explained in the book that black income generation is a process that needs to be eliminated, and demonetization does not do that. Black money is not a stock that can be taken care of once and for all by using some silver bullet. It is also explained that wealth is a portfolio of assets consisting of many things—shares, landed property, jewellery, bank balances, fixed deposits and so on, with cash being one tiny component of it. Even if some of the black cash is extinguished, it would be quickly replenished because the black-income-generation process continues.

It was also explained that most of the cash is not held by households but by businesses, and they can usually explain it away as working capital, which is a legitimate requirement. Cash is also needed by households for their requirements, so very little of the Rs 15.44 lakh crore of demonetized high-denomination currency notes would have been black cash.

It has been repeatedly emphasized in the book that it is a common mistake to think that 'black means cash'. It was not only the government which erred in this regard, but also the common

---

[1] Kumar, 1999.

[2] Now the RBI has confirmed in its Annual Report in September 2017 that 99 per cent of the old notes have come back.

man. Most believe that those with black money hold crores of rupees as cash. And the public bought the line that if cash is squeezed out of the system, black money would disappear. The results of Demonetization 2016 are now clear, and it has once again been shown that both theoretically and empirically this did not happen. It is also the case that cash is coloured neither black nor white, so it is available to circulate both black and white incomes. Clearly, once cash is available for the white economy it becomes equally available for the black economy. Hence, black cash cannot be eliminated once and for all. Even if cash is made scarce for some reasons, it can be replaced by gold, foreign exchange and so on. These are the near-money forms that can be used to carry on the black economic activities, including black income circulation.

The government's other reasons for announcing demonetization were to tackle counterfeit currency and its financing of terrorism. But even the RBI data show that counterfeit currency, if it was all in high-denomination notes, amounted to a mere 0.03 per cent of the demonetized notes. One does not cause a huge disruption of an economy for such a small amount. Just as it was done earlier, such notes could have been eliminated by changing the currency notes over a period of time.

If counterfeit notes were financing terrorism, that would continue since new counterfeit notes made their appearance shortly after the introduction of the new currency notes. The reason pointed out was that state actors were involved in this activity and demonetization does not impact them so they will not stop. What is needed is a diplomatic and political approach, and better enforcement. Further, terrorism is also financed by smuggling, drug trafficking, *havala*, use of dollars, and the like. These conduits would continue even if Indian currency becomes scarce for a while. Neither has counterfeiting stopped nor has terrorist activity come down.

Changing Goalposts: Cashless Economy and Digitization

It is argued in the book that it became clear to the government that it was not going to be successful in achieving its initially announced goals, and so it shifted ground. Within fifteen days, it started talking of creating a cashless society. And then, realizing its mistake in claiming too much, it again shifted ground to say it aimed for a 'less cash' economy. But, as argued in this book, even this aim is not easy to achieve since it requires a lot of preparation. Extensive and good-quality infrastructure is needed for this, and that is not in place. Even many advanced countries with robust infrastructure have not been able to achieve this goal as yet and still work with a lot of cash in the economy. Since black is not cash, the problem is not one of more or less cash; the cause of the black economy is what needs to be eliminated. It is argued that in the same way that India was pushed into demonetization without preparation, a similar mistake is being made by pushing the country too fast towards a 'less cash' economy. It requires financial literacy, cybersecurity, regulation and reliable infrastructure, and we are far from having all this in place. The danger is that if problems emerge, the move towards a 'less cash' economy would get discredited.

Most importantly, it is pointed out that there is no link between demonetization and a 'less cash' economy. One can be done independently of the other, and that is the way it should be, given the complexity involved in both and the preparation needed for both.

The talk again shifted to how a 'less cash' economy would push the economy towards digitization, which in turn would lead to formalization of the informal activities in the economy. It was argued that digitization would help check the flow of black incomes. The book, however, suggests that this is a reflection of the 'expert mentality' of putting faith in technology to solve the problem of the black economy. People and their convenience do not matter. Their transformation into less alienated citizens is not material. However, implementation of new technology without preparation also leads to new forms of black income generation even if some of the older ways are eliminated or become redundant. It is pointed out that cybercrime is rising fast, with hacking and phishing going on at an increasing rate. It is the person behind the technology that matters, perhaps more than the technology itself.

Faith in technology rather than in people is a sure way of weakening democracy and increasing alienation. In the long run, this can only result in greater social and political instability. Any policy has to be mindful of the long term and not just think of the short run, as was the case with the announcement of demonetization. The costs may turn out to be far greater than any temporary benefits that may accrue to the nation.

Shortage of Money in an Economy Is a Serious Matter

The book discusses the sudden demonetization in 2016 that created a shortage of cash for transactions in the economy. It then discusses why this is a serious matter.

It was shown that, overnight, valid currency in circulation dropped to 14 per cent of the pre-demonetization amount. This shortage led to currency hoarding. Both money supply and velocity of circulation dropped. Since money is needed for transactions, the number of transactions suddenly declined, and that impacted the income-generation process. The impact was more on those sectors which use cash than on the sectors which also use banking transactions and electronic money. So, the unorganized sector was impacted far more than the organized sector.[3]

In the organized sector, more transactions took place through the banking system and velocity of circulation may

---

[3] Kumar, 2017b.

have increased. But discretionary demand declined and people hoarded currency, so that would have countered the trend of increase for the organized sector. The transactions in this sector may have declined to begin with and later picked up. So, the income-generation process was impacted to begin with, but would have picked up over time as demand rose but did not reach the earlier extent.

In the unorganized sector, due to a sharp drop in the money supply and the velocity of circulation, activity almost came to a halt. Transactions declined sharply and the income-generation process was badly affected. Some in this sector went in for banking transactions and electronic transfers, but this was a small minority. The drop in incomes in this sector may have been 60 to 80 per cent, to begin with. That is what the initial reports suggested in November and December 2016. Cash availability picked up slowly with remonetization, but was short for at least eight months. So, the impact was long term.

The shortage of notes continued for a long time because of a variety of factors, like printing capacity, shortage of paper and ink, hoarding of currency, the requirement to print smaller-denomination notes and so on. The more damaging part of demonetization was that the autonomy of RBI has been dented. The RBI needed to give proper advice to the government about the pros and cons of the sudden and unplanned demonetization. The importance of adequate availability of currency in the economy was not appreciated in taking the decision.

Economic Costs

The book demonstrates that demonetization immediately impacted the economy adversely and especially its unorganized component. The enormous shortage of cash meant that transactions could not go through and the income-generation process slowed down especially for the unbanked, who are mostly the poor. The impact on the economy is that the marginalized have become more marginalized because of demonetization.

The economy consists of the vast unorganized sector and the small organized sector. The former employs 93 per cent of the workforce and produces 45 per cent of the output. It lacks access to bank facilities and works on cash. So the cash shortage, hit it hard. The organized sector was less affected, but it too suffered as is pointed out in the book quoting from various reports in November 2016 to January 2017. This increased the already existing divide between these two sectors of the economy and worked against the policy of inclusive growth that various governments have been announcing and claiming to work towards in the last ten years.

The above-mentioned impact on the economy is not yet visible in the data. They show only a minor decline in the growth rate of the economy for 2016-17. It has been pointed out that this is because the data are only available for a part of the organized sector. The unorganized-sector data becomes available with a huge time lag. So, the official data assume that this component of the economy is behaving in a way similar to the organized sector. This is clearly erroneous. Demonetization led to a clear divergence in the growth of the organized and the unorganized sectors. A new methodology is required to understand the impact of the big shock to the economy. It has been pointed out that the rate of growth of the economy for 2016-17 became negative or was close to zero. The economy showed recessionary tendencies.

So, an economy that was functioning well till 8 November 2016 suddenly went into a tailspin. The government had claimed that India was the fastest-growing economy in the world and that its macro-parameters were robust. The fiscal deficit, current account deficit and inflation were low. On the negative side, credit off-take had plunged to a historic fifty-year low, and capacity utilization in industry was around 75 per cent. Consequently, investment in the economy was low, at around 30 per cent. It was private investment that had declined. Large NPAs in public-sector banks were a huge cause of worry, and since these NPAs belonged to infrastructure companies, these companies were not only not able to invest, but more seriously, they were in danger of going bankrupt. To boost the economy, the government needed to step up its expenditures, but that was constrained by the credit rating agencies monitoring the fiscal deficit. In other words, the economic policies under the NDA were similar to those of the UPA,[4] and that is why the economy was in a trap. This book points out that demonetization increased these macroeconomic problems.

Demonetization led to a collapse in demand, especially in the unorganized sectors. This led to a decline in output and employment in the economy, and a fall in investment. The agriculture sector also suffered a blow due to the collapse in prices of vegetables and lentils. This reflected in a low rate of inflation, but for the farmers who were just recovering from two droughts, this meant another drop in income. This hit them hard because demonetization induced a rise in costs on account of the higher cost of borrowing for the inputs bought with old notes or bought on credit from the retailers. This is likely to create problems for the banks whose NPAs will rise. And also for the farmers who will find it difficult to borrow from the banks for the next crop because of the difficulty of repaying past loans. There have been large-scale agitations demanding farm loan waivers. This is likely to have fiscal implications for the states and the Centre.

Demonetization was expected to boost the government's resources, both because of its supposed impact on the black economy and declaration of higher incomes and also because of a possible windfall gain for the RBI. Neither has happened. In fact, it is likely that given the uncertainty about production

[4] Kumar, 2015.

and prices, planning for the Budget 2017-18 became difficult, and the figures contained therein may turn out to be erroneous, upsetting policy goals.

The difficulties set into motion by demonetization which led to a cash shortage will dissipate slowly. However, the long-term impact which set in with the cash shortage has given way to the initiation of recessionary conditions due to fall in output, employment and investment. These will take quite a while to go away because of the change in expectations.

If the note shortage had reversed in a few days, there would have been only a temporary dip in the economy followed by a fast recovery. Unfortunately, the cash shortage continued for at least eight months, and this has led to a more permanent impact on the economy. The problem has been converted from one of note shortage to one of deepening recessionary conditions. Recovery from this would take several years. The government had hoped for a quick recovery (which it called a V-shaped recovery) but that is not in sight.

The advice to reverse the note ban quickly, since it was clear from the beginning that it would not succeed in its main goal, was not accepted. To be fair, governments of all hues are loath to admit their mistakes and like to put a spin on the bad news. But this was no ordinary mistake and should have been corrected. However, that was not done, reflecting an authoritarian streak in the government. Even the group, Arthakranti, which had apparently suggested demonetization to Modi in 2013, advised the government that demonetization had not been the correct thing to do. The old notes were still with the public and in the banks, and if their use was allowed till the time adequate new notes were printed, it would have eased the situation. The government possibly thought it would be embarrassing to admit a mistake and correct it, so it kept giving spin after spin and changed the goalposts several times.

Steps to Tackle the Black Economy: Demonetization Not the First

Demonetization was like a bolt from the blue. It was argued by the proponents that secrecy was required for its success, and while the secrecy was achieved, the primary goal of tackling the black economy was not. The move was unplanned, and that led to a host of problems in the implementation of the scheme. Repeated course changes were required to meet the emerging crises among farmers and the unorganized sectors.

The government and the ruling party gave the spin that the daily, and at times hourly, changes they were making were a sign of a responsive government. However, it is the citizens who had to bear the enormous hardship caused by the government's unplanned action. Those who had little or no role in generating black incomes were put into hardship, standing in long queues, losing their jobs, facing difficulties in getting medical treatment for their family members, struggling to conduct weddings that had been scheduled, and so on. The real culprits who generate large sums of black money escaped, converting most of their black money into new currency in connivance with the corrupt in the system.

It is undoubtedly the case that the black economy is the single biggest problem facing the nation. It was argued that it impacts the economic, political and social aspects of the citizens' lives even for those citizens who do not generate black incomes. It is the cause of widespread policy failure and the inability of the government to deliver on policies. The result is substandard living conditions, especially for the poor. It affects all the macro-parameters and leads to greater poverty and inequality, higher inflation, lower rate of growth and employment than is potentially possible in the economy.[5]

---

[5] See Kumar, 2017a and Kumar, 1999.

Since Independence, it has been felt that the black economy needs to be checked, even though to begin with it was small compared with what it is now. Many steps have been taken from time to time to tackle the growing black economy. Demonetization 2016 is certainly not the first step against the black economy. It is not that this step was not taken ever before or that the analysis of what it may do to the black and the white economy was not available. Indeed, demonetization was announced earlier, in 1978 and also in 1946, with the aim of checking the black economy, but it made no dent in it. One needed to learn from those experiences, if not from the advice of experts in the field.

It has been argued that high-denomination notes are the culprits in the generation of black incomes because it is easy to transact in cash using them. So their demonetization would help control the black economy. It is shown in this book that the growth of high-denomination notes in India is consistent with the growth of the economy and with the need for high-value transactions in a large economy. Also, the use of cash in India is not out of line with practices in many other economies where the black economy is small. Further, when the black economy is taken into account, the cash-to-GDP ratio, dips from 12 per cent to 7.5 per cent, which is not too high by international comparisons. Finally, for Japan this ratio is 18 per cent but it has little corruption, while for Nigeria this ratio is 1.4 per cent but it has a higher level of corruption.

Political Gambit

In life, the economic, social and political are intertwined and not separate. Usually, good economics and good politics go hand in hand. Of course, the definition of good politics may differ for different people. The demonetization decision also had a large political content, and that needs to be understood.

The current NDA government has taken many steps against the black economy since coming to power in 2014. However, these steps have yielded little, and that was embarrassing since Modi had promised to bring back the trillions of dollars of black money held abroad and had said that there would be enough to give each Indian family Rs 15 lakh by bringing this money back.

The prime minister was being taunted on his government's failure to keep the promise. He needed a big bang, and demonetization was seen as the solution. Politically, he succeeded, even if economically he had failed. The common man believed this was a genuine step to control the black economy. It created a Robin Hood image for Modi, somewhat similar to the image Indira Gandhi had created with her 'Garibi Hatao' slogan. His image as a pro-rich, pro-corporate politician has been largely erased. Demonetization's political success in spite of the economic failure can be seen in the ruling dispensation's victory in several elections, but most importantly in the UP assembly elections in 2017.

People believed the PM when he said that demonetization would help unearth black money and that would help them. Demonetization was in that sense more a political than an economic policy step. No political party has mobilized the people effectively against this misstep because they have been a part of the black economy and feel threatened by the government.

The reason for the failure of the earlier steps, as well as demonetization, to tackle the black economy lies in the lack of understanding as to what is the root cause of the problem. It is pointed out in the book that a 'triad' of corrupt businessmen, politicians and the executive (bureaucracy, police and judiciary) runs the black economy. If this is not dismantled, the black economy will continue to flourish. But this is a tough job. It requires a change in consciousness among the public.[6]

---

[6] See Kumar, 2017a. It is argued there that change in consciousness requires movements over a sustained period of time.

The ruling circles and the technocratic advisers are always impatient, and believe they have all the solutions. They want a quick fix and not to have to worry about the crucial social change necessary. They neither have the understanding as to how to strengthen democracy nor the patience with such endeavours. They think they can take some technical steps and solve the problem with some narrow economic measures, such as demonetization or raids or digitization. It is as though they have a silver bullet to quickly fix the problem. They lack the understanding that the problem is political and requires a change in consciousness of the citizens and the rulers, and this can only be brought about gradually through movements.

The government branded the opponents of demonetization as having black money or being anti-national. The opposition parties, most of whom deal with black money for not only their party work but also for their leaders' personal wealth, got bullied into silence. This is the surest way of undermining democracy. Institutions like Parliament, the Cabinet and the RBI seem to have been undermined. The PM refused to answer questions in Parliament or to face a press conference. All this leads to undermining of accountability, which is the bedrock of democracy.

The black economy must be treated as a political issue and has to be tackled politically. No magic wand exists that can help solve the problem. In the long run, a strong accountable system of politics and economics is required to tackle India's basic problems. In the short run, steps can be taken to tackle *havala*, check banking secrecy, strengthen the RTI and whistle blowers Bills, and simplify direct taxes via Direct Tax Code.[7]

It is also argued by the proponents of demonetization that this has initiated a long-term trend of change to make the country more honest. It is said that more steps will be taken,

---

[7] See Kumar, 2017a.

that demonetization is only the first of many. As already argued, hundreds of steps have been taken in the past, and tough ones at that, without making a dent in the black economy which has continued to grow since Independence. Faith is put in the functioning of the markets but one has been moving in that direction for long with little effect on the black economy. So, these arguments are clever political ploys to divert attention from a big failure of an ill-conceived policy. It is an attempt to divert attention from the present to a golden future ahead.

In the end, one can say, the cost of demonetization far outweighs any perceived benefits in the near or distant future. To catch a few, a large number of those who never generated black incomes were inconvenienced while the culprits got off lightly. Does one chop off one's nose to cure a cold?

Acknowledgements

I was in the US to give a lecture on India's black economy when, on 8 November 2016, I saw news on the Internet that India had demonetized its high denomination currency notes. I could not believe that this was happening. Also, that was the day of the US presidential election and counting of votes, so attention was on the results of this crucial election. Being pre-occupied, I did not look at the details of what had been announced. My mind could not accept that this was happening in India.

Soon my wife called from India asking whether I had seen the news, and that there was a great deal of consternation all around as to what this would mean. She mentioned that there was panic all around because people did not understand what this would imply. She also passed on the request from *Hindustan Times'* edit page editor for a quick short article on the subject. The penny dropped, and I realized that demonetization had been announced by the PM and it was a major move by the government.

This topic has been widely discussed and commented on since 8 November 2016. So, a lot of material has been generated and needs to be digested. This has also confused the public since the government and its supporters have been putting out arguments in favour of demonetization whereas critics like myself have been strongly arguing why demonetization has been a failure and it has needlessly put the citizens to a lot of trouble.

Lohit from Penguin first got in touch with me in December 2016. I was at that point writing a short popular book on black economy, the primary reason for demonetization. We again met in February 2017, and he persuaded me to write this book. He asked if demonetization would remain relevant after some months when most of the demonetized notes would have been replaced with new ones. In the articles I had written for the popular press, I had argued that the effect of demonetization would be felt for a long time, and it would be a case study for economists the world over to study the impact of a sudden withdrawal from a major world economy. So, in April it was decided that we would go ahead with this book on demonetization.

One of the reasons for writing this book was to try to sort out the widespread confusion about the benefits and the costs of demonetization. The government has in a variety of ways tried hard to enumerate the benefits of demonetization—tackling the black economy in one shot to creating a cashless society to formalizing the informal economy to making the population more honest in the long term. The ground has been shifting and that has confused the citizens.

Demonetization became the main topic of discussion among citizens and in the media because it affected the lives of a vast majority. Many important economists, journalists and politicians spoke and wrote on the subject but that did not help clarify matters since most of them had never analysed the black economy seriously and therefore they created more confusion. To most economists, black economy is a nuisance which is best ignored. To politicians and media, it is anecdotal—to be referred to whenever a new scam breaks out. A lot was written and spoken for more than two months. The material was scattered all over the place and needed to be put together in one place and this book tries to do that.

I have tried to produce a book that should be accessible to a lay intelligent reader. While simplifying the presentations of the various concepts, I have tried to ensure accuracy so that the reader does not get short-changed. Money and black economy are deceptively simple concepts at one level but very complex in reality, and I hope the reader of this volume will derive some clarity on these matters. The macroeconomic impact of demonetization also appears to be deceptively simple but needs understanding. The book presents a lot of data to support the various arguments and also gives details that are needed by the reader to understand what was going on. All this is in annexures so as to not break the flow of reading. There is some repetition in the book across chapters but that was necessary for the sake of continuity so that the reader does not have to switch back and forth which often breaks the flow of reading.

My own analysis got enriched as I participated in daily debates on TV and read what others had to say. I got help in data work for this book from Ankur Verma, an M.Phil student of JNU, who acted as a research assistant for over two months. I also discussed the matter with my former PhD students and got help in their area of expertise. This sharpened the analysis, and I must mention Prof Saumen Chattopadhyay, Dr Astha Ahuja, Dr Pawan Kumar and Mr Prafulla Prusty. This list is long and I am grateful to all those people who contributed to my understanding in direct and indirect ways. I have always believed that in social sciences ideas evolve and are not the original product of any one person.

I am grateful to Lohit of Penguin for the patience and constant encouragement during the work on this book. I must express my gratitude to the team in Penguin for their hard work in producing this work. I must specifically mention Saloni Mital, the editor, who patiently and meticulously worked to polish this work. Her suggestions at various places help clarify matters and make them readable and accessible to a lay reader.

My father passed away nineteen years ago, and I always remember him for inculcating in me the desire to be independent and to withstand pressures. I have been overly preoccupied in the last eleven months and given less time to the family who bore with me for my mental absence and the postponement of the pending work at home. My mother, Neerja, and Nakul deserve a major part of the credit for this work.

8 October 2017   Arun Kumar

Bibliography

Ali, M. 2015. '23 lakh Apply for 368 Peon Posts in Uttar Pradesh'. *The Hindu*. 17 September. http://www.thehindu.com/news/national/other-states/23-lakh-apply-for-368-peon-posts-in-uttar-pradesh/article7660341.ece.

ANI. 2016. 'Ludhiana Hosiery Industry Badly Hit by Demonetization'. 21 November. *Business Standard*. http://www.business-standard.com/article/news-ani/ludhiana-hosiery-industry-badly-hit-by-demonetization-116112100092_1.html. Accessed 16 July 2017.

Arthakranti. 2016. 'What Was Arthakranti Proposal to PM Narendra Modi?'. http://www.arthakranti.org/news-events/159-what-was-arthakranti-proposal-to-pm-narendra-modi. Accessed 11 July 2017.

Ashraf, A. 2016. 'Interview: Demonetisation Has Hit 80% of Small Businesses, the Sector Is Staring at Apocalypse'. Scroll.in. 6 December. https://scroll.in/article/823231/interview-demonetisation-has-hit-80-of-small-businesses-the-sector-is-staring-at-apocalypse. Accessed 16 July 2017.

Birch, D. 2017. 'India's Demonetization a Fascinating Case Study of Cash-reform Shock Therapy'. Disruptive Asia. 12 January. https://disruptive.asia/india-demonetization-cash-shock-therapy/. Accessed 17 September 2017.

Bhattacharya, A. and S. Varma. 2017. 'Note Ban: Trade Slows to a Trickle at MP Mandi's Busiest Time of Year'. *The Times of India*. 10 January. http://timesofindia.indiatimes.com/

india/note-ban-trade-slows-to-a-trickle-at-mp-mandis-busiest-time-of-year/articleshow/56431171.cms.

Bhattacharya, K., S. Mitra, S. Pal and B. Saha. 2017. 'Reviving the Informal Sector from the Throes of Demonetization'. South Asia @ LSE Blog. 28 February. http://eprints.lse.ac.uk/74565/1/blogs.lse.ac.uk-Reviving%20the%20informal%20sector%20from%20the%20throes%20of%20demonetisation.pdf. Accessed 5 July 2017.

Bhayani, R. 2017. 'Note Ban Hits New Investment in Quarter 3: CMIE'. *Business Standard*. 3 January. http://www.business-standard.com/article/economy-policy/note-ban-hits-new-investment-in-quarter-3-cmie-117010200648_1.html. Accessed 1 July 2017.

Biswas, P.S. 2016. 'Amid Cash Crunch, Only 17% of Rabi Crop Loans Disbursed'. 21 December. *The Indian Express*. http://indianexpress.com/?s=Amid+Cash+Crunch%2C+Only+17%25+of+Rabi+Crop+Loans+Disbursed. Accessed 16 July 2017.

Catch News. 2016. 'After 50 Days, Troubles of Honest Will Reduce, Problems of Dishonest Will Increase: PM Modi'. Catch News. 24 December. http://www.catchnews.com/national-news/after-50-days-troubles-of-honest-will-reduce-problems-of-dishonest-will-increase-pm-modi-1482591360.html. Accessed 18 June 2017.

Chauhan, N. 2016. 'Fake Notes Worth Rs 400 Crores in Circulation'. *The Times of India*. 11 May. http://timesofindia.indiatimes.com/india/Fake-notes-worth-Rs-400-crores-in-circulation/articleshow/52214965.cms. Accessed 11 July 2017.

Christopher, N. 2016. 'The Worst Cyber Attacks of 2016'. *The Economic Times*. 28 December. http://economictimes.indiatimes.com/small-biz/security-tech/security/the-worst-cyber-attacks-of-2016/articleshow/56212448.cms.

CMIE. 2016. 'Transaction Cost of Demonetisation Estimated at Rs. 1.28 Trillion'. https://www.cmie.com/

kommon/bin/sr.php?kall=warticle&dt=2016-11-21%20
15:12:31&msec=360. Accessed 29 June 2017.

Dasgupta, D. 2016. 'Theoretical Analysis of Demonetisation'. *Economic & Political Weekly*. Vol. 51, Issue 51. 17 December.

Dash, D.K. 2016. 'Ramdev Welcomes Government's Move on High Value Currency Notes'. *The Times of India*. 8 November. http://timesofindia.indiatimes.com/india/Ramdev-welcomes-governments-move-on-high-value-currency-notes/articleshow/55319345.cms. Accessed 20 September 2017.

Debroy, B. 2017. '12 Reasons Why'. *The Indian Express*. 3 May.

Desai, J.P. 2012. *Accountability: Angst, Awareness, Action*, Delhi: Pearson.

Devara, R. 2016. 'Crisis of Credit: An Omission Most Untimely and Unfair'. *The Indian Express*. 9 December. http://indianexpress.com/article/business/banking-and-finance/demonetisation-scheme-banking-sector-post-offices-rural-economy-4417973/. Accessed 16 July 2017.

DNA. 2017. 'Raghuram Rajan Stepped Down because of Demonetization: P. Chidambaram'. *DNA*. 11 February. http://www.dnaindia.com/money/report-raghuram-rajan-stepped-down-because-of-demonetization-p-chidambaram-2319589. Accessed 11 July 2017.

Dua, H.K. (Ed). 2017. *Demonetisation in the Detail*. New Delhi: Palimpsest.

ET Bureau. 2017. 'Slowdown in New Investments Post Demonetisation: CMIE'. The *Economic Times*. 3 January. https://economictimes.indiatimes.com/news/economy/finance/slowdown-in-new-investments-post-demonetisation-cmie/articleshow/56302642.cms.

Gandhi, J. 2016. 'Give Me 50 days Over Scrapped Notes, Punish Me if Problems Persist: Modi'. *The Hindustan Times*. 13 November. http://www.hindustantimes.com/india-news/modi-turns-emotional-as-he-speaks-on-demonetisation-says-has-more-such-steps-in-mind/story-naFFmlHrFbhqbdUrj6ALBK.html. Accessed 18 June 2017.

Gandhi, M. K. *Hind Swaraj*. Navjivan Press.

Government of India. 1956. *Direct Tax Reform: Report of a Survey*. (Chairperson: Kaldor).

Government of India, Ministry of Finance. 2012. *Black Money Report*.

Government of India, Ministry of Statistics and Programme Implementation. 2013. 'Methodology for Estimating Quarterly GDP'. http://mospiold.nic.in/Mospi_New/upload/Methodology_doc_for_compilation_qrt_GDP_14aug13.pdf. Accessed 30 June 2017.

Government of India, Ministry of Statistics and Programme Implementation. 2015. 'Consumer Price Index: Changes in Revised Series Base Year 2012 = 100'. http://164.100.34.62:8080/PDFile/CPI-Changes_in_the_Revised_Series.pdf.

Government of India, Ministry of Finance. 2016a. *Economic Survey 2015-16: Statistical Appendix*. New Delhi: Oxford University Press India.

Government of India, Ministry of Finance. 2016b. Committee on Digital Payments. 'Medium Term Recommendations to Strengthen Digital Payments Ecosystem'. December. http://pibphoto.nic.in/documents/rlink/2016/dec/p2016122801.pdf.

Government of India, Press Information Bureau. 2016c. 'Government Takes Various Steps in Last Two Years to Curb the Menace of Black Economy Both Within and Outside the Country'. 10 May. http://pib.nic.in/newsite/PrintRelease.aspx?relid=145129.

Government of India, Ministry of Finance, CBDT. 2016d. 'Inflow of Funds into Jan Dhan Accounts'. 7 December 2016. http://www.incometaxindia.gov.in/Lists/Press%20Releases/Attachments/562/Inflow-of-Funds-into-

Jan-Dhan-Accounts-8-12-2016.pdf. Accessed 7 July 2017.

Government of India, Department of Agriculture, Cooperation and Farmers Welfare, Ministry of Agriculture and Farmers Welfare. 2017a. 'Minutes of the Meetings of the Crop Weather Watch Group Held on 27.01.2017'. http://agricoop.nic.in/sites/default/files/Minutes-27-Jan-2017%28for%20mail%29.pdf.

Government of India, Ministry of Commerce and Industry. 2017b. 'Key Economic Indicators'. http://www.eaindustry. nic.in/key_economic_indicators/Key_Economic_ Indicators.pdf.

Government of India, Ministry of Finance. 2017c. *Economic Survey 2016-17*. New Delhi: Oxford University Press India.

Government of India, Ministry of Finance. 2017d. 'Union Budget of India, 2017-18'. http://indiabudget.nic.in/budget.asp.

Government of India, Ministry of Finance. 2017e. 'Pradhan Mantri Jan Dhan Yojana Progress Reports Archive'. https://www.pmjdy.gov.in/Archive. Accessed 7 July 2017.

Government of India, Ministry of Rural Development. 2017f. 'MNREGS Website: MIS Reports'. http://mnregaweb4. nic.in/netnrega/MISreport4.aspx?fin_year=2013-2014&rpt=RP.

Government of India, Ministry of Statistics and Programme Implementation. 2017g. 'Second Advance Estimates of National Income, 2016-17 and Quarterly Estimates of Gross Domestic Product for the Third Quarter Oct-Dec'. 28 February. http://pib.nic.in/newsite/PrintRelease. aspx?relid=158734.

Government of India, Ministry of Finance, Controller General of Accounts. 2017h. 'Union Government Accounts at a Glance: Monthly Accounts'. http://www.cga.nic.in/.

Government of India, Ministry of Statistics and Programme Implementation. 2017i. 'National Account Statistics'. Various Issues.

Government of India. NITI Aayog. 2017j. 'Interim Report of the Committee of Chief Ministers on Digital Payments'. January. http://niti.gov.in/content/interim-report-committee-cms-digital-payments.

Government of India. 2017k. Telecom Regulatory Authority of India (TRAI). 'Indian Telecom Services Performance Indicators, October–December 2016'. April. http://www.trai.gov.in/release-publication/reports/performance-indicators-reports.

Government of India, Ministry of Commerce and Industry, Office of the Economic Adviser. 'Wholesale Price Index Data'. Various Issues. http://www.eaindustry.nic.in/home.asp.

Government of India, Department of Publication. 'The Gazette of India', Various Notifications. http://egazette.nic.in.

IANS. 2016a. 'How Demonetisation Has Hit Small Traders Hard'. *The New Indian Express*. 15 November. http://www.newindianexpress.com/nation/2016/nov/15/how-demonetisation-has-hit-small-traders-hard-1538869.html. Accessed 16 July 2017.

IANS. 2016b. 'Widespread Distress as Demonetisation Hits Small, Medium Businesses Hard'. *Millennium Post*. 24 November. http://www.millenniumpost.in/widespread-distress-as-demonetisation-hits-small-medium-businesses-hard-171300?NID=334531. Accessed 16 July 2017.

IMF. 2016. 'Financial Access Survey'. International Monetary Fund. http://data.imf.org/regular.aspx?key=61063966.

Janardhan, A. 2017. 'Demonetisation: 35 Per Cent Job Losses, 50 Per Cent Revenue Dip, Says Study by Largest Organisation of Manufacturers'. *The Indian Express*. 9 January. http://indianexpress.com/article/india/demonetisation-35-per-

cent-job-losses-50-per-cent-revenue-dip-says-study-by-
largest-organisation-of-manufacturers-4465524/.

Jha, N. 2016. 'Note Demonetisation: What of Women Who
Hide Cash to Feed Their Children or to Escape Abuse'.
Scroll.in. 12 November. https://scroll.in/article/821255/
note-demonetisation-what-of-the-women-who-hide-
cash-to-feed-their-children-or-to-escape-abuse. Accessed
7 July 2017.

Joseph, T. 2016. 'The Real Reasons for Demonetisation Might
Be Hiding in Plain Sight'. *The Indian Express*. 19 December.
http://indianexpress.com/article/blogs/demonetisation-
implementation-cash-crunch-digital-payments-cashless-
transactions-4435312/.

Kerala State Planning Board. 2016. *Interim Report of the
Committee to Study the Impact of Demonetisation on the State
Economy of Kerala*. December.

Krishnan, D. and S. Siegel. 2016. 'Survey of the Effects of
Demonetisation on 28 Slum Neighbourhoods in Mumbai'.
Economic & Political Weekly. Vol. 52, Issue No. 3. 21 January
2017.

Kumar, A. 1985. 'The Chequered Economy in Black & White
[Review of *The Black Economy in India* by K.N. Kabra]'.
Economic & Political Weekly. 30 March.

- 1987. 'Surplus, Services and Black: The Growing Triad'.
  Mimeo, paper presented at the conference on Resource
  Mobilisation, organized at NIPFP, New Delhi.

- 1999. *The Black Economy in India*. New Delhi: Penguin
  India.

- 2002. *The Black Economy in India*, Second Edition, New
  Delhi: Penguin India.

- 2005. 'India's Black Economy: The Macroeconomic
  Implications'. South Asia: *Journal of South Asian Studies*.
  Vol. 28, No. 2. August. Pp. 249–263.

- 2006. 'The Flawed Macro Statistics: Overestimated Growth and Underestimated Inflation'. Chapter in the Alternative Economic Survey Group (Ed.) *Alternative Economic Survey, India 2005-06: Disempowering Masses*. Pp. 29-44. New Delhi: Daanish Books.
- 2013. *Indian Economy Since Independence: Persisting Colonial Disruption*. New Delhi: Vision Books.
- 2015. 'Union Budget 2015-16: Continuity with the Past Framework'. *Mainstream*. Vol. LIII, No. 11. 7 March.
- 2016a. 'Curbing the Black Economy. Good Intentions Will Not Suffice'. *Economic & Political Weekly*. 3 September. Vol. LI, No. 36. Pp. 25–28.
- 2016b. 'Demonetisation: Counting the Cost of an Economic Risk'. *The Hindustan Times*. 14 November. http://m.hindustantimes.com/analysis/demonetisation-counting-the-cost-of-an-economic-risk/story-jHD9bOBSwUDCdqAUz5ft4M.html.
- 2016c. 'Estimation of the Size of the Black Economy in India, 1996–2012'. *Economic & Political Weekly*. Vol. 51, No. 48. Pp 36–42.
- 2017a. *Understanding Black Economy and Black Money in India: An Enquiry into Causes, Consequences and Remedies*. New Delhi: Aleph.
- 2017b. 'Economic Consequences of Demonetisation: Money Supply and Economic Structure'. *Economic & Political Weekly*. Vol. 52, No. 1. 7 January.
- 2017c. 'Curbing the Black Economy: Demonetisation Not the Way'. *The Mainstream*. Vol. LV, No. 1. 24 December 2016.
- 2017d. 'Unusual times, Usual Ways'. *The Indian Express*. 9 March.
- 2017e. 'Painting It All Black'. *The Hindu*. 6 April.
- 2017f. 'Policy Making and Autonomous Intellectuals: Who Wants Genuine Debates?'. Catch News. 30 May.

- 2017g. 'Not Worth the Tax'. *The Indian Express*. 14 June.
- 2017h. 'An Embarrassment of Riches'. *The Indian Express*. 1 August.
- 2017i. 'Demonetisation Is a Clear Case of How Public Policy Should Not Be Made'. The Wire. 4 September. https://thewire.in/173595/demonetisation-is-a-clear-case-of-how-public-policy-should-not-be-made. Accessed 4 September 2017.
- 2017j. 'Calling Black White'. *The Indian Express*. 8 September.
- 2017k. 'With the Post-GST Trend of Rising Prices, Has the Government Taken the Public for a Ride?'. The Wire. 20 September. https://thewire.in/179281/gst-and-price-rise-public-taken-for-a-ride/.

Kumar, A. and A. Verma. 2017. 'What Do We Know about Remonetisation? Analysis of Available Data till April 2017'. *Economic & Political Weekly*. Vol. 52, No. 24. 17 June.

Kumar, A. and S. Chattopadhyay. 2013. 'Estimation of Capital Flight from India: 1948–2012'. Mimeo, paper presented at the Black Economy conference, organized by CESP, JNU in 2013 and 2015.

Kumar, A.P. 2016. 'Demonetisation and the Rule of Law'. *Economic & Political Weekly*. Vol. 51, No. 50. 10 December.

Lele, A. and N. Anand. 2016. '10% Interest Rates: Money Lenders Make a Comeback Due to Currency Shortage'. *Business Standard*. 27 December. http://www.business-standard.com/article/economy-policy/10-interest-rates-money-lenders-make-a-comeback-due-to-currency-shortage-116122601048_1.html. Accessed 7 July 2017.

Lok Sabha. 2016a. 'ISI Study on Counterfeit Currency'. Unstarred Question No. 3285. http://164.100.47.190/loksabhaquestions/annex/9/AU3285.pdf.
- 2016b. Unstarred Question No. 2526, Answered on 30/11/2016 (Data for Cyber Security Incidents)

http://164.100.47.190/loksabhaquestions/annex/10/AU2526.pdf.

- 2017a. Unstarred Question No. 806, Answered on 7/2/2017 (Data for Govt Websites hacked during 2013-16). http://164.100.47.190/loksabhaquestions/annex/11/AU806.pdf.

- 2017b. Unstarred Question No. 1084, Answered on 8/2/2017 (Data for all websites hacked). http://164.100.47.190/loksabhaquestions/annex/11/AU1084.pdf.

Lokayat and Janata Trust. 2017. 'Demonetisation: Yet Another Fraud on the People'. http://indianculturalforum.in/2017/01/11/demonetisation-yet-another-fraud-on-the-people/. Accessed 2 July 2017.

Mehra, P. 2016. 'The Black Economy Now Amounts to 75% of GDP'. *The Hindu*. 19 December 2016. http://www.thehindu.com/news/national/black-economy-now-amounts-to-75-of-gdp/article6278286.ece.

Menon, S. 2016. 'Banning Notes Will Not Curb Black Money, Says Think Tank that Called for Demonetization'. *The Economic Times*. 22 November. http://economictimes.indiatimes.com/news/economy/policy/banning-notes-will-not-curb-black-money-says-thinktank-that-called-for-demonetisation/articleshow/55550552.cms. Accessed 11 July 2017.

Mishra, A. 2017. 'Demonetisation: On Nov 7, It Was Govt which "Advised" RBI to "Consider" Note Ban, Got RBI Nod Next Day'. *The Indian Express*. 10 January. http://indianexpress.com/article/business/economy/demonetisation-on-november-7-it-was-govt-which-advised-rbi-to-consider-note-ban-got-rbi-nod-the-next-day-rajya-sabha-4467235/.

MoneyControl. 2017. 'Cash Crunch Pushed Factory Activity into Contraction in December'. *MoneyControl*. 3 January. http://www.moneycontrol.com/news/business/

economy/cash-crunch-pushed-factory-activity-into-contractiondecember-939356.html. Accessed 16 July 2017.

Mukherjee, S. 2016. 'Rabi Sowing: Acreage More than 2015, but Slowing Pace Slows Further'. *Business Standard*. 26 November. http://www.business-standard.com/article/economy-policy/rabi-sowing-acreage-more-than-2015-but-sowing-pace-slows-further-116112501152_1.html.

Nag, A. 2016. 'Lost Due to Demonetisation'. *Economic & Political Weekly*. Vol. 51, No. 48. 26 November.

Nair, S. 2016. 'Demonetisation Impact: Vegetables, Fruits Trade Halves in Mumbai'. Firstpost. 21 November. http://www.firstpost.com/india/demonetisation-vegetable-vendors-farmers-affected-as-trade-slowdown-cripples-them-3112794.html. Accessed 16 July 2017.

Nair, S. 2017. 'As Rural Hands Return, NREGA Demand Spikes Over 60 Per Cent'. *The Indian Express*. 9 January. http://indianexpress.com/article/india/as-rural-hands-return-nrega-demand-spikes-over-60-per-cent-4465577/. Accessed 7 July 2017.

Naqvi, S. 2016. 'Textile Market in Tirupur Badly Hit Post-Demonetisation'. *CMIE*. 3 December. https://www.cmie.com. Accessed 16 July 2017.

National Crime Records Bureau. 2016. *Crime in India–2015*. http://ncrb.nic.in/StatPublications/CII/CII2015/cii2015.asp.

Nikkei PMI Report. http://asia.nikkei.com/Markets/Nikkei-PMI/December-India-manufacturing-PMI-falls-on-demonetization.

NIPFP. 1985. *Aspects of Black Economy in India*. New Delhi: NIPFP.

NIPFP Tax Research Team. 2016. 'Demonetisation: Impact on the Economy'. Working Papers Id:11481. eSocialSciences. https://ideas.repec.org/p/ess/wpaper/id11481.html. Accessed 4 July 2017.

PHD Research Bureau. 2017. 'Impact of Demonetization on Economy, Businesses and People: Suggestive Measures for Remonetization'. New Delhi: PHD Chamber Of Commerce and Industry. http://phdcci.in/image/data/Research%20Bureau-2014/Economic%20Developments/paper/Study%20on%20Impact.pdf. Accessed 2 July 2017.

Philipose, P. 2016. 'At Delhi's Azadpur Mandi, Lack of Money Is Slowly Choking Business and Also Workers'. The Wire. 18 November. https://thewire.in/82831/backstory-money-demonetisation-talks-media-listen/. Accessed 16 July 2017.

PRS. 2015a. 'The Undisclosed Foreign Income and Assets [Imposition of Tax] Bill, 2015'. 20 April. http://www.prsindia.org/uploads/media/Black%20Money/Bill%20Summary%20--%20Undisclosed%20Foreign%20Income.pdf.

    - 2015b. 'Bill Summary: The Benami Transactions [Prohibition] Amendment Bill, 2015'. 29 May. http://www.prsindia.org/uploads/media/Benami/Bill%20Summary-%20Benami%20Transactions.pdf.

Pricewaterhouse Coopers. 2014. 'Disrupting Cash: Accelerating Electronic Payments in India'. https://www.pwc.in/assets/pdfs/publications/2015/disrupting-cash-accelerating-electronic-payments-in-india.pdf.

PTI. 2016. 'Vegetables Growers Hard Hit by Demonetisation'. Business Standard. 8 December. http://www.business-standard.com/article/pti-stories/vegetables-growers-hard-hit-by-demonetisation-116120801457_1.html. Accessed 16 July 2017.

PTI. 2015. 'Opposition Targets Amit Shah for Black Money Remark.' The Times of India. 5 February. http://timesofindia.indiatimes.com/india/Opposition-targets-Amit-Shah-for-black-money-remark/articleshow/46136285.cms. Accessed 17 September 2017.

Rajakumar, J.D. and S.L. Shetty. 2016. 'Demonetisation 1978, the Present and the Aftermath.' *Economic & Political Weekly*. Vol. LI, No. 48. 26 November.

Rajya Sabha. 2017. 'Questions and Answers'. Unstarred Questions 543 and 547. http://164.100.47.5/qsearch/qsearch.aspx.

Ram, N. 2017. *Why Scams Are Here to Stay: Understanding Political Corruption in India*. New Delhi: Aleph.

Rao, V.K. 2016. 'Demonetisation: Small Businesses Hit Hard'. *The Times of India*. 5 December. http://timesofindia. indiatimes.com/city/visakhapatnam/Demonetisation-Small-businesses-hit-hard/articleshow/55804448.cms. Accessed 16 July 2017.

Ray, P. 2013. *Monetary Policy*. New Delhi: Oxford University Press.

Raza, G. 'Survey of Impact of Demonetization across India'. Mimeo.

Reddy, C.R. 2017. *Demonetisation and Black Money*. Delhi: Orient BlackSwan.

Reserve Bank of India. 1978. *Annual Report 1977-78*.

  -2005. *History of RBI* (reprint). Pp. 706-709. https://rbidocs. rbi.org.in/rdocs/content/PDFs/89654.pdf.

  - 2016. 'Currency Management'. *Annual Report, 2015-16*. Pp. 91-92.

  - 2017a. *Database on Indian Economy*. https://dbie.rbi.org. in/DBIE/dbie.rbi?site=statistics.

  - 2017b. 'All You Wanted to Know from RBI about Withdrawal of Legal Tender Status of Rs 500 and Rs 1000 Notes'. https://www.rbi.org.in/scripts/bs_ viewcontent.aspx?Id=3270. Accessed 7 July 2017.

  - 2017c. 'Macroeconomic Impact of Demonetisation: A Preliminary Assessment'. 10 March. https:// rbidocs.rbi.org.in/rdocs/Publications/PDFs/ MID10031760E85BDAFEFD497193995BB1B6DBE602. PDF.

- 2017d. Quarterly Order Books, Inventories and Capacity Utilisation Survey. OBICUS. Various Rounds. https://www.rbi.org.in/scripts/QuarterlyPublications. aspx?head=Quarterly%20Order%20Books,%20 Inventories%20and%20Capacity%20Utilisation%20Survey.
- 2017e. Weekly Statistical Supplement. https://www.rbi. org.in/scripts/BS_ViewWSS.aspx.
- 2017f. *Annual Report 2016-17*.

Rogoff, K. 2014. 'Costs and Benefits to Phasing Out Paper Currency'. Mimeo, paper presented at NBER Macroeconomics Annual Conference. https://scholar.harvard. edu/files/rogoff/files/c13431.pdf. Accessed 22 June 2017.

Rogoff, K. 2017. *The Curse of Cash*. Princeton, USA: Princeton University Press.

Samrat. 2017. 'Malicious and Unjust: Powerful Media Houses vs Journalists'. *Economic & Political Weekly*. Vol. LII, No. 4. 28 January.

Saxena, D. 2016. 'Gwalior Farmers Pay Kids' School Fees in Paddy'. *The Times of India*. December 25. http:// timesofindia.indiatimes.com/city/bhopal/gwalior-farmers- pay-kids-school-fees-in-paddy/articleshow/56163293.cms.

SBI. 2017a. *Ecowrap*. 10 January. No. 71. FY 17.

SBI. 2017b. *Ecowrap*. 27 June. No. 15. FY 18.

Shah, A. 2016. 'A Monetary Economics View of the De-monetisation'. *Business Standard*. 14 November. http://www.business-standard.com/article/opinion/ ajay-shah-a-monetary-economics-view-of-the- demonetisation-116111300767_1.html. Accessed 5 July 2017.

Shukla, S. and P. Bhakta. 2016. '3.2 Million Debit Cards Compromised; SBI, HDFC, ICICI, Yes Bank and AXIS Worst Hit'. *The Economic Times*. 20 October. http://economictimes.indiatimes.com/industry/banking/ finance/banking/3-2-million-debit-cards-compromised-

sbi-hdfc-bank-icici-yes-bank-and-axis-worst-hit/
articleshow/54945561.cms.

Singh, R., M. Seth and I. Mishra. 2016. 'Demonetisation
on a Shoestring: How UP Leather Industry Is Hit by
Cash Crunch'. *The Indian Express*. 25 December. http://
indianexpress.com/article/india/demonetisation-on-a-
shoestring-how-up-leather-industry-is-hit-by-cash-
crunch-4443645/. Accessed 16 July 2017.

Singh, S., V. Sharma, M. Mohanty and D.P. Bhattacharya.
2016. 'RBI's No Exchange Rule for Cooperative Banks
Hits Farmers'. *The Economic Times*. 18 November.
http://economictimes.indiatimes.com/news/economy/
agriculture/rbis-no-exchange-rule-for-cooperative-
banks-hits-farmers/articleshow/55484261.cms. Accessed
16 July 2017.

Silvia, M. 2016. 'Demonetisation and Information Poverty:
Insights from Slum Areas in Bangalore and Mumbai'. South
Asia @ LSE Blog. 5 December. http://blogs.lse.ac.uk/
southasia/2016/12/05/demonetisation-and-information-
poverty-insights-from-slum-areas-in-bangalore-and-
mumbai/. Accessed 4 July 2017.

South Asia Terrorism Portal. 2017. 'India Database: Fatalities
1994-2017'.   http://www.satp.org/satporgtp/countries/
india/database/indiafatalities.htm.

Sunder, S. 2016. 'What Are the Consequences of India's
Currency Reform?'. *Yale Insights*. 13 December.
http://insights.som.yale.edu/insights/what-are-the-
consequences-of-india-s-currency-reform. Accessed 17
September 2017.

Ray, S. 2017. 'Higher Tax Collection Show No Impact of Note
Ban: Jaitley'. *The Hindustan Times*. 9 January. http://www.
hindustantimes.com/business-news/tax-figures-show-
demonetization-had-little-impact-on-economy-says-arun-
jaitley/story-NxPefmW9mGVeX8uQzuflLI.html.

TRAI. 2017. 'Indian Telecom Services Performance Indicators, October–December, 2016'. 7 April. http://www.trai.gov.in/sites/default/files/Indicator_Reports_Dec_16_07042017.pdf.

The Hindu. 2017. 'Jan Dhan Deposits Double to Rs 87,000 cr., Come Under I-T Lens'. *The Hindu.* 2 January. http://www.thehindu.com/news/national/Jan-Dhan-deposits-double-to-Rs.-87000-cr.-come-under-I-T-lens/article16975200.ece. Accessed 7 July 2017.

The Indian Express. 2017. 'Sowing of Seeds Much Higher This Year than Last Year: Radha Mohan Singh'. *The Indian Express.* 13 February. http://indianexpress.com/article/india/sowing-of-seeds-much-higher-this-year-than-last-year-radha-mohan-singh-4522586/. Accessed 30 June 2017.

The Times of India. 2016a. 'Maharashtra: Fishing Business Grinds to a Halt Due to Shortage of Cash'. *The Times of India.* 6 December. http://timesofindia.indiatimes.com/city/kolhapur/Fishing-business-grinds-to-a-halt-due-to-shortage-of-cash/articleshow/55842158.cms.

- 2016b. 'Illegal Exchange of Old Notes: CBI Arrests 2 RBI Officials in Bengaluru'. *The Times of India.* 17 December. http://timesofindia.indiatimes.com/india/illegal-exchange-of-old-notes-cbi-arrests-2-rbi-officials-in-bengaluru/articleshow/56035940.cms. Accessed 11 July 2017.

The Wire. 2016. 'Five Reasons Why the Recent Demonetisation May Be Legally Unsound'. The Wire. 20 November. https://thewire.in/81325/demonetisation-legally-unsound/. Accessed 18 June 2017.

Vaishnav, M. 2017. *When Crime Pays: Money and Muscle in Indian Politics.* Noida, India: HarperCollins Publisher.

Varma, S. and A. Bhattacharya. 2017. 'Two Months On, Rural Jobs in UP Still in Freeze Frame'. *The Times of India.* 11 January. http://timesofindia.indiatimes.com/india/

two-months-on-rural-jobs-in-up-still-in-freeze-frame/
articleshow/56463862.cms.

Wilts, A. 2017. 'US Data Leak: 198 Million Americans'
Personal Information Accidentally Released'. *Independent*.
19   June.   http://www.independent.co.uk/news/world/
americas/us-politics/us-leak-data-americans-personal-
information-deep-root-analytics-republican-national-
committee-a7798251.html. Accessed 4 October 2017.

World Atlas. 2017. 'Top Countries Using Digital Money
For Cashless Transactions'. http://www.worldatlas.com/
articles/which-are-the-world-s-most-cashless-countries.
html . Accessed 2 July 2017.

Annexures

Introduction

ANNEXURE 1

Text of Prime Minister Narendra Modi's Address to the Nation

8 November 2017
(http://pib.nic.in/newsite/pmreleases.aspx?mincode=3&speech=S.
Accessed 17 May 2017)

My dear citizens,

I hope you ended the festive season of Diwali with joy and new hope. Today, I will be speaking to you about some critical issues and important decisions. Today I want to make a special request to all of you. You may recall the economic situation in May 2014 when you entrusted us with an onerous responsibility. In the context of BRICS, it was being said that the 'I' in BRICS was shaky. Since then, we had two years of severe drought. Yet, in the last two and a half years with the support of 125 crore Indians, India has become the 'bright spot' in the global economy. It is not just we who are saying this; it is being stated by the International Monetary Fund and the World Bank.

In this effort for development, our motto has been '*Sab Ka Saath Sab Ka Vikas*': We are with all citizens and for development of all citizens. This Government is dedicated to the poor. It will remain dedicated to them. In our fight against poverty, our main thrust has been to empower the poor, and make them active participants in the benefits of economic progress.

The Pradhan Mantri Jan Dhan Yojana, the Jan Suraksha Yojana, the Pradhan Mantri Mudra Yojana for small enterprises, the Stand-up India program for Dalits, Adivasis and women, the Pradhan Mantri Ujjwala Scheme for gas connections in the homes of the poor, the Pradhan Mantri Fasal Beema Yojana and Pradhan Mantri Krishi Sinchai Yojana to protect the income of farmers, the Soil Health Card Scheme to ensure the best possible yield from farmers' fields, and the e-NAM National Market Place scheme to ensure farmers get the right price for their produce—these are all reflections of this approach.

In the past decades, the spectre of corruption and black money has grown. It has weakened the effort to remove poverty. On the one hand, we are now no. 1 in the rate of economic growth. But on the other hand, we were ranked close to one hundred in the global corruption perceptions ranking two years back. In spite of many steps taken, we have only been able to reach a ranking of seventy-six now. Of course, there is improvement. This shows the extent to which corruption and black money have spread their tentacles.

The evil of corruption has been spread by certain sections of society for their selfish interest. They have ignored the poor and cornered benefits. Some people have misused their office for personal gain. On the other hand, honest people have fought against this evil. Crores of common men and women have lived lives of integrity. We hear about poor auto-rickshaw drivers returning gold ornaments left in the vehicles to their rightful owners. We hear about taxi drivers who take pains to locate the owners of cell phones left behind. We hear of vegetable vendors who return excess money given by customers.

There comes a time in the history of a country's development when a need is felt for a strong and decisive step. For years, this country has felt that corruption, black money and terrorism are festering sores, holding us back in the race towards development.

Terrorism is a frightening threat. So many have lost their lives because of it. But have you ever thought about how these terrorists get their money? Enemies from across the border run their operations using fake currency notes. This has been going on for years. Many times, those using fake 500 and 1,000 rupee notes have been caught and many such notes have been seized.

Brothers and sisters,

On the one hand is the problem of terrorism; on the other is the challenge posed by corruption and black money. We began our battle against corruption by setting up an SIT headed by a retired Supreme Court judge, immediately upon taking office. Since then a law was passed in 2015 for disclosure of foreign black money;

- agreements with many countries, including the USA, have been made to add provisions for sharing banking information;
- a strict law has come into force from August 2016 to curb *benami* transactions, which are used to deploy black money earned through corruption;
- a scheme was introduced for declaring black money after paying a stiff penalty.

My dear countrymen,

Through all these efforts, in the last two and a half years, we have brought into the open nearly 1 lakh 25 thousand crore rupees of black money belonging to the corrupt. Honest citizens want this fight against corruption, black money, benami property, terrorism and counterfeiting to continue. Which honest citizen would not be pained by reports of crores worth of currency notes stashed under the beds of government officers? Or by reports of cash found in gunny bags?

The magnitude of cash in circulation is directly linked to the level of corruption. Inflation becomes worse through the deployment of cash earned in corrupt ways. The poor have to bear the brunt of this. It has a direct effect on the purchasing power of the poor and the middle class. You may yourself have experienced when buying land or a house, that apart from the amount paid by cheque, a large amount is demanded in cash. This creates problems for an honest person in buying property. The misuse of cash has led to artificial increase in the cost of goods and services like houses, land, higher education, healthcare and so on.

High circulation of cash also strengthens the *hawala* trade which is directly connected to black money and illegal trade in weapons. Debate on the role of black money in elections has been going on for years.

Brothers and sisters,

To break the grip of corruption and black money, we have decided that the 500 rupee and 1,000 rupee currency notes presently in use will no longer be legal tender from midnight tonight, that is 8th November 2016. This means that these notes will not be acceptable for transactions from midnight onwards. The 500 and 1,000 rupee notes hoarded by anti-national and antisocial elements will become just worthless pieces of paper. The rights and the interests of honest, hard-working people will be fully protected. Let me assure you that notes of 100, 50, 20, 10, five, two and one rupee and all coins will remain legal tender and will not be affected.

This step will strengthen the hands of the common man in the fight against corruption, black money and fake currency. To minimize the difficulties of citizens in the coming days, several steps are being taken.

1. Persons holding old notes of 500 or 1,000 rupees can deposit these notes in their bank or post office accounts from 10th November till close of banking hours on 30th December 2016 without any limit.

2. Thus you will have 50 days to deposit your notes and there is no need for panic.

3. Your money will remain yours. You need have no worry on this point.

4. After depositing your money in your account, you can draw it when you need it.

5. Keeping in mind the supply of new notes, in the first few days, there will be a limit of 10,000 rupees per day and 20,000 rupees per week. This limit will be increased in the coming days.

6. Apart from depositing your notes in your bank account, another facility will also be there.

7. For your immediate needs, you can go to any bank, head post office or sub post office, show your identity proof like Aadhaar card, voter card, ration card, passport, PAN card or other approved proofs, and exchange your old 500 or 1,000 rupee notes for new notes.

8. From 10th November till 24th November the limit for such exchange will be 4,000 rupees. From 25th November till 30th December, the limit will be increased.

9. There may be some who, for some reason, are not able to deposit their old 500 or 1,000 rupee notes by 30th December 2016.

10. They can go to specified offices of the Reserve Bank of India up to 31st March 2017 and deposit the notes after submitting a declaration form.

11. On 9th November and in some places on 10th November also, ATMs will not work. In the first few days, there will be a limit of 2,000 rupees per day per card.

12. This will be raised to 4,000 rupees later.

13. 500 and 1,000 rupee notes will not be legal tender from midnight. However, for humanitarian reasons, to reduce hardship to citizens, some special arrangements have been made for the first 72 hours, that is till midnight on 11th November.

14. During this period, government hospitals will continue to accept 500 and 1,000 rupee notes for payment.

15. This is for the benefit of those families whose members may be unwell.

16. Pharmacies in government hospitals will also accept these notes for buying medicines with doctors' prescription.

17. For 72 hours, till midnight on 11th November, railway ticket booking counters, ticket counters of government buses and airline ticket counters at airports will accept the old notes for purchase of tickets. This is for the benefit of those who may be travelling at this time.

18. For 72 hours, 500 and 1,000 rupee notes will be accepted also at

- Petrol, diesel and CNG gas stations authorized by public sector oil companies
- Consumer co-operative stores authorized by State or Central Government
- Milk booths authorized by State governments
- Crematoria and burial grounds.

These outlets will have to keep proper records of stock and collections.

19. Arrangements will be made at international airports for arriving and departing passengers who have 500 or 1,000 rupee notes of not more than 5,000 rupees, to exchange them for new notes or other legal tender.

20. Foreign tourists will be able to exchange foreign currency or old notes of not more than Rs 5,000 into legal tender.

21. One more thing I would like to mention, I want to stress that in this entire exercise, there is no restriction of any kind on non-cash payments by cheques, demand drafts, debit or credit cards and electronic fund transfer.

Brothers and sisters,

In spite of all these efforts there may be temporary hardships to be faced by honest citizens. Experience tells us that ordinary citizens are always ready to make sacrifices and face difficulties for the benefit of the nation. I see that spirit when a poor widow gives up her LPG subsidy, when a retired schoolteacher contributes his pension to the Swachh Bharat mission, when a poor Adivasi mother sells her goats to build a toilet, when a soldier contributes 57,000 rupees to make his village clean. I have seen that the ordinary citizen has the determination to do anything, if it will lead to the country's progress.

So, in this fight against corruption, black money, fake notes and terrorism, in this movement for purifying our country, will our people not put up with difficulties for some days? I have full confidence that every citizen will stand up and participate in this 'mahayagna'. My dear countrymen, after the festivity of Diwali, now join the nation and extend your hand in this *Imandaari ka Utsav*, this *Pramanikta ka Parv*, this celebration of integrity, this festival of credibility.

I am sure that all political parties, all governments, social services organizations, the media and indeed all sections of the society, will take part in this with enthusiasm and make it a success.

My dear countrymen,

Secrecy was essential for this action. It is only now, as I speak to you, that various agencies like banks, post offices, railways, hospitals and others are being informed. The Reserve Bank, banks and post offices have to make many arrangements at very short notice. Obviously, time will be needed. Therefore all banks will be closed to the public on 9th November. This may cause some hardship to you. I have full faith that banks and post offices will successfully carry out this great task of national importance. However, I appeal to all of you to help the banks and post offices to meet this challenge with poise and determination.

My dear citizens,

From time to time, based on currency needs, the Reserve Bank with the approval of the Central Government brings out new notes of higher value. In 2014, the Reserve Bank sent a recommendation for issue of 5,000 and 10,000 rupee notes. After careful consideration, this was not accepted. Now as part of this exercise, RBI's recommendation to issue 2,000 rupee notes has been accepted. New notes of 500 rupees and 2,000 rupees, with completely new design, will be introduced. Based on past experience, the Reserve Bank will hereafter make arrangements to limit the share of high-denomination notes in the total currency in circulation.

In a country's history, there come moments when every person feels he too should be part of that moment, that he too should make his contribution to the country's progress. Such moments come but rarely. Now, we again have an opportunity where every citizen can join this *mahayagna* against the ills of corruption, black money and fake notes. The more help you give in this campaign, the more successful it will be.

It has been a matter of concern for all of us that corruption and black money tend to be accepted as part of life. This type of thinking has afflicted our politics, our administration and our society like an infestation of termites. None of our public institutions is free from these termites.

Time and again, I have seen that when the average citizen has to choose between accepting dishonesty and bearing inconvenience, they always choose to put up with inconvenience. They will not support dishonesty.

Once again, let me invite you to make your contribution to this grand sacrifice for cleansing our country, just as you cleaned up your surroundings during Diwali.

Let us ignore the temporary hardship.

Let us join this festival of integrity and credibility.

Let us enable coming generations to live their lives with dignity.

Let us fight corruption and black money.

Let us ensure that the nation's wealth benefits the poor.

Let us enable law-abiding citizens to get their due share.

I am confident in the 125 crore people of India and I am sure our country will get success.

Thank you very much. Thanks a lot.

Namaskar.

Bharat Mata Ki Jai.

ANNEXURE 2

Table 1: Notifications/Press Releases Regarding Demonetization from 8 November 2016 to 30 March 2017

S. NO	Date	Title	Issued By
1	08-11-16	Cancellation of the legal tender character of the high-denomination banknotes of Rs 500 and Rs 1000 denominations issued by RBI	Ministry of Finance
2	08-11-16	RBI Instructions to Banks—exchange of old notes up to Rs 4,000, withdrawal of up to Rs 10,000 per day (Rs 20,000 per week), ATM withdrawal up to Rs 2,000 per day	RBI

(Contd)

S. NO	Date	Title	Issued By
3	08-11-16	Issue of Rs 2,000 banknotes	RBI
4	08-11-16	Closure of ATM Operations—Non-dispensing of Old High-Denomination Notes	RBI
5	09-11-16	RBI Instructions to Banks for changes in ATMs—Recalibration of ATMs to dispense Rs 100 and Rs 50 banknotes through ATMs	RBI
6	09-11-16	Banks to remain open for public on Saturday, Nov 12 and Sunday, Nov 13, 2016	RBI
7	09-11-16	Government suspends payment of fees on all toll plazas on National Highways till midnight of 11.11.2016	Ministry of Road Transport and Highways
8	09-11-16	Instructions to Authorized Persons—specified banknotes shall continue to be legal tender until Nov 11 at international airports and for foreign tourists up to Rs 5,000	RBI
9	10-11-16	Replies given by Revenue Secretary Dr. Hasmukh Adhia on the questions relating to action by Income Tax Department in respect of old currency deposited in banks	Ministry of Finance
10	10-11-16	Old demonetized Rs 500 and 1,000 notes accepted for making payments towards fees, charges, taxes and penalties payable to the Central and State Governments including Municipal and local bodies; This facility available only till midnight of 11 November, 2016.	Ministry of Finance
11	10-11-16	Cash Limits not applicable for Banks (withdrawal from another bank), Post Offices, Money Changers operating at international airports, operators of White Label ATMs	RBI

(Contd)

S. NO	Date	Title	Issued By
12	10-11-16	Payment Systems (NEFT, RTGS, cheque clearing) to remain open on Saturday, Nov 12 and Sunday, Nov 13, 2016	RBI
13	11-11-16	Exemptions in payment of court fees, utility bills (of households) using old notes extended until the expiry of Nov 14, 2016	Ministry of Finance
14	11-11-16	Enough cash is available, RBI reassures; urges public to exercise patience and exchange notes at convenience	RBI
15	11-11-16	Issue of pre-paid instruments to foreign tourists	RBI
16	11-11-16	Reporting and Monitoring—report daily position on exchange of specified banknotes (in cash as well as credit to account) and detection of counterfeit notes	RBI
17	11-11-16	Relaxation for government departments—may withdraw more than Rs 10,000 a day, only in exceptional cases	RBI
18	11-11-16	Exemption of fee on National Highways extended till 14 November	Ministry of Road Transport and Highways
19	11-11-16	Action taken by Ministry of Railways on demonetization of Rs 500 and Rs 1000	Railways
20	12-11-16	Ministry of Finance advised RBI to set up a Special Cell to monitor the receipt of fake currency notes and inform such instances	Ministry of Finance
21	12-11-16	MoF reviewed the cash availability and issuance to the public and assured that there is sufficient cash available with banks and RBI.	Ministry of Finance

(Contd)

S. NO	Date	Title	Issued By
22	12-11-16	Public are encouraged to switch over to alternative modes of payment, such as pre-paid cards, Rupay/Credit/Debit cards, mobile banking and internet banking	RBI
23	13-11-16	Review of the position regarding availability and distribution of notes and decisions: Increase in the exchange limit from 4,000 to 4,500, cash withdrawal limit from 2,000 to 2,500, weekly withdrawal limit from 20,000 to 24,000; advice to banks to increase the usage of debit/credit cards and mobile wallets	Ministry of Finance
24	13-11-16	Revision in limits for cash as above; separate queue for senior citizens	RBI
25	13-11-16	Advice: Don't draw and hoard; enough cash in small denominations available at RBI and banks: RBI	RBI
26	13-11-16	Issue of Rs 500 banknotes inset letter 'L' in Mahatma Gandhi (New) Series	RBI
27	13-11-16	Reporting and Monitoring - information on issuance of banknotes over the counter/ATMs	RBI
28	14-11-16	Usage of ATMs - waiver of customer charges	RBI
29	14-11-16	Exemption of fee on National Highways extended across the country till midnight of 18.11.16	Ministry of Road Transport and Highways
30	14-11-16	Expanding the distribution locations for deposit and withdrawal of cash - micro ATMs and mobile vans for people in remote areas, opening account of plantation workers; current account holders allowed withdrawal of up to Rs 50,000 a week.	RBI

(Contd)

S. NO	Date	Title	Issued By
31	14-11-16	Applicability of the scheme to District Central Cooperative Banks - can allow customers to withdraw money up to Rs 24,000 a week but no exchange or deposit	RBI
32	15-11-16	RBI asks Cooperative Banks to ensure strict compliance of its instructions	RBI
33	15-11-16	Standard Operating Procedure (SOP) for putting indelible ink on the finger of the customers coming to a bank branch for SBNs	RBI
34	16-11-16	Daily reporting by banks - send daily data before 2300 hrs every day to RBI	RBI
35	16-11-16	Compliance with provisions of 114B of the Income Tax Rules, 1962 - requirement of a copy of PAN card for depositing more than Rs 50,000	RBI
36	16-11-16	Govt. announces decisions to facilitate farmers, small traders, group C employees in the aftermath of the cancellation of the legal tender character of the old Rs 500 and Rs 1,000 notes. Reduce the limit of exchange from Rs 4,500 to Rs 2,000 w.e.f. 18 Nov, 2016; also withdrawal up to Rs 2,50,000 for weddings	Ministry of Finance
37	16-11-16	Limit for exchange over the counter revised from Rs 4,500 to Rs 2,000	RBI
38	17-11-16	Transactions in relation to which quoting PAN is mandatory—quoting of PAN will now also be mandatory in respect of cash deposits aggregating to rupees two lakh fifty thousand or more during the period 09th November, 2016 to 30th December, 2016	Ministry of Finance

(Contd)

S. NO	Date	Title	Issued By
39	17-11-16	Exemption of fee on National Highways extended	Ministry of Road Transport and Highways
40	17-11-16	RBI reiterates: Supply of Notes Sufficient; Do Not Panic or Hoard Currency	RBI
41	18-11-16	Cash dispensing facility operational at 686 retail outlets	Ministry of Petroleum & Natural Gas
42	18-11-16	Cash withdrawal at PoS - withdrawal limits and customer fee/charges - Relaxed	RBI
43	20-11-16	Withdrawal limits from ATMs unchanged - not increased from 2,500	RBI
44	21-11-16	Central Government constitutes Committees of Addl. Secretaries/Joint Secretaries/Directors for visiting States/UTs and reporting about the status of implementation of its decision cancelling the legal tender character of high-denomination banknotes of Rs 500 and Rs 1,000.	Ministry of Finance
45	21-11-16	To further support the farmers for the current Rabi crop, farmers allowed to purchase seeds with the old high-denomination banknotes of Rs 500 from designated centres	Ministry of Finance
46	21-11-16	Revisions for farmers/traders registered with APMC/mandis - farmers allowed 25,000 per week and traders 50,000 per week from their current account	RBI
47	21-11-16	Cash withdrawal for purpose of celebration of wedding – Rs 2,50,000 only if the date of marriage is on or before Dec 30, 2016	RBI

(Contd)

S. NO	Date	Title	Issued By
48	21-11-16	Prudential Norms on Income Recognition, Asset Classification and Provisioning pertaining to Advances - consequent upon withdrawal of the legal tender status of the existing Rs 500 and Rs 1,000 notes (SBN): Small borrowers may need some more time to repay their loans due. Additional 60 days allowed before designating a loan account as substandard.	RBI
49	21-11-16	Cash Withdrawal Limit Facility for Overdraft/Cash Credit Accounts - holders of current / overdraft / cash credit accounts, which are operational for the last three months or more, may now withdraw up to Rs 50,000 in cash, in a week.	RBI
50	22-11-16	PM invites views from the people, on decision taken regarding demonetization of currency notes of Rs 500 and Rs 1,000	PMO
51	22-11-16	Special Measures to incentivize Electronic Payments – (i) Enhancement in Issuance Limits for PPIs in India (ii) Special measures for merchants	RBI
52	22-11-16	Cash Withdrawal for purpose of Celebration of Wedding – Modification. A detailed list of persons to whom the cash withdrawn is proposed, together with a declaration that they do not have a bank account, where the amount proposed to be paid is Rs 10,000 or more. The list should indicate the purpose of proposed payments.	RBI
53	22-11-16	Making Cash available for Rabi Crop Season – Advisory to Banks. Banks with currency chests advised to ensure adequate cash supply to DCCBs and RRBs. Branches in APMCs may also be given adequate cash to facilitate procurement.	RBI

(Contd)

S. NO	Date	Title	Issued By
54	22-11-16	Fraudulent Practices - banks are advised to ensure that fraudulent practices are stopped forthwith through enhanced vigilance and take stern action against officials involved in such activities.	RBI
55	23-11-16	The Central Government takes various decisions for the benefit of farmers in the current Rabi season and to promote digital payments in the economy. Indian Railways decided not to levy service charges of Rs 20 for second class and Rs 40 for upper classes on purchase of reserved E-tickets up to 31st December, 2016. TRAI decided to reduce the USSD charges from the current Rs 1.50 per session to Rs 0.50 per session for transactions relating to banking and payments. All Government organizations, public-sector undertakings and other Government authorities advised to use only digital payment methods	Ministry of Finance
56	23-11-16	Deposit of specified banknotes in Small Savings Schemes - banks are advised not to accept SBNs for deposits in Small Saving Schemes with immediate effect.	RBI
57	24-11-16	The Union Finance Minister Shri Arun Jaitley holds video conferencing with banks for major push to cashless transactions; Banks to now focus on stepping up transactions in mission mode through alternate banking channels such as NEFT, mobile wallets, pre-paid cards, QR codes, pay-roll cards, debit and credit cards and Unified Payments Interface (UPI) among others	Ministry of Finance

(Contd)

S. NO	Date	Title	Issued By
58	24-11-16	No over-the-counter exchange of old Rs 500 and Rs 1000 notes after midnight of 24.11.2016. Certain other exemptions continued till 15th December, 2016 with certain additions and modifications (School and college fees and other previous services continued)	Ministry of Finance
59	24-11-16	Discontinuation of over-the-counter exchange of SBN after midnight of Nov, 24	RBI
60	24-11-16	Withdrawal of Specified Bank Notes: banks advised to take appropriate steps for cash requirements of pensioners and Armed Forces Personnel	RBI
61	24-11-16	Deposit under Guarantee Scheme to decongest the storage facilities at banks - Banks may deposit SBNs directly with the offices of RBI under whose jurisdiction they are located.	RBI
62	25-11-16	Exchange Facility at RBI to continue	RBI
63	25-11-16	Withdrawal of cash – weekly limit (continuance of Rs 24,000 per week)	RBI
64	25-11-16	Exchange facility to foreign citizens - exchange foreign exchange for Indian currency notes up to a limit of Rs 5,000 per week till December 15, 2016	RBI
65	26-11-16	Section 42(1A) requirement for maintaining additional CRR - on a review of the current liquidity conditions, banks to maintain with the Reserve Bank of India, effective from the fortnight beginning November 26, 2016, an incremental CRR of 100 per cent on the increase in NDTL between September 16, 2016 and November 11, 2016.	RBI

(Contd)

S. NO	Date	Title	Issued By
66	27-11-16	Chest Guarantee Scheme for Specified Bank Notes (SBNs) – CGSS. New scheme for depositing SBNs with designated currency chest at the district level, under guarantee agreement similar to the current facility available at RBI offices.	RBI
67	28-11-16	Withdrawal of cash from bank deposit accounts – Relaxation. To allow withdrawals of deposits made in current legal tender notes on or after November 29, 2016 beyond the current limits.	RBI
68	28-11-16	Chest Guarantee Scheme for Specified Bank Notes (SBNs) – CGSS. To expand the ambit of the CGSS, it has been decided that banks operating currency chests may be allowed to operate CGSS if they have additional space in their existing currency chest or additional storage space at the same centre which is nearly as safe and secure as that of a currency chest.	RBI
69	29-11-16	Accounts under PMJDY - Precautions - limit of Rs 10,000 per month for KYC-compliant PMJDY accounts (further withdrawals after ascertaining the genuineness; Rs 5,000 per month for non-KYC accounts	RBI
70	29-11-16	Point of Sale (PoS) Devices and Goods required for their manufacture exempted from Central Excise Duty till March 31, 2017.	Ministry of Finance
71	29-11-16	Chest Balance Limit / Cash Holding Limit - in the wake of deposits of SBNs in massive quantity, SBNs deposited in the currency chests, since November 10, 2016 will be considered as part of the chest balance in the soiled note category but such deposits will not be reckoned for calculating Chest Balance Limit / Cash Holding Limit.	RBI

(Contd)

S. NO	Date	Title	Issued By
72	01-12-16	Toll collection to resume on National Highways from midnight of 2 December	Ministry of Road Transport and Highways
73	01-12-16	With effect from midnight of 2 December, 2016, old Rs 500 banknotes will not be accepted at petrol, diesel and gas outlets of public-sector oil and gas marketing companies as well as for purchase of air tickets at airports. Supply of LPG continues to be in the exempted category for the purpose of payment through old Rs 500 banknotes.	Ministry of Finance
74	01-12-16	Shri Dharmendra Pradhan, Minister Petroleum, launches digital awareness campaign to educate the people about cashless transactions.	Ministry of Petroleum & Natural Gas
75	02-12-16	Action taken in cases of bank officials involved in carrying out irregular transactions, in violation of RBI's instructions post demonetization of Specified Bank Notes by the Government w.e.f. midnight of 8 November 2016.	Ministry of Finance
76	02-12-16	Allocation of banknotes - to ensure that adequate allocation of banknotes are made for the rural branches, post offices and DCCBs.	RBI
77	05-12-16	Any payment above Rs 5000 to suppliers, contractors, grantee/loanee institutions, etc. by Government Departments to be now made through e-payment to attain the goal of complete digitization of Government payments.	Ministry of Finance

(Contd)

S. NO	Date	Title	Issued By
78	06-12-16	Income Tax (IT) Department carries out swift investigations in more than 400 cases since the demonetization of Old High Denomination (OHD) currency on 8 November, 2016; More than Rs 130 crore in cash and jewellery seized and approximately Rs 2,000 crore of undisclosed income admitted by the taxpayers; IT Department refers large number of cases with serious irregularities detected post demonetization to Enforcement Directorate (ED) & CBI.	Ministry of Finance
79	06-12-16	In order to facilitate the move towards cashless transactions, the Government has directed the banks to install an additional one million new PoS terminals by 31st March, 2017; 2,73,919 camps organized to open bank accounts for unorganized labour in which 24.54 lakh accounts opened.	Ministry of Finance
80	07-12-16	Withdrawal of the Incremental CRR effective beginning Dec 10.	RBI
81	08-12-16	Government waives service tax charged while making payments through credit card, debit card, charge card or any other payment card; waiver limited to payments up to Rs 2,000 in a single transaction.	Ministry of Finance
82	08-12-16	Package for Promotion of Digital and Cashless Economy.	Ministry of Finance
83	09-12-16	Committee on Digital Payments headed by Shri Ratan P. Watal, Principal Adviser, NITI Aayog and former Finance Secretary submits its Final Report to the Union Finance Minister.	Ministry of Finance

(Contd)

S. NO	Date	Title	Issued By
84	09-12-16	Government withdraws exemptions given for the use of Rs 500 old notes, from midnight of December 9, 2016, for making payments at railway ticketing counters, ticket counters of Government or public-sector undertakings buses for purchase of tickets; for making payments to catering services on board, during travel by rail; and for making payments for purchasing tickets for travel by suburban and metro rail services.	Ministry of Finance
85	12-12-16	Distribution of Mahatma Gandhi (New) Series Banknotes – Records: In the wake of reported seizures by Income Tax Department and other law-enforcement agencies of large quantities of high-denomination banknotes it has been felt necessary to put in place an appropriate reporting system to keep track of issuance of these banknotes by the currency chests.	RBI
86	12-12-16	Detection of counterfeit notes in Specified Bank Notes (SBNs) - Reporting: Banks are advised to send branch-wise report on detection of counterfeit notes.	RBI
87	13-12-16	Shri R. Gandhi and Shri S.S. Mundra, RBI Deputy Governors brief agencies on currency issues	RBI
88	13-12-16	Preservation of CCTV recordings: banks are further advised to preserve CCTV recordings of operations at bank branches and currency chests for the period from November 08 to December 30, 2016, until further instructions, to facilitate coordinated and effective action by the enforcement agencies in dealing with matters relating to illegal accumulation of new currency notes.	RBI

(Contd)

S. NO	Date	Title	Issued By
89	15-12-16	NITI Aayog announces launch of the schemes - Lucky Grahak Yojana and Digi-Dhan Vyapar Yojana - for incentivizing digital payment.	NITI Aayog
90	16-12-16	Taxation Laws (Second Amendment) Act, 2016, came into force yesterday, i.e., 15th December, 2016 and rules notified today and placed in public domain; The Taxation and Investment Regime for Pradhan Mantri Garib Kalyan Yojana, 2016	Ministry of Finance
91	16-12-16	Pradhan Mantri Garib Kalyan Deposit Scheme (PMGKDS), 2016 - Operational Guidelines.	RBI
92	16-12-16	Exchange facility to foreign citizens of Rs 5,000 per week extended till Dec 31	RBI
93	16-12-16	Special measures up to March 31, 2017: Rationalization of Merchant Discount Rate (MDR) for transactions up to Rs 2,000 (For transactions up to Rs 1,000, MDR shall be capped at 0.25% of the transaction value. For transactions above Rs 1,000 and up to Rs 2,000, MDR shall be capped at 0.5% of the transaction value.)	RBI
94	16-12-16	Special Measures up to March 31, 2017: Rationalization of customer charges for Immediate Payment Service (IMPS), Unified Payment Interface (UPI) & Unstructured Supplementary Service Data (USSD) - no charges on customers for transactions up to Rs 1,000 settled on the Immediate Payment Service (IMPS), USSD-based *99# and Unified Payment Interface (UPI) systems.	RBI

(Contd)

S. NO	Date	Title	Issued By
95	17-12-16	Statement by Finance Minister Shri Arun Jaitley: Political parties have not been granted any exemption post demonetization and introduction of Taxation Laws (Second Amendment) Act, 2016 which came into force on 15th December, 2016	Ministry of Finance
96	19-12-16	Deposit of Specified Bank Notes (SBNs) into bank accounts: Tenders of SBNs in excess of Rs 5,000 into a bank account will be received for credit only once during the remaining period till December 30, 2016. The credit in such cases shall be afforded only after questioning tenderer, on record, in the presence of at least two officials of the bank, as to why this could not be deposited earlier and receiving a satisfactory explanation.	RBI
97	20-12-16	Measures for Promoting Digital Payments & Creation of Less-Cash Economy: Benefit of lower rate of income tax on digital turnover for small businesses.	Ministry of Finance
98	21-12-16	In order to further promote digital and card payments, Department of Financial Services, Ministry of Finance issues direction in public interest to all Public Sector Banks (PSBs) not to charge fees for transactions settled on Immediate Payment Service (IMPS) and Unified Payments Interface (UPI) in excess of rates charged for National Electronic Funds Transfer (NEFT) for transactions above Rs 1,000, with service tax being charged at actual rate.	Ministry of Finance

(Contd)

S.NO	Date	Title	Issued By
99	21-12-16	Deposit of Specified Bank Notes (SBNs) into bank accounts - Modification: provisions of the above circular at sub para (i) and (ii) will not apply to fully KYC-compliant accounts.	RBI
100	22-12-16	Ministry of Electronics and Information Technology (MEITY) organizes national workshop on 'Electronic Government Payments & Receipts'	Ministry of Electronics and I-T
101	23-12-16	Payments towards Tax, Penalty, Surcharge and Deposit under PMGKY 2016 in old Demonetized Currency allowed till 30th December, 2016	Ministry of Finance
102	23-12-16	Reporting Cash Transactions under Rule 114E of Income Tax Rules, 1962	Ministry of Finance
103	25-12-16	Government of India kick-starts the awards of the Lucky Grahak Yojana and Digi-Dhan Vyapar Yojana	NITI Aayog
104	26-12-16	Interest Subvention Scheme for Short Term Crop Loans during the year 2016-17 - grant of grace period of 60 days beyond due date - in view of the constraints faced by farmers for timely repayment of loan dues on account of withdrawal of legal tender status of Specified Bank Notes (SBNs), it has been decided by the GoI to provide an additional grace period of 60 days for prompt repayment incentive of 3% to those farmers whose crop loan dues are falling due between 1st November, 2016 and 31st December, 2016.	RBI
105	28-12-16	It is decided to provide 30 days, in addition to the 60 days provided for crop loans; term loans for business purposes including agriculture loans.	RBI

(Contd)

S. NO	Date	Title	Issued By
106	29-12-16	Sanction of Additional Working Capital Limits to Micro and Small Enterprises (MSEs) - some MSEs are facing temporary difficulties in carrying out their normal business due to cash flow mismatches, banks are advised that they may use the facility of providing above 'additional working capital limit' to their MSE borrowers, to overcome the difficulties arising out of such cash flow mismatches also. This would be a one-time measure up to March 31, 2017.	RBI
107	30-12-16	Cash withdrawal from ATMs – enhancement of daily limits from Rs 2,500 to Rs 4,500 (weekly limit unchanged).	RBI
108	30-12-16	The President of India approves the Promulgation of the Specified Bank Notes (Cessation of Liabilities) Ordinance, 2016	Ministry of Finance
109	30-12-16	Closure of the scheme of exchange of Specified Bank Notes (SBNs) at banks on December 30 2016 - accounting and SBNs cannot form part of banks' cash balances from the close of business as on December 31, 2016	RBI
110	30-12-16	White Label ATM Operators (WLAOs) - sourcing of cash from retail outlets	RBI
111	30-12-16	Facility for exchange of Specified Bank Notes (SBNs) during Grace Period – verification of KYC and account details - a facility for exchange of SBNs is made available for the resident and non-resident citizens who could not avail the facility from November 10 to December 30, 2016 on account of their absence from India during the aforementioned period.	RBI

(Contd)

S. NO	Date	Title	Issued By
112	30-12-16	Ministry of Agriculture & Farmers Welfare decides to extend the cut-off date for crop insurance during Rabi 2016-17 under Pradhan Mantri Fasal Bima Yojana up to 10th January, 2017.	Ministry of Agriculture and Farmers Welfare
113	31-12-16	RBI introduces facility for citizens and NRIs who were abroad for exchange of SBNs.	RBI
114	03-01-17	Allocation of cash for rural areas - at least 40% banknotes are supplied to rural areas.	RBI
115	03-01-17	Exchange facility to foreign citizens - foreign citizens allowed to exchange foreign exchange for Indian currency notes up to a limit of Rs 5,000 per week till Jan 31, 2017	RBI
116	05-01-17	Clarification regarding Specified Bank Notes - The periodical SBN figures released were based on aggregation of accounting entries done at the large no. of currency chests all over the country. The scheme has come to an end on December 30, 2016, these figures would need to be reconciled with the physical cash balances to eliminate accounting errors/possible double counts, etc.	RBI
117	16-01-17	Enhancement of withdrawal limits from ATMs (from Rs 4,500 to Rs 10,000 per day per card) and Current Accounts (from Rs 50,000 to Rs 1,00,000 per week)	RBI
118	30-01-17	Limits on cash withdrawals from bank accounts and ATMs - restoration of status quo ante (limits on savings bank accounts will continue for the present)	RBI

(Contd)

S. NO	Date	Title	Issued By
119	07-02-17	Amendment to Pradhan Mantri Garib Kalyan Deposit Scheme	RBI
120	08-02-17	Removal of limits on withdrawal of cash from savings bank accounts - effective February 20, 2017, the limits on cash withdrawals from the savings bank accounts will be enhanced to Rs 50,000 per week (from the current limit of Rs 24,000 per week); and effective March 13, 2017, there will be no limits on cash withdrawals from savings bank accounts.	RBI
121	13-02-17	Chest Balance Limit / Cash Holding Limit - SBNs deposited in the currency chests, since November 10, 2016, will be considered as part of the chest balance in the soiled note category but such deposits will not be reckoned for calculating Chest Balance Limit / Cash Holding Limit.	RBI
122	16-02-17	Reimbursement of Merchant Discount Rate - (GoI) has decided to absorb the Merchant Discount Rate (MDR) charges in respect of debit card transactions while making payments to GoI.	RBI
123	30-03-17	Rationalization of Merchant Discount Rate (MDR) for Debit Card Transactions – Continuance of Special Measures - special measures for debit card transactions (including for payments made to Government) were introduced for a temporary period starting January 1, 2017 through March 31, 2017. Till the issuance of final instructions on MDR for debit card transactions, the instructions shall continue.	RBI

Source: RBI Website, Ministry of Finance Website and pib.nic.in

Table 2: Frequency of Issuance of Notifications Regarding Demonetization

S. No	Week	No. of Notifications
1	8 Nov–13 Nov	28
2	14 Nov–20 Nov	16
3	21 Nov–27 Nov	23
4	28 Nov–4 Dec	10
5	5 Dec–11 Dec	8
6	12 Dec–18 Dec	11
7	19 Dec–25 Dec	8
8	26 Dec–31 Dec	10
9	Later	10
Total		124

Source: Based on Table 1 (Notifications Regarding Demonetization)

Graph 1: Frequency of Issuance of Notifications Regarding Demonetization

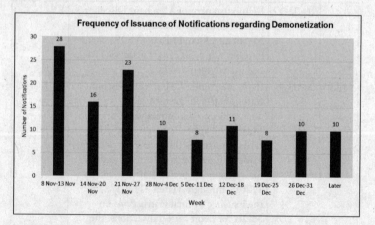

Source: Based on Table 1 (Notifications Regarding Demonetization)

ANNEXURE 3

Table 3: Places Where/Activities and Period for Which Old Notes Were Allowed to Be Used

S. No	Description	Time Period
1	At government hospitals for medical treatment and at pharmacies in govt hospitals for buying medicines against doctors' prescriptions	9 Nov–15 Dec
2	Purchases at railway ticket counters	9 Nov–9 Dec
3	Purchase of tickets at counters of govt or public-sector bus services	9 Nov–9 Dec
4	Purchase of tickets at airline ticket counters	9 Nov–2 Dec
5	Purchase of ticket for suburban and metro rail travel	9 Nov–9 Dec
6	Purchases at consumer cooperative stores operated under authorization of central or state governments (limited to Rs 5000 at a time from 24 Nov)	9 Nov–15 Dec
7	Purchases at milk booths operating under authorization of Central or state government	9 Nov–15 Dec
8	Purchase of petrol, diesel and gas at the stations operating under authorization of public-sector oil marketing companies	9 Nov–2 Dec
9	Purchase of LPG gas cylinders	9 Nov–15 Dec
10	Expenses at crematoriums and burial grounds	9 Nov–15 Dec
11	Exchange of foreign currency for up to Rs 5000 at international airports, for arriving and departing passengers	9 Nov–15 Dec
12	Availing of on-board catering during travel by rail	9 Nov–9 Dec
13	Purchase of entry tickets for monuments maintained by Archaeological Survey of India	9 Nov–15 Dec
14	Payments towards any fees, charges, taxes or penalties payable to the Central or state governments, including municipal and local bodies	10 Nov–15 Dec
15	Payments towards utility charges, including water and electricity (for households only; no advance payment permitted)	10 Nov–15 Dec

(Contd)

S. No	Description	Time Period
16	Payment of court fees	11 Nov–15 Dec
17	Purchase of seeds from designated outlets	21 Nov–15 Dec
18	Payment of school fees up to Rs 2000 per student in Central government, state government, municipality and local body schools	24 Nov–15 Dec
19	Payment of fees in Central or state government colleges	24 Nov–15 Dec
20	Purchase of pre-paid mobile top-up, up to a limit of Rs 500 per top-up	24 Nov–15 Dec
21	Payment towards tax, penalty, surcharge and deposit under PMGKY 2016	22 Dec–30 Dec

Source: Press Information Bureau
Note: After 24 November 2016, exempted transactions were allowed in old notes of Rs 500 only

ANNEXURE 4

Table 4: Changes in Rules Related to Demonetization

Change	S. No	Date	Description
Time period allowed for deposit of old notes	1	8 Nov	'An opportunity will be given for those who are unable to exchange/deposit their notes on or before 30 December . . . at specified offices of the RBI on later dates along with necessary documentation.'
		30 Dec	'Grace period available only for the resident and non-resident citizens who could not avail the facility from November 10 to December 30, 2016 on account of their absence from India during the aforementioned period.'

(Contd)

Change	S. No	Date	Description
Limit on amount allowed to be deposited	2	8 Nov	'No limit on the quantity or value of the old notes to be credited to the account maintained with the bank. However, maximum Rs 50,000 can be deposited in accounts where compliance with KYC not complete.'
		15 Nov	Cash deposit limit on Jan Dhan accounts at Rs 50,000.
	3	19 Dec	'Amounts exceeding Rs 5000 in old notes can be deposited only once between now [19 Dec] and 30th December, 2016 plus subject to satisfactory response on late deposit . . .'
		21 Dec	Notification withdrawn
Exchange of old notes for new notes	4	8 Nov	Exchange up to Rs 4000 by a person at any bank branch/offices of RBI/post offices till 30 December
		24 Nov	Exchange over the counter stopped (more than a month earlier than promised)
	5	8 Nov	Exchange allowed up to Rs 4000 per person
		13 Nov	Exchange limit over the counter increased to Rs 4500
		15 Nov	Rule of using indelible ink
		18 Nov	Exchange limit again decreased to Rs 2000; allowed only once per person before stopping it altogether on 24 November
ATM withdrawal	6	8 Nov	Withdrawal limit Rs 2000 per day per ATM card; limit was to be raised to Rs 4000 per day per card from 19 November onwards
		13 Nov	Withdrawal limit increased to Rs 2500
			Withdrawal limit not raised to Rs 4000 on 19 November, as was promised
		30 Dec	Withdrawal limit increased to Rs 4500
		16 Jan	Daily withdrawal limit increased to Rs 10,000
		13 Mar	Removal of all limits

(Contd)

Change	S. No	Date	Description
Cash withdrawal from banks	7	8 Nov	Cash withdrawal from bank account restricted to Rs 10,000 per day subject to an overall limit of Rs 20,000 per week until 24 November
		13 Nov	Weekly limit increased to Rs 24,000; daily limit removed
		30 Nov	Withdrawals from Jan Dhan accounts limited to Rs 10,000 per month
		30 Jan	Cash withdrawal limits removed on current accounts
		20 Feb	Cash withdrawal limit on savings accounts enhanced to Rs 50,000 per week
		13 Mar	Removal of all cash withdrawal limits
Continuous extension of time period for use of old notes	8	8 Nov	Government allows use of old currency notes at hospitals, for railway/bus/airline tickets, petrol pumps, etc., for seventy-two hours, i.e., till 11 November. The list was later extended to included public utility bills and taxes
		11 Nov	Government extended the use of old currency notes for payments in exempted transactions by another seventy-two hours, i.e., till 14 November
		14 Nov	Time limit for use of old currency notes in exempted categories again extended, till 24 November
		24 Nov	Government decided to continue the exemptions further, up to 15 December. The Rs 1000 note was no longer to be used for payments in the list of exemptions

(Contd)

Change	S. No	Date	Description
Deadline preponed compared to the earlier deadline	9	1 Dec	Use of old Rs 500 notes for purchase of air tickets, petrol, diesel and gas stopped from 2 December as against the earlier promised date of 15 December
	10	9 Dec	Use of old Rs 500 notes for railway/bus/metro tickets and catering services was to continue till 15 December; this date was revised to 10 December, and then the provision was stopped one day earlier
	11	2 Dec	No highway tolls till 2 December 2016. The Rs 500 note was allowed to be used at tolls on national highways from 2 December up to 15 December, but facility withdrawn on 2 December itself

Source: RBI Press Releases and Notifications and Press Information Bureau

ANNEXURE 5

India's Recent Economic Performance

Graph 2: Annual Growth Rate of Real GDP at Factor Cost (2003-04 to 2016-17)

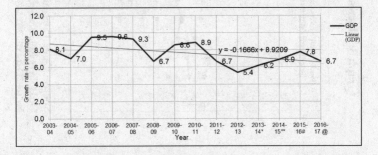

Source: Central Statistical Organization (Economic Survey), CSO Press Releases
Note: Data from 2012–13 based on New Series (2011-12) Estimates
*GVA at Basic Prices from 2012-13
*Third Revised Estimates, **Second Revised Estimates, #First Revised Estimates, @Advanced Estimates

Graph 3: Macroeconomic Quarterly Data for the Indian Economy

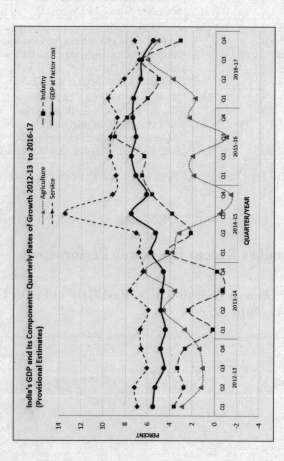

India's GDP and Its Components: Quarterly Rates of Growth 2012-13 to 2016-17 (Provisional Estimates)

Source: Central Statistical Office, Ministry of Statistics and Programme Implementation, GoI (Press Releases—Q1: 31 August, Q2: 30 November, Q3: 28 Feb, Q4: 31 May)
Note: *Data till 2014–15 based on 2004–05 base prices, and afterwards on 2011–12 prices

Graph 4: Inflation, Fiscal Deficit and Current Account Deficit to GDP (Quarterly Data), 2012-13 to 2016-17

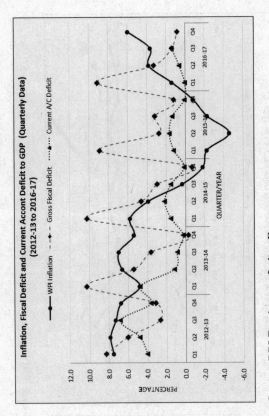

Source: RBI Database on Indian Economy

Note: 1. Gross fiscal deficit calculated from monthly data (until July 2016 from RBI and Controller General of Accounts for subsequent months)

   2. For WPI Inflation: RBI Database on Indian Economy, Statistics, Real Sector, Prices and Wages

   3. For Current Account: RBI Database on Indian Economy—India's Overall Balance of Payments, Quarterly, Rupees

Graph 5: India's External Trade and Its Deficits, Quarterly Data, 2012–13 to 2016–17

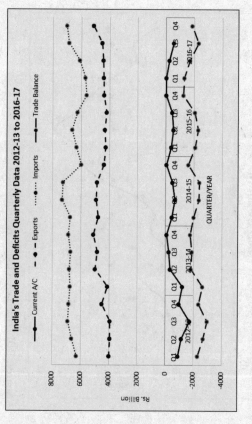

India's Trade and Deficits Quarterly Data 2012-13 to 2016-17

● Current A/C   ● Exports   ····●···· Imports   ● Trade Balance

Rs. Billion

QUARTER/YEAR

Source: RBI Database on Indian Economy—India's Foreign Trade, Monthly

Chapter I

ANNEXURE 6

Money in Relation to GDP

Table 5: Currency in Circulation and Nominal GDP (GDP$_{MP}$ at Current Prices)

(Rs Billion)

Year	Currency in Circulation	GDP at Market Prices	Growth Rate (CIC)	Growth Rate (Nominal GDP)	Decadal Growth Rate (%) CIC	Decadal Growth Rate (%) GDP
1950-51	-	104.01	-	-		
1951-52	12.92	110.54	-	6.28		
1952-53	12.73	108.50	-1.5	-1.85		
1953-54	13.30	118.10	4.5	8.85		
1954-55	14.17	111.70	6.5	-5.42		
1955-56	16.14	113.71	13.9	1.80		
1956-57	16.68	135.47	3.3	19.14		
1957-58	17.20	139.51	3.1	2.98		
1958-59	18.46	155.51	7.3	11.47		
1959-60	20.01	163.84	8.4	5.36	5.7	5.4
1960-61	21.54	179.42	7.6	9.51		
1961-62	22.56	190.10	4.7	5.95		
1962-63	24.39	204.29	8.1	7.46		
1963-64	26.70	234.62	9.5	14.85		

(Contd)

Year	Currency in Circulation	GDP at Market Prices	Growth Rate (CIC)	Growth Rate (Nominal GDP)	Decadal Growth Rate (%)	
					CIC	GDP
1964-65	28.41	273.67	6.4	16.64		
1965-66	31.12	288.57	9.5	5.44		
1966-67	32.89	326.69	5.7	13.21		
1967-68	34.68	382.61	5.4	17.12		
1968-69	37.94	405.12	9.4	5.88		
1969-70	41.60	446.05	9.6	10.10	7.6	10.6
1970-71	45.57	476.38	9.5	6.80		
1971-72	50.06	509.99	9.9	7.06		
1972-73	56.80	562.14	13.5	10.23		
1973-74	65.95	684.20	16.1	21.71		
1974-75	67.01	807.70	1.6	18.05		
1975-76	70.53	867.07	5.3	7.35		
1976-77	82.88	934.22	17.5	7.74		
1977-78	91.52	1058.48	10.4	13.30		
1978-79	108.35	1146.47	18.4	8.31		
1979-80	123.82	1257.29	14.3	9.67	11.6	11.0
1980-81	143.07	1496.42	15.5	19.02		
1981-82	154.11	1758.05	7.7	17.48		
1982-83	176.39	1966.44	14.5	11.85		
1983-84	206.43	2290.21	17.0	16.46		
1984-85	238.75	2566.11	15.7	12.05		
1985-86	265.24	2895.24	11.1	12.83		
1986-87	299.13	3239.49	12.8	11.89		
1987-88	351.22	3682.11	17.4	13.66		
1988-89	401.19	4368.93	14.2	18.65		
1989-90	482.86	5019.28	20.4	14.89	14.6	14.9
1990-91	552.82	5862.12	14.5	16.79		
1991-92	637.38	6738.75	15.3	14.95		
1992-93	713.26	7745.45	11.9	14.94		
1993-94	853.96	8913.55	19.7	15.08		

(Contd)

Year	Currency in Circulation	GDP at Market Prices	Growth Rate (CIC)	Growth Rate (Nominal GDP)	Decadal Growth Rate (%)	
					CIC	GDP
1994-95	1046.81	10455.90	22.6	17.30		
1995-96	1225.69	12267.25	17.1	17.32		
1996-97	1372.17	14192.77	12.0	15.70		
1997-98	1510.56	15723.94	10.1	10.79		
1998-99	1758.46	18033.78	16.4	14.69		
1999-00	1970.61	20231.30	12.1	12.19	15.2	15.0
2000-01	2182.05	21774.13	10.7	7.63		
2001-02	2509.74	23558.45	15.0	8.19		
2002-03	2824.73	25363.27	12.6	7.66		
2003-04	3270.28	28415.03	15.8	12.03		
2004-05	3686.61	32422.09	12.7	14.10		
2005-06	4295.78	36933.69	16.5	13.92		
2006-07	5040.99	42947.06	17.3	16.28		
2007-08	5908.01	49870.90	17.2	16.12		
2008-09	6911.53	56300.63	17.0	12.89		
2009-10	7995.49	64778.27	15.7	15.06	15.1	12.4
2010-11	9496.59	77841.15	18.8	20.17		
2011-12	10672.30	87360.39	12.4	12.23		
2012-13	11909.75	99466.36	11.6	13.86		
2013-14	13010.74	112366.35	9.2	12.97		
2014-15	14483.12	124451.28	11.3	10.75		
2015-16	16634.63	136820.35	14.9	9.94		
2016-17*	17,977.0	151837.09	8.1	10.98	13.6	13.5

Source: RBI Database on Indian Economy (Components of Money Stock—Annual and Macroeconomic Aggregates at Current Prices)
Note: For GDP at Current Prices, Base Year is 2004–05 for the years prior to 2011–12, and Base Year is 2011–12 for the years 2011–12 and later
* Currency in circulation just before demonetization

Table 6: Currency in Circulation, High-Denomination Notes and Nominal GDP (GDP$_{MP}$ at Current Prices)

Year	Currency in Circulation	Change in CIC	GDP at Market Prices	High Denomination Notes (Value)	Change in HD Notes (Value)	Change in HD Notes/Change in CIC	Growth Rate (%)		
							CIC	Nominal GDP	HD Notes
2000-01	2182.0	-	21774.13	566.6			-	-	-
2001-02	2509.7	327.7	23558.45	756.9	190.3	0.581	15.0	8.2	33.6
2002-03	2824.7	315.0	25363.27	1097.8	340.9	1.082	12.6	7.7	45.0
2003-04	3270.3	445.6	28415.03	1504.1	406.3	0.912	15.8	12.0	37.0
2004-05	3686.6	416.3	32422.09	1948.1	444.0	1.066	12.7	14.1	29.5
2005-06	4295.8	609.2	36933.69	2466.8	518.7	0.851	16.5	13.9	26.6
2006-07	5041.0	745.2	42947.06	3190.8	724.0	0.972	17.3	16.3	29.3
2007-08	5908.0	867.0	49870.90	4043.3	852.5	0.983	17.2	16.1	26.7
2008-09	6911.5	1003.5	56300.63	5000.9	957.6	0.954	17.0	12.9	23.7
2009-10	7995.5	1084.0	64778.27	6027.3	1026.4	0.947	15.7	15.1	20.5
2010-11	9496.6	1501.1	77841.15	7480.2	1452.9	0.968	18.8	20.2	24.1
2011-12	10672.3	1175.7	87360.39	8596.9	1116.6	0.950	12.4	12.2	14.9
2012-13	11909.8	1237.5	99466.36	9658.5	1061.6	0.858	11.6	13.9	12.3
2013-14	13010.7	1101.0	112366.35	10783.9	1125.4	1.022	9.2	13.0	11.7

(Contd)

Year	Currency in Circulation	Change in CIC	GDP at Market Prices	High Denomination Notes (Value)	Change in HD Notes (Value)	Change in HD Notes/ Change in CIC	Growth Rate (%)		
							CIC	Nominal GDP	HD Notes
2014-15	14483.1	1472.4	124451.28	12176.4	1392.5	0.946	11.3	10.8	12.9
2015-16	16634.6	2151.5	136820.35	14179.4	2003.1	0.931	14.9	9.9	16.5
2016-17*	17977.0	1342.4	151837.09	15440.0	1260.6	0.939	8.1	11.0	8.9
Average Growth Rate							14.1	13.3	22.7

Source: RBI Database on Indian Economy (1. Components of Money Stock—Annual, 2. Macroeconomic Aggregates at Current Prices, 3. Notes and Coins in Circulation)

Note: For GDP at Current Prices, Base Year is 2004–05 for the years prior to 2011–12, and Base Year is 2011–12 for the years 2011–12 and later

* Currency in Circulation and High-Denomination Notes Value as on 4 November 2016. For the rest of the years, the figures are as on 31 March of that year

High-denomination notes include Rs 500 and Rs 1000 notes

Graph 6: Growth in Currency and GDP, 1951-52 to 2016-17

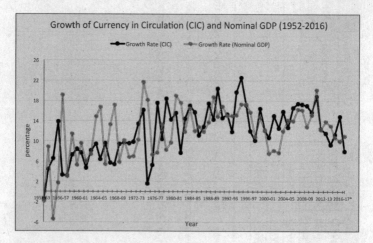

Source: Table 6

Graph 7: Growth of Currency in Circulation (CIC), High-Denomination (HD) Notes and Nominal GDP (2001–02 to 2016–17)

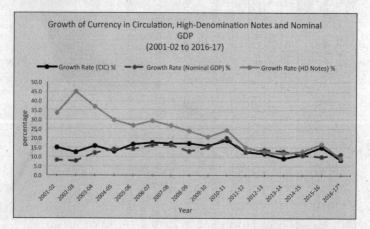

Source: Table 6

Graph 8: Growth of Currency in Circulation and Nominal GDP (2001–02 to 2016–17)

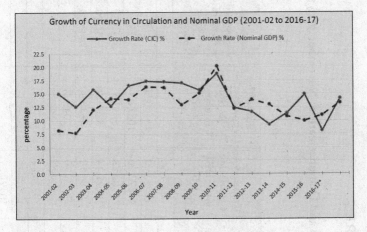

Source: Table 6

Graph 9: Growth of Currency in Circulation, High-Denomination Notes and Nominal GDP (2011–12 to 2016–17)

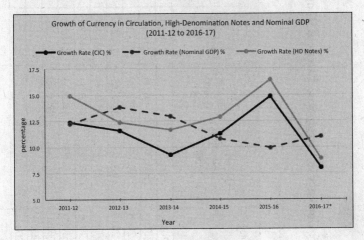

Source: Table 6

ANNEXURE 7

Table 7: Currency in Circulation: Extent of Remonetization and Demonetization, November 2016 to April 2017

(Rs Billion)

Date	Small-Denomination Old Notes (A)	New Currency Issued (B)	Coins (C)	Total Valid Currency as per Our Calculations (A+B+C) (D)	Currency in Circulation as per RBI (E)	Old High-Denomination Notes Still in Circulation (E-D) (F)	Amount Deposited in Banks as per RBI/ Reports (G)	Amount Returned to RBI as per Our Calculations (H)
Nov 8, 2016	2301.50		235.10	17977.00	17977.00			
Nov 9, 2016	2301.50	0.00	235.10	2536.60	17977.00	15440.50		0.00
Nov 18, 2016	2301.50	1363.22	235.10	3899.82	14272.26	10372.44	5115.65	5068.06
Nov 27, 2016	2301.50	2505.65	241.80	5048.95	11502.88	6453.93	8110.33	8986.57
Dec 7, 2016	2301.50	4276.84	241.80	6820.14	10027.44	3207.30	11550.00	12233.20
Dec 10, 2016	2301.50	4610.00	241.80	7153.30	9786.10	2632.80	12440.00	12807.70
Dec 19, 2016	2301.50	5926.13	246.10	8473.73	9523.10	1049.37		14391.13
Jan 13, 2017	2301.50	6780.00	246.10	9327.60	9508.03	180.43		15260.07
Jan 20, 2017					9874.84			
Jan 27, 2017					10167.20			
Feb 3, 2017					10491.25			

(Contd)

Date	Small-Denomination Old Notes (A)	New Currency Issued (B)	Coins (C)	Total Valid Currency as per Our Calculations (A+B+C) (D)	Currency in Circulation as per RBI (E)	Old High-Denomination Notes Still in Circulation (E-D) (F)	Amount Deposited in Banks as per RBI/ Reports (G)	Amount Returned to RBI as per Our Calculations (H)
Feb 10, 2017					10972.65			
Feb 17, 2017					11314.06			
Feb 24, 2017					11644.80			
Mar 3, 2017					11984.12			
Mar 10, 2017					12461.50			
Mar 17, 2017					12806.00			
Mar 24, 2017					13130.72			
Mar 31, 2017					13352.66			
Apr 7, 2017					13616.56			
Apr 14, 2017					13897.03			
Apr 21, 2017					14174.79			
Apr 28, 2017					14320.37			

Sources: 1. RBI Database on Indian Economy

2. RBI Press Releases (21 November, 28 November, 8 December, 21 December)

3. Rajya Sabha Question and Answers (for New Currency figures for 13 January & Amount Deposited for 10 December) (Unstarred Question -547, 7/2/17)

4. Statement by deputy governor of RBI, R. Gandhi, in post-policy media interaction (for amount deposited till 7 December)

Table 8: How Many of the Old Notes Are Back?

Date	Amount Returned to RBI as per Our Calculations (%)	Old High-Denomination Notes Still in Circulation (%)
9 Nov 2016	0.0	100.0
18 Nov 2016	32.8	67.2
27 Nov 2016	58.2	41.8
7 Dec 2016	79.2	20.8
10 Dec 2016	82.9	17.1
19 Dec 2016	93.2	6.8
13 Jan 2017	98.8	1.2

Source: Data in Columns H and F in Table 7

Graph 10: Currency in Circulation (Total Currency and Valid Currency)

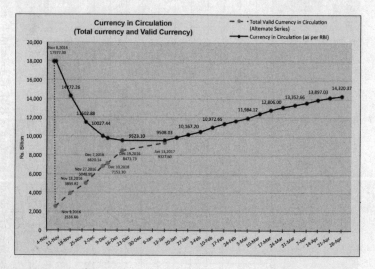

Source: Data in Table 7

Chapter II

ANNEXURE 8

Money Supply Measures during Demonetization Period

Table 9: Components of Money Stock—Demonetization Period

(Rs Billion)

Date	Currency with the Public	M⁰	Deposit Money of the Public	M¹	Post Office Savings Deposits	M²	Time Deposits with Banks	M³	Total Post Office Deposits	M⁴
				(A+C)		(D+E)		(D+G)		(H+I)
	(A)	(B)	(C)	(D)	(E)	(F)	(G)	(H)	(I)	(J)
Apr 28, 2017	13539.7	19290.6	12495.6	26035.3	930.9	26966.2	100170.6	126205.9	2542.2	128748.0
Apr 14, 2017	13286.6	18726.1	12326.1	25612.8	930.9	26543.7	101408.6	127021.4	2542.2	129563.5
Mar 31, 2017	12637.1	19004.9	14317.2	26954.3	930.9	27885.2	101489.5	128443.9	2542.2	130986.0
Mar 17, 2017	12138.3	17529.7	12899.8	25038.0	930.9	25968.9	100064.2	125102.2	2542.2	127644.4
Mar 3, 2017	11312.3	16795.0	12132.1	23444.5	930.9	24375.4	100867.1	124311.6	2542.2	126853.7
Feb 17, 2017	10638.6	16060.2	11955.1	22593.6	930.9	23524.5	100492.5	123086.1	2542.2	125628.3

(Contd)

Date	Currency with the Public	M^0	Deposit Money of the Public	M^1	Post Office Savings Deposits	M^2	Time Deposits with Banks	M^3	Total Post Office Deposits	M^4
				(A+C)		(D+E)		(D+G)		(H+I)
	(A)	(B)	(C)	(D)	(E)	(F)	(G)	(H)	(I)	(J)
Feb 3, 2017	9804.9	15342.8	12022.9	21827.9	930.9	22758.8	101167.5	122995.3	2542.2	125537.5
Jan 20, 2017	9128.7	14659.9	11933.4	21062.1	930.9	21993.0	100500.8	121562.9	2542.2	124105.1
Jan 6, 2017	8112.3	13754.3	12102.5	20214.8	937.5	21152.3	101237.3	121452.1	2549.6	124001.7
Dec 23, 2016	7843.1	14207.4	12161.5	20004.6	937.5	20942.1	100501.9	120506.5	2549.6	123056.1
Dec 9, 2016	7819.2	18392.2	12135.1	19954.3	925.6	20879.8	101297.6	121251.9	2521.9	123773.9
Nov 25, 2016	9128.8	16490.4	12109.4	21238.2	925.6	22163.7	100573.2	121811.4	2521.9	124333.3
Nov 11, 2016	15265.3	22493.3	10981.8	26247.1	720.6	26967.6	97566.6	123813.7	2277.9	126091.5
Oct 28, 2016	17022.1	22398.2	10565.0	27587.1	720.6	28307.6	96062.0	123649.1	2277.9	125926.9

Source: RBI, Database on Indian Economy (Money Stock—Components and Sources)

Notes: 1. Currency with the public = currency in circulation – cash on hand with banks

2. M^0 = currency with the public + cash on hand with banks + 'other' deposits with RBI + bankers' deposits with RBI

3. M^1 = currency with the public + deposit money of the public; (deposit money of the public = demand deposits with banks + 'other' deposits with Reserve Bank)

4. $M^2 = M^1$ + post office savings deposits

5. $M^3 = M^1$ + time deposits with banks

6. $M^4 = M^3$ + total post office deposits

Graph 11: Deposit Money of the Public (Demand Deposits)

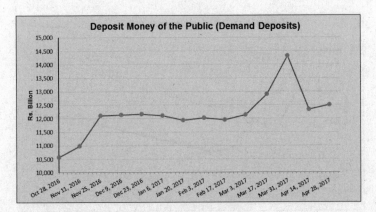

Source: RBI Database on Indian Economy

Graph 12: Time Deposits with the Banks

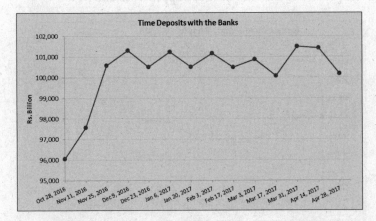

Source: RBI Database on Indian Economy

Graph 13: Measures of Money Supply—M0, M1 and M2

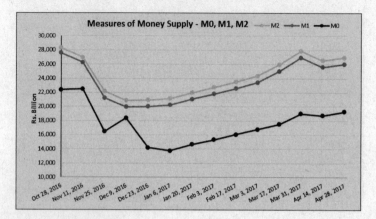

Source: RBI Database on Indian Economy

Graph 14: Measures of Money Supply—M3 and M4

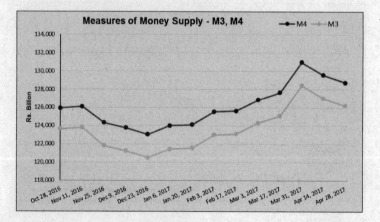

Source: RBI Database on Indian Economy

ANNEXURE 9

High Denomination Currency Notes

Table 10: Banknotes of Different Denominations in Circulation, 2014–16

Denomination Rs	Volume (million pieces)			Value (Rs billion)		
	March 2014	March 2015	March 2016	March 2014	March 2015	March 2016
2 and 5	11,698	11,672	11626	46	46	45
	(15.1)	(13.9)	(12.9)	(0.4)	(0.3)	(0.3)
10	26,648	30,304	32015	266	303	320
	(34.5)	(36.3)	(35.5)	(2.1)	(2.1)	(1.9)
20	4285	4350	4924	86	87	98
	(5.5)	(5.2)	(5.4)	(0.7)	(0.6)	(0.6)
50	3448	3487	3890	172	174	194
	(4.5)	(4.2)	(4.3)	(1.3)	(1.2)	1.2)
100	14,765	15,026	15,778	1476	1503	1578
	(19.1)	(18)	(17.5)	(11.5)	(10.5)	(9.6)
500	11,405	13,128	15,707	5702	6564	7854
	(14.7)	(15.7)	(17.4)	(44.4)	(46)	(47.8)
1,000	5081	5612	6326	5081	5612	6326
	(6.6)	(6.7)	(7)	(39.6)	(39.3)	(38.6)
Total	77,330	83,579	90,266	12,829	14,289	16,415

Source: RBI Annual Report, 29 August 2016
Note: Figures in parentheses represent the percentage share in total

Table 11: Distribution of Different Denomination Currency Notes in March 2016

Denomination Rs	Volume (%)	Value (%)
2 and 5	12.9	0.3
10	35.5	1.9
20	5.4	0.6

(Contd)

Denomination Rs	Volume (%)	Value (%)
50	4.3	1.2
100	17.5	9.6
500	17.4	47.8
1000	7	38.6

Source: Data from Table 10

Table 12: Large-Denomination Notes on 4 November 2016

	Rs Billion	%
Total Currency in Notes (as on November 4, 2016) =	17,742.00	100.0
Currency in Small-Denomination Notes =	2301.5	13.0
Currency in Large-Denomination Notes =	15,440.5	87.0

Note: The total currency in circulation as on 4 November was Rs 17,977 billion, out of which Rs 235.12 billion was in coins. So the value of notes in circulation is Rs 17,977 billion - Rs 235 billion = Rs 17,742 billion

Also, based on the information from Questions and Answers, Rajya Sabha (06/12/16), there were 17,165 million notes of Rs 500 and 6858 million notes of Rs 1000

Table 13: Demonetization Amounts: 1946, 1978 and 2016

(Rupees Crores)

	1946	1978	2016
Total Notes in Circulation	1151.79	8070	17,74,200
Amount of Notes Demonetized	143.97	145.42	15,44,050
% of Notes Demonetized	12.5	1.8	87.0
Amount Returned/Tendered for Conversion	134.9	124.25	15,26,007
% Amount Returned	93.7	85.4	98.8

Sources: 1. History of RBI, Vol. I, 1935–1951, pp. 708, 853
2. RBI Annual Report, 1977–78
3. Handbook of Statistics on Indian Economy, 2016, RBI
4. Kumar and Verma, 2017

Graph 15: Banknotes of Different Denominations in Circulation, March 2016

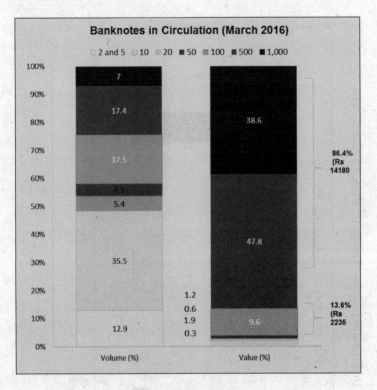

Source: RBI Annual Report, 29 August 2016

Graph 16: Demonetization Amounts: 1946, 1978 and 2016

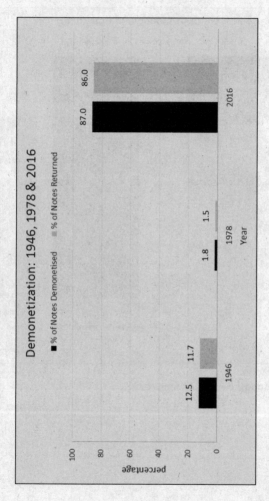

Source: Data in Table 13

Chapter III

ANNEXURE 10

Table 14: Fatalities (since 2011) from Terrorism in India

Years	Civilians	Security Force Personnel	Terrorists	Total
2011	429	194	450	1073
2012	252	139	412	803
2013	303	193	388	884
2014	407	161	408	976
2015	181	155	386	722
2016	202	180	516	898
2017*	109	114	202	425

Source: South Asia Terrorism Portal (SATP)
*Data till 25 June 2017

Chapter IV

ANNEXURE 11

Table 15: Assets and Liabilities of Household Sector for Year 2015-16

(at current prices)

Item Description	S. No	Rs Crore	% of Gross Financial Savings	% of Gross Household Savings	% of Net Household Savings
currency	1.1	200518	13.24	6.59	7.68
deposits	1.2	662815	43.77	21.79	25.40
shares and debentures	1.3	41317	2.73	1.36	1.58
claims on government	1.4	66639	4.40	2.19	2.55
insurance funds	1.5	266063	17.57	8.75	10.19
provident and pension funds	1.6	276854	18.28	9.10	10.61
gross financial savings	1	1514207	100.00	49.78	58.02
savings in physical assets	2	1483539		48.77	56.84
savings in form of gold and silver ornaments	3	43930		1.44	1.68
gross household savings	1+2+3	3041676		100.00	116.54
financial liabilities	4	431755			16.54
net household savings	1+2+3-4	2609921			100.00

Source: National Accounts Statistics, 2017, MOSPI

#Gross financial savings & liabilities for household sector includes gross financial savings and liabilities for quasi-corporate sector

Graph 17: Assets and Liabilities of Household Sector for the Year 2015-16

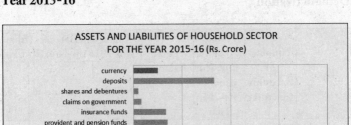

Source: National Accounts Statistics, 2017, MOSPI

ANNEXURE 12

Graph 18: Balance in Jan Dhan Accounts, November 2016 to February 2017

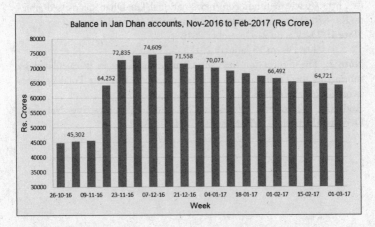

Source: GoI, 2017e

Table 16: Amount Deposited in Jan Dhan Accounts during Demonetization

Date	Number of Accounts (in crore)	New Accounts Opened (from 9 Nov 2016 till date)	Total Balance (Rs Crores)	Change in Balances (from 9 Nov 2016 till date) (Rs Crore)		
				Deposits	Withdrawal	Net
9 Nov 16	25.51	-	45636.6	-	-	-
16 Nov 16	25.58	0.07	64252.2	20206#	1590	18616
23 Nov 16	25.68	0.16	72834.7	31553#	4355	27198
30 Nov 16	25.78	0.27	74321.6	36420#	7735	28685
23 Dec 16	26.03*	0.52*	71557.9*	41523##	15602	25921*
20 Jan 17	27.11**	1.60**	68237.7**	50481	27880@	22601**

Source: GoI, 2017e

@ Rajya Sabha Q/As No. 543, Answered on 7/2/2017 (Deposits and Withdrawal from Jan Dhan Accounts) (For the period 13 November 2016 to 20 January 2017)

Inflow of Funds into Jan Dhan Accounts, CBDT Press Release (7 December 2016)

http://www.thehindu.com/news/national/Jan-Dhan-deposits-double-to-Rs.-87000-cr.-come-under-I-T-lens/article16975200.ece

Note 1: *Data as on 21 December 2016
        **Data as on 18 January 2017

Note 2: The figures for the Net Change in Balances is calculated by subtracting the Total Balances on a particular date from the Total Balances as on 9 November 2016

And, the Withdrawal figures are calculated by subtracting Net from Deposits (Deposits - Withdrawals = Net)

ANNEXURE 13

Reserve Bank of India Balance Sheet

Table 17: Reserve Bank of India, Balance Sheet (as on 30 June 2016)

(Rs Billion)

Liabilities	Amount	Assets	Amount
Capital	0.05	**Assets of Banking Department (BD)**	
Reserve Fund	65	Notes, rupee coin, small coin	0.14
Other Reserves	2.24	Gold Coin and Bullion	662.23
Deposits	5065.28	Investments-Foreign-BD	6727.84
Other Liabilities and Provisions	10,220.38	Investments-Domestic-BD	7022.85
		Bills Purchased and Discounted	0
		Loans and Advances	520.41
		Investment in Subsidiaries	23.2
		Other Assets	396.28
Liabilities of Issue Department		**Assets of Issue Department (ID)**	
Notes issued	17,077.16	Gold Coin and Bullion (as Backing for Note Issue)	729.07
		Rupee Coin	1.71
		Investment-Foreign-ID	16,335.92
		Investment-Domestic-ID	10.46
		Domestic Bills of Exchange and other Commercial Papers	0
Total Liabilities	32,430.11	**Total Assets**	32,430.11

Source: RBI Annual Report, 2015-16

Table 18: Reserve Bank of India, Income Statement for 2014-15 and 2015-16 (ending June)

(Amount in Rs Billion)

INCOME	2014-15	2015-16
Interest	744.82	749.24
Others	47.74	59.46
Total	792.56	808.70
EXPENDITURE		
Printing of Notes	37.62	34.21
Expense on Remittance of Currency	0.98	1.09
Agency Charges	30.45	47.56
Interest	0.01	0.01
Employee Cost	40.58	44.77
Postage and Telecommunication Charges	0.91	0.78
Printing and Stationery	0.34	0.33
Rent, Taxes, Insurance, Lighting, etc.	1.14	1.40
Repairs and Maintenance	1.04	1.01
Directors' and Local Board Members' Fees and Expenses	0.03	0.02
Auditors' Fees and Expenses	0.03	0.03
Law Charges	0.04	0.07
Miscellaneous Expenses	7.97	6.42
Depreciation	2.42	2.20
Provisions	10.00	10.00
Total	133.56	149.90
Available Balance	659.00	658.80
Less:		
a) Contribution to:		
i) National Industrial Credit (Long Term Operations) Fund	0.01	0.01
ii) National Housing Credit (Long Term Operations) Fund	0.01	0.01

(Contd)

b) Transferable to NABARD:		
i) National Rural Credit (Long Term Operations) Fund*	0.01	0.01
ii) National Rural Credit (Stabilization) Fund*	0.01	0.01
Surplus payable to the Central Government	**658.96**	**658.76**

Source: RBI Annual Report, 2015-16
* These funds are maintained by the National Bank for Agriculture and Rural Development (NABARD)

Table 19: Reserve Bank of India, Liabilities and Assets, 2016 to 2017

(Rs Billion)

Item	03-Apr-15	01-Apr-16	04-Nov-16	30-Dec-16	31-Mar-17
1 Notes Issued	14,293.63	16,415.71	17,742.00	9137.80	13,101.93
1.1 Notes in Circulation	14,293.53	16,415.58	17,741.87	9137.63	13,101.81
1.2 Notes Held in Banking Department	0.10	0.13	0.13	0.17	0.12
2 Deposits					
2.1 Central Government	0.54	1.00	1.01	1.01	50.00
2.2 Market Stabilization Scheme	–	–	–	4989.55	–
2.3 State Governments	8.10	0.42	0.42	0.42	0.42
2.4 Scheduled Commercial Banks	3681.98	4746.08	4094.72	4495.75	5087.73
2.5 Scheduled State Co-operative Banks	42.04	38.93	33.89	37.76	55.13
2.6 Other Banks	216.19	240.60	237.00	276.25	298.41
2.7 Others	2867.77	2522.68	1375.97	4088.35	4897.74
3 Other Liabilities	7993.85	9659.61	9216.64	9529.95	8411.18
TOTAL LIABILITIES	29,104.11	33,625.04	32,701.65	32,556.83	31,902.54

(Contd)

Item	03-Apr-15	01-Apr-16	04-Nov-16	30-Dec-16	31-Mar-17
1 Foreign Currency Assets	20,164.85	22,474.82	23,155.98	23,134.05	22,685.84
2 Gold Coin and Bullion	1191.60	1334.29	1367.94	1369.35	1288.27
3 Rupee Securities (including Treasury Bills)	5256.16	6159.58	7562.44	7745.32	7494.91
4 Loans and Advances					
4.1 Central Government	–	–	–	–	–
4.2 State Governments	7.94	0.88	43.06	15.29	12.62
4.3 NABARD	–	–	–	–	–
4.4 Scheduled Commercial Banks	2198.45	3264.04	371.03	154.75	218.10
4.5 Scheduled State Co-op Banks	–	–	–	–	–
4.6 Industrial Development Bank of India	–	–	–	–	–
4.7 Export-Import Bank of India	–	–	–	–	–
4.8 Others	135.92	177.83	53.97	35.94	39.91
5 Bills Purchased and Discounted					
5.1 Commercial	–	–	–	–	–
5.2 Treasury	–	–	–	–	–
6 Investments	13.20	23.20	23.20	23.20	33.20
7 Other Assets	135.98	190.39	124.03	78.93	129.69
TOTAL ASSETS	29,104.10	33,625.03	32,701.65	32,556.83	31,902.54

Source: Reserve Bank of India, Weekly Statistical Supplements

ANNEXURE 14

Table 20: Number of Income Tax Assesses and Income Shown in Different Categories

Category	Number		
Organized-sector employment	4.2 crore persons	filing return for salary income, 1.74 crore	
Individuals filing tax returns in 2015-16	3.7 crore	*Showing income of: (per annum)*	
	99 lakh	Below Rs 2.5 lakh	
	1.95 crore	Rs 2.5–5 lakh	
	52 lakh	Rs 5–10 lakh	
	24 lakh	Above Rs 10 lakh	
	1.72 lakh	More than Rs 50 lakh	
	76 lakh	Above Rs 5 lakh	
	56 lakh	Salaried class	
Cars bought	1.25 crore cars bought	(in last five years)	Why not audit them?
No. who flew abroad	2 crore	(in 2015)	How many workers?
Informal-sector individual enterprises and firms	5.6 crore	Returns filed, 1.81 crore	
Companies registered in India	13.94 lakh	Returns filed, 5.97 lakh in AY 2016-17	
	2.76 lakh	Showed losses or zero income	
	2.85 lakh	Profit before tax of less than Rs 1 crore	
	28,667	PBT between Rs 1 crore and Rs 10 crore	
	7781	PBT more than Rs 10 crore	

(Contd)

Category	Number		
During demonetization, no. of accounts showing deposits of Rs 2 lakh to Rs 80 lakh	1.09 crore	Average deposit size, Rs 5.03 lakh	Total deposits, Rs 5.48 lakh crore
Accounts in which more than Rs 80 lakh was deposited	1.48 lakh	Average deposit size, Rs 3.31 crore	Total deposits, Rs 4.9 lakh crore

Source: GoI, 2017d

ANNEXURE 15

Situation of Rural Areas

Table 21: Gross Area Sown under Rabi, 2010-11 to 2016-17

(Million Hectares)

Crop	2010-11	2011-12	2012-13	2013-14	2014-15	2015-16	2016-17	2016-17 (Area Sown as % of Normal)	2016-17 (% Change over Average)
Cereals	40.2	39.4	39.8	41.1	41.0	37.8	39.4	97.4	-
% change over last year	-	-2.0	1.0	3.3	-0.2	-7.8	4.2	-	2.3
Pulses	14.1	13.3	13.3	14.9	13.3	14.3	15.9	115.3	-
% change over last year	-	-5.7	0.0	12.0	-10.7	7.5	11.2	-	8.5
Oilseeds	9.0	7.9	8.2	8.4	7.4	7.8	8.4	98.9	-
% change over last year	-	-12.2	3.8	2.4	-11.9	5.4	6.7	-	-0.3
Total Area Sown under Rabi Crops	63.3	60.6	61.3	64.4	61.7	59.9	63.7	101.5	-
% change over last year	-	-4.3	1.2	5.1	-4.2	-2.9	6.2	-	3.4

Sources: 1. GoI, 2016a up to year 2014-15
2. Minutes of the Meeting of the Crop Weather Watch Group Held on 27 January 2017, Department of Agriculture, Cooperation and Farmers Welfare (Ministry of Agriculture & Farmers Welfare)

Graph 19: Total Area Sown under Rabi in Various Years

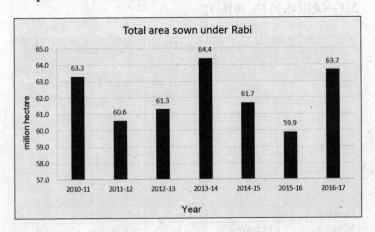

Total area sown under Rabi

Source: Data in Table 21

Table 22: Price Index of Key Agricultural Products (September 2016–March 2017)

Item	Sep-16	Nov-16	Jan-17	Mar-17
Cereals	142.6	145.5	146.3	145.2
Pulses	198.7	214.5	182.7	154.0
Fruits	153.4	135.9	130.7	139.3
Vegetables	144.7	143.3	106.2	118.4
Potato	229.8	201.8	102.5	91.1
Peas (Green)	-	263.5	102.8	121.2
Tomato	116.6	114.4	91.4	126.1
Onion	107.8	120.6	117.8	110.6

Source: Office of the Economic Adviser, GoI, Ministry of Commerce & Industry (DIPP)

Table 23: Work Demand and Employment Provided under MGNREGS in FY 2016-17

Month	Work Demand		Employment Provided	
	No. of Persons	% Change from Last Month	Person Days	% Change from Last Month
April	27600808	-	129342646	-
May	37282903	35.1	198000112	53.1
June	39857531	6.9	220451160	11.3
July	23548326	-40.9	174096928	-21.0
August	18208933	-22.7	141740257	-18.6
September	14194352	-22.0	149199363	5.3
October	10403909	-26.7	147859955	-0.9
November	10785056	3.7	143047798	-3.3
December	15054129	39.6	232776450	62.7
January	19712221	30.9	284736203	22.3
February	24839128	26.0	304213839	6.8
March	26701939	7.5	225881759	-25.7

Source: GoI, 2017f

Graph 20: Growth in Work Demand and Employment Provided under MGNREGS, 2016-17

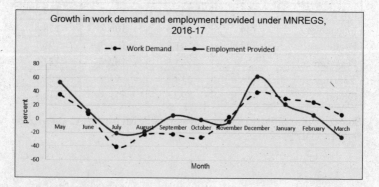

Source: Table 23

Chapter V

ANNEXURE 16

Employment and Output Across Sectors, and Organized, Unorganized

Table 24: Distribution of Workforce in Organized and Unorganized Sectors, 2011-12

Sector	Total Workforce (%)	Total Workforce (millions)	Workforce in Organized Sector (millions)	Workforce in Unorganized Sector (millions)	% of Workforce in Unorganized Sector	% of Workforce in Organized Sector
Agriculture	48.90	231.84	1.39	230.45	99.40	0.60
Industry	24.26	115.02	9.65	105.37	91.61	8.39
Services	26.86	127.35	18.23	109.12	85.68	14.32
Total	100.00	474.11	29.27	444.84	93.83	6.17

Source: Rajya Sabha, Unstarred Question 1621 for Total Workforce Data and Table 3.1: Employment in Organized Sector, in GoI, 2016a

Graph 21: Distribution of Workforce in Organized and Unorganized Sectors, 2011-12

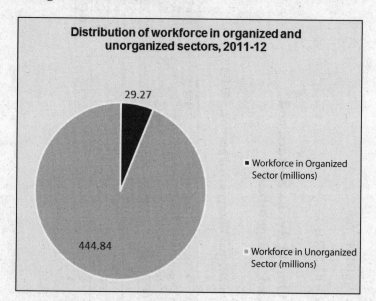

Source: Table 24

Table 25: Incomes Across Different Sectors, 2014-15 (current prices)

(Rs Crore)

Sector	GVA at Basic Prices
Public non-financial corporations	758761
Private non-financial corporations	3783578
Public financial corporations	318419
Private financial corporations	331941
General Government	1144744
Households including NPISHs	5134966
Total	11472409

Source: GoI, 2017i

Note: NPISH stands for Non-profit Institutions Serving Households

Graph 22: Incomes Across Different Sectors, 2014-15 (current prices)

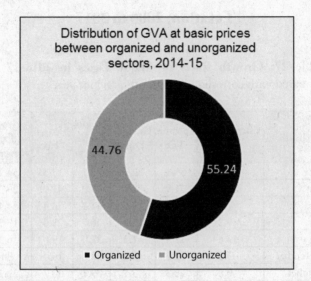

Distribution of GVA at basic prices between organized and unorganized sectors, 2014-15

44.76

55.24

■ Organized   ■ Unorganized

Source: National Accounts Statistics, 2016

Table 26: GVA at Basic Prices by Sector and Unorganized Sector, 2014-15 (current prices)

Sector	Total GVA at Basic Prices (Rs Crore)	GVA from Household Sector (Rs Crore)	% of Household Sector or Unorganized Sector
Agriculture	1995253	1888354	94.6
Industry	3442680	1100876	32.0
Services	6034480	2145737	35.6

Source: National Accounts Statistics, 2016

ANNEXURE 17

Taxation, 2000 to 2017

Table 27: Growth Rates of Major Taxes in 2016-17 (as compared with corresponding month previous year)

Month	Corporation Tax	Income Tax	Custom Duty	Union Excise Duty	Service Tax	Gross Tax Revenue
April	-34.8	55.1	22.2	-85.1	13.3	54.2
May	-60.2	21.9	22.7	65.0	41.0	29.2
June	7.4	78.3	9.6	41.1	26.4	24.4
July	-9.2	34.4	-13.6	46.7	22.0	17.3
August	-12.6	-15.4	-1.3	38.0	19.0	6.3
September	5.3	-12.2	-0.2	37.8	16.0	5.8
October	30.8	28.3	3.1	39.1	30.7	27.1
November	164.3	40.7	20.0	43.4	44.3	54.6
December	-3.6	18.3	-8.0	30.5	9.2	5.3
January	-38.9	11.9	7.7	36.6	13.6	11.8
February	10.2	35.3	5.1	22.7	3.0	16.3
March	15.3	39.3	33.9	6.5	17.0	19.0
Year	6.7	24.7	7.4	32.7	20.4	17.9

Source: GoI, 2017h

Table 28: Central Tax-to-GDP Ratio, 2000-01 to 2016-17

Year	Revenue (Rs Crore)			% Annual Growth Rate			GDP$_{MP}$ at Current Prices (Rs Crore)	Tax/GDP Ratio		
	Direct	Indirect	Total	Direct	Indirect	Total		Direct	Indirect	Total
2000-01	68305	119814	188119	-	-	-	2177413	3.1	5.5	8.6
2001-02	69198	117318	186516	1.3	-2.1	-0.9	2355845	2.9	5.0	7.9
2002-03	83088	132608	215696	20.1	13.0	15.6	2536327	3.3	5.2	8.5
2003-04	105088	148608	253696	26.5	12.1	17.6	2841503	3.7	5.2	8.9
2004-05	132771	170396	303167	26.3	14.7	19.5	3242209	4.1	5.3	9.4
2005-06	165216	199348	364564	24.4	17.0	20.3	3693369	4.5	5.4	9.9
2006-07	230181	242066	472247	39.3	21.4	29.5	4294706	5.4	5.6	11.0
2007-08	314330	279031	593361	36.6	15.3	25.6	4987090	6.3	5.6	11.9
2008-09	333818	269433	603251	6.2	-3.4	1.7	5630063	5.9	4.8	10.7
2009-10	378063	245367	623430	13.3	-8.9	3.3	6477827	5.8	3.8	9.6
2010-11	446935	345127	792062	18.2	40.7	27.0	7784115	5.7	4.4	10.2
2011-12	493959	391738	885697	10.5	13.5	11.8	8736039	5.7	4.5	10.1
2012-13	558658	474482	1033140	13.1	21.1	16.6	9946636	5.6	4.8	10.4
2013-14	638543	497060	1135603	14.3	4.8	9.9	11236635	5.7	4.4	10.1
2014-15	695744	544772	1240516	9.0	9.6	9.2	12445128	5.6	4.4	10.0
2015-16	741945	709825	1451770	6.6	30.3	17.0	13682035	5.4	5.2	10.6
2016-17	847097	851869	1698966	14.2	20.0	17.0	15183709	5.6	5.6	11.2

Source: MOSPI for data up to 2012-13 and Budget Documents (Tax Revenue) for subsequent years; GDP$_{MP}$ from RBI Database on Indian Economy (Macroeconomic Aggregates at Current Prices)

Graph 23: Growth Rate of Gross Tax Revenue of Central Government

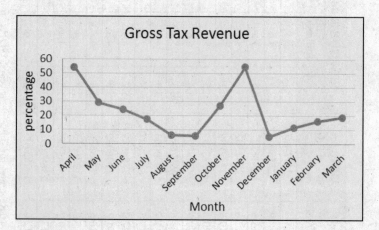

Source: Table 27

Graph 24: Growth Rate of Corporation Tax

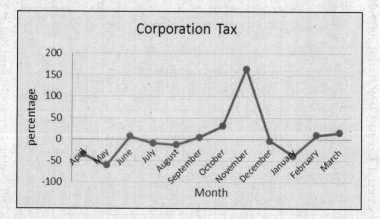

Source: Table 27

Graph 25: Growth Rate of Income Tax

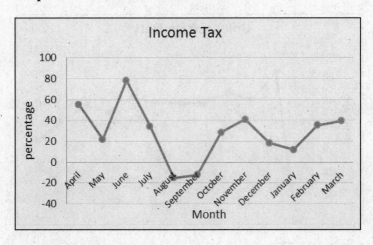

Source: Table 27

Graph 26: Growth Rate of Customs Duty

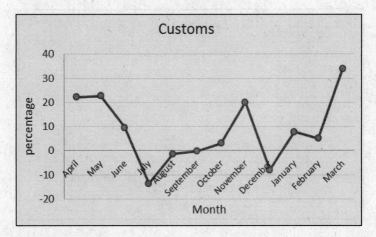

Source: Table 27

Graph 27: Growth Rate of Union Excise Duty

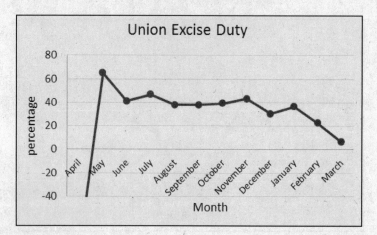

Source: Table 27

Graph 28: Growth Rate of Service Tax

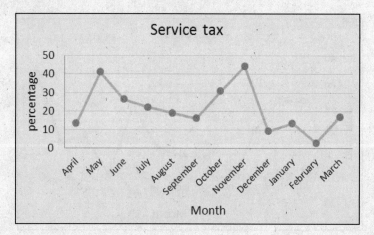

Source: Table 27

Graph 29: Growth Rate of Other Taxes

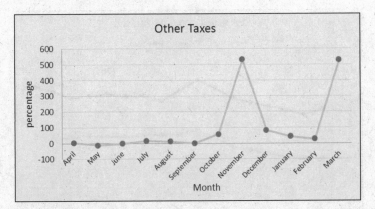

Source: GoI, 2017h

Note: Includes Securities Transaction Tax, Banking Cash Transaction Tax, Fringe Benefit Tax, Wealth Tax, etc.

Graph 30: Central Tax Revenue—Annual Growth Rate

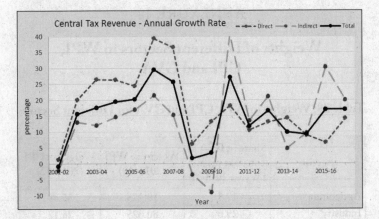

Source: MOSPI till 2012-13 and Budget Documents (Tax Revenue) for subsequent years

Graph 31: Central Tax-to-GDP Ratio, 2000-01 to 2016-17

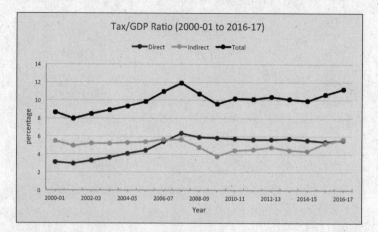

Source: MOSPI for data up to 2012-13 and Budget Documents (Tax Revenue) for subsequent years; GDP$_{MP}$ from RBI Database on Indian Economy (Macroeconomic Aggregates at Current Prices)

ANNEXURE 18

Weights of Different Sectors in WPI, CPI and GVA

Table 29: Weights in WPI, CPI and GVA for Different Sectors

Sector	Share in GVA at constant prices* for year 2015-16	Weight in WPI (2011-12)	Weight in CPI (2011-12)
Agriculture	17.5	19.375	35.49
Industry*	29.6	80.625	26.12
Services	53	0	38.38

Source: GoI (DIPP) Key Economic Indicators
*Industry also includes Construction, which, too, is not considered in WPI

Graph 32: Weights of Different Sectors in WPI, CPI and GVA

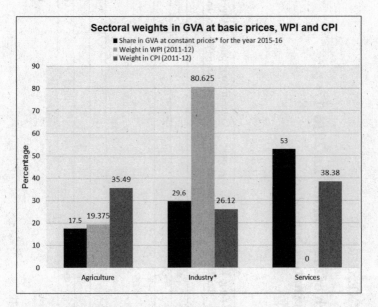

Sectoral weights in GVA at basic prices, WPI and CPI

- Share in GVA at constant prices* for the year 2015-16
- Weight in WPI (2011-12)
- Weight in CPI (2011-12)

	Agriculture	Industry*	Services
Share in GVA	17.5	29.6	53
Weight in WPI	19.375	80.625	0
Weight in CPI	35.49	26.12	38.38

Source: Data in Table 29

ANNEXURE 19

Likely Rate of Growth of the Economy for 2016–17: Two Alternative Scenarios

Scenario 1

Sector	GDP Share	r.o.g. April to October (%)	r.o.g. Nov to Jan (%)	r.o.g. Feb to March (%)	Sectoral r.o.g. post demonetization (%)	Overall r.o.g. post demonetization (%)	Overall r.o.g. for the year (%)
Organized	0.55	7.7	0	3	1		
Agriculture	0.14	7.7	4	4	4		
Unorganized rest	0.31	7.7	-60	-30	-48	-14	-1.2

Scenario 2

Sector	GDP Share	r.o.g. April to October (%)	r.o.g. Nov to Jan (%)	r.o.g. Feb to March (%)	Sectoral r.o.g. post demonetization (%)	Overall r.o.g. post demonetization (%)	Overall r.o.g. for the year (%)
Organized	0.55	7.7	2	5	3		
Agriculture	0.14	7.7	4	4	4		
Unorganized rest	0.31	7.7	-50	-20	-38	-9	0.55

Note: Assumptions on growth as given in the text in Chapter V

ANNEXURE 20

Sectors and Industries Affected by Demonetization

1. Gauhar Raza-led Survey Across India by NGOs

Thirty-two organizations enthusiastically participated in the project. The survey started in the first week of January 2017, and it took about a month and a half to collect data through interviews. The total number of valid questionnaires used for analysis is 3647.

While almost all the states were represented, more than 50 per cent of the respondents were from Delhi and Maharashtra. This was a weakness of the survey.

56.5 per cent	said wholesale trade was affected
60.7 per cent	said farmers were affected
53.8 per cent	felt '*karobar*' has come to a halt
50.0 per cent	reported loss of job
64.9 per cent	reported they knew someone sick who faced a problem
59.9 per cent	reported knowing someone who died and their family facing a problem
65.2 per cent	reported they knew a family which faced wedding-related problems
55.6 per cent	reported things had not normalized even after fifty days had elapsed

2. Krishnan, D. and S. Siegel. 2016. 'Survey of the Effects of Demonetisation on 28 Slum Neighbourhoods in Mumbai'

The authors summarize that there was an 'immediate impact of and reaction to demonetisation'. The survey was based on 'around 200 families living in 28 slum or lower-income neighbourhoods in Mumbai in early December 2016'. The survey reported a) 'a drop in family income . . . with wide variation across different groups and occupation types' and b) 'A drop in consumption as well as changes in the families' savings in November'.

3. SBI PMI Report
SBI, 2017b

SBI Yearly and Monthly Composite Index

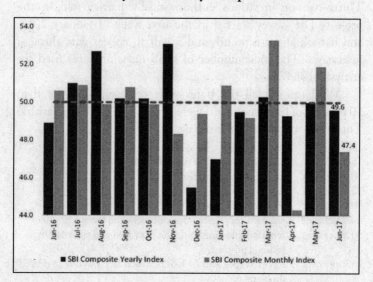

It can be seen from the chart above that the Purchase Managers' Index (PMI) has been mostly below the 50 mark, which implies a contraction for most of the time between November 2016 and June 2017. This indicates low level of activity, including negative growth, in many months in this period. Compared with the five months prior to November 2016, the level of activity is definitely lower. This indicates the mostly adverse impact of demonetization on business activity.

4. SBI Survey of Industries
SBI, 2017a

The SBI 'decided to do a primary survey to understand the nuances of demonetization'. The survey was conducted between 30 December 2016 and 7 January 2017. 'The survey reveals that 69% of the respondents did affirm that their business has been impacted.'

'Overall the decline in business is less than 50% for the majority of the businesses that were impacted. Construction sector and the informal road-side vendors seem to be the worst hit. Less impact was seen on automobile and chemist shops that already had digital modes of transaction.

Within the textile sector, shopkeepers dealing with retail segment have been more impacted than those in the wholesale segment. The gems and jewellery sector has also been hit with declining sales.'

Extent of Impact on Businesses

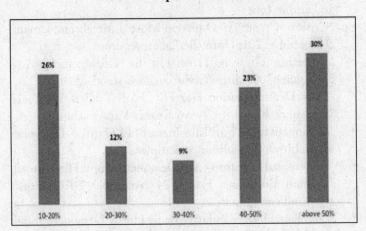

SBI Survey, 30 December 2016 to 7 January 2017

Data in the chart above suggest that 72 per cent of the businesses were affected to the extent of more than 30 per cent. Further, 30 per cent of the businesses were impacted by more than 50 per cent.

5. Lokayat and Janata Trust, 2017

It lists the following reports of adverse impact on the farming sector and small businesses:

- 'Amid Cash Crunch, Only 17% of Rabi Crop Loans Disbursed', 21 December 2016, http://indianexpress.com
- 'At Delhi's Azadpur Mandi, Lack of Money Is Slowly Choking Business and Also Workers', 18 November 2016, http://thewire.in
- 'Demonetisation Impact: Vegetables, Fruits Trade Halves in Mumbai', 19 November 2016, http://www.firstpost.com
- 'RBI's No Exchange Rule for Cooperative Banks Hits Farmers', 18 November 2016, http://economictimes. indiatimes.com
- 'Crisis of Credit: An Omission Most Untimely and Unfair', 9 December 2016, http://indianexpress.com
- 'Vegetable Growers Hard Hit by Demonetisation', 8 December 2016, http://www.business-standard.com
- 'How Demonetisation Has Hit Small Traders Hard', 15 November 2016, http://www.financialexpress.com
- 'Demonetisation: Small Businesses Hit Hard', 5 December 2016, http://timesofindia.indiatimes.com
- 'Widespread Distress as Demonetisation Hits Small, Medium Businesses Hard', 24 November 2016, http:// www.millenniumpost.in
- 'Ludhiana Hosiery Industry Badly Hit by Demonetization', 21 November 2016, http://www.business-standard.com

- Ajaz Ashraf, 'Interview: Demonetisation Has Hit 80% of Small Businesses, the Sector Is Staring at Apocalypse', 6 December 2016, https://scroll.in
- Saher Naqvi, 'Textile Market in Tirupur Badly Hit Post-Demonetisation', 3 December 2016, https://www.cmie.com
- 'Cash Crunch Pushed Factory Activity into Contraction in December', 3 January 2017, http://www.moneycontrol.com

6. PHD Research Bureau, 2017

The report is based on 'a survey covering 700 business firms from MSMEs and large enterprises, operating in different states and sectors and received feedback from around 2,000 people'.

It argues that Indian businesses have been impacted 'directly or indirectly in terms of impact on demand'. It adds that small businesses and labour-intensive sectors have been impacted heavily 'since a major portion of transactions involve cash for the purchase of raw materials and payment to daily wage labourers'.

The survey reported that in the MSME sector, '73% Respondents are facing huge cash crunch due to demonetization as they are unable to fulfil their daily requirements.'

Regarding the impact on people, the report says, 'Demonetization has affected the short-term consumption needs of the people basically belonging to the lower and middle-class families.' Further, a big impact is noticed 'on those who live in remote areas of the country, having no bank accounts and no identification proofs'.

The business firms surveyed were broadly from the following sectors :

Sector	Respondents reporting adverse impact
1) Retail	88 per cent
2) Agriculture	81 per cent
3) Real Estate	77 per cent
4) Construction	74 per cent
5) Media and Entertainment	68 per cent
6) Gems and Jewellery	65 per cent
7) Tourism, Hospitality and Wellness	61 per cent
8) Leather	56 per cent
9) Mining	56 per cent
10) Textile and Garments	56 per cent
11) Automobiles	52 per cent

The major impact of currency crunch on people regarding:

1. Inability to fulfil daily needs   92 per cent
   (Difficulty in purchase of eatables, dairy products and
   other necessities)
2. Difficulty in transportation   76 per cent
3. Difficulty in getting healthcare and wellness   68 per cent
4. Difficulty in getting beauty and cosmetics-related
   goods and services   43 per cent
5. Entertainment   40 per cent
6. Tourism   37 per cent
7. Shopping   34 per cent

7.   RBI Report on Impact of Demonetization (RBI, 2017e)

This report said the growth of gross value added (GVA) is expected to have been impacted. The construction sector and some of the labour-intensive manufacturing sectors such as textiles, leather, gems and jewellery, and transportation engage casual/migrant labourers extensively. The loss of wage income for workers is also expected to have caused a drag on consumption demand. It found that there was a:

(i) Decline in the sales of fast-moving consumer goods (FMCG) (as per the Nielsen survey) and automobiles in all the months from November to January;

(ii) Contraction in the manufacturing purchasing managers' index (PMI) in December for the first time in 2016;

(iii) Deceleration in export growth during November;

iv) Contraction in auto sales of 4.7 per cent in January 2017;

v) Big impact on the two-wheeler segment, especially in rural pockets;

vi) Impact on the sales performance of the consumer-durables industry. Manufacturers also cut production due to rising inventories;

Growth in Consumer-durable Segments

(per cent)

Category	Volume Growth		Value Growth	
	October 2016	November 2016	October 2016	November 2016
Microwave	90.6	-53.0	90.7	-51.5
Refrigerator	74.0	-41.2	73.4	-40.3
Air Conditioner	1.8	-34.0	4.0	-33.8
Washing Machine	116.7	-31.7	113.1	-34.4
Flat Panel TV	94.7	-30.4	99.4	-26.6

Source: Retail sales data by GFK-Nielsen

vii) Slowdown in domestic demand for apparels and other end-products of the textile industry;

viii) Sharp fall in the services PMI 54.5 in October to 46.7 and 46.8 in November and December, respectively, entering contraction territory for the first time after June 2015. Despite improvement in January to 48.7, it remained in contraction mode;

ix) Sharp deceleration in production of cement, one of the main indicators for the construction sector in November, and by 8.7 per cent and 13.3 per cent in December 2016 and January 2017, respectively; and

x) Contraction in sales of commercial vehicles—an indicator of transportation activity—by 11.6 per cent in November, 5.1 per cent in December 2016, and 0.7 per cent in January 2017, against an average growth of 6.9 per cent during April-October 2016.

8. Summary of Sectors/Industries Affected by Demonetization:

1. Auto: Maruti, tractor makers, two-wheeler makers Bajaj, Hero MotoCorp
2. Housing/Realty
3. Travel and Tourism
4. Trade
5. Construction
6. Plantation Industry
7. Media and Entertainment
8. Leather
9. Mining
10. Textiles
11. Hospitality and Wellness Industry
12. FMCG
13. Gold
14. Jewellery Industry
15. Microwave Ovens
16. Refrigerators
17. Air Conditioners
18. Washing Machine
19. Flat Panel TV
20. Brassware Industry
21. Lock Industry
22. Hosiery Industry

23. Cycle Industry
24. Cement
25. Commercial Vehicles
26. Smartphone Sales
27. Sugar Industry (less demand from Soft Drinks)
28. HFCs
29. Emami
30. ShopClues
31. L & T
32. Hindustan Unilever
33. ICICI
34. Jet Airways
35. Coke
36. Nestle
37. Coal India Limited
38. Britannia
39. Sun Pharma
40. PepsiCo

Source: Based on a) reports in select newspapers: *The Hindu, Times of India, Economic Times* and *Indian Express* in the months January to March 2017 and b) the above-mentioned reports in this Annexure

ANNEXURE 21

Table 30: Capacity Utilization in Industry

Quarter	CU (in the latest survey round) (percentage)
2014-15: Q1	70.2
2014-15: Q2	73.6
2014-15: Q3	71.7
2014-15: Q4	74.0

(Contd)

Quarter	CU (in the latest survey round) (percentage)
2015-16: Q1	72.0
2015-16: Q2	71.1
2015-16: Q3	72.2
2015-16: Q4	74.6
2016-17: Q1	73.6
2016-17: Q2	73.1
2016-17: Q3	72.7

Source: RBI, 2017d, Quarterly Order Books, Inventories and Capacity Utilization Survey (OBICUS), Various Rounds

Graph 33: Capacity Utilization in Industry

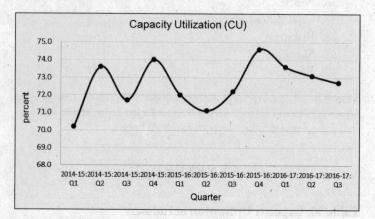

Source: RBI, 2017d

ANNEXURE 22

NPAs of Banks

Table 31: Gross Advances and NPAs of Scheduled Commercial Banks

(Amount in Rs Crore)

Year*	All Scheduled Commercial Banks			Public Sector Banks		
	Gross Loans and Advances	Gross NPAs	Gross NPAs to Gross Advances (%)	Gross Loans and Advances	Gross NPAs	Gross NPAs to Gross Advances (%)
2008-09	3038254	68328	2.25	2283473	44957	1.97
2009-10	3544965	84698	2.39	2733458	59926	2.19
2010-11	4012079	97900	2.44	3079804	74600	2.42
2011-12	4648808	142903	3.07	3550389	117839	3.32
2012-13	5971820	194053	3.25	4560169	165606	3.63
2013-14	6875748	263372	3.83	5215920	227264	4.36
2014-15	7560666	323345	4.28	5616718	278468	4.96
2015-16 Q1	7493890	344161	4.59	5502390	297428	5.41
2015-16 Q2	7550869	361734	4.79	5580281	315213	5.65
2015-16 Q3	7909576	463929	5.87	5691123	404677	7.11
2015-16 Q4	8173121	611619	7.48	5823907	539968	9.27
2016-17 Q1	8087071	668441	8.27	5684608	592246	10.42
2016-17 Q2	8183658	720812	8.81	5714271	630321	11.03

Source: RBI, 2017a

*Figures as at the end of the period

Graph 34: Gross NPAs of All Scheduled Commercial Banks

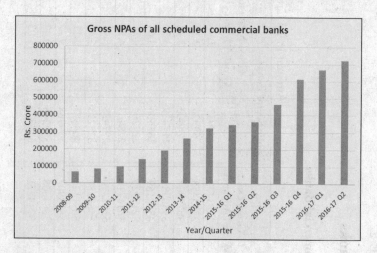

Source: RBI, 2017a

Graph 35: Gross NPAs to Gross Advances Ratio

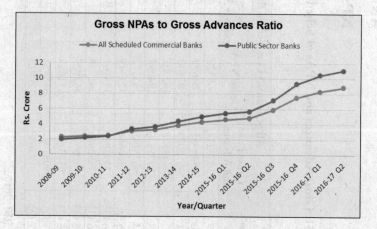

Source: RBI, 2017a

Chapter VI

ANNEXURE 23

Cashlessness in Different Countries

Table 32: Which Are the World's Most Cashless Countries?

Rank	Country	Non-cash Payments' Share of Total Value of Consumer Payments	% of Population with a Debit Card
1	Belgium	93	86
2	France	92	69
3	Canada	90	88
4	United Kingdom	89	88
5	Sweden	89	96
6	Australia	86	79
7	The Netherlands	85	98
8	United States	80	72
9	Germany	76	88
10	South Korea	70	58

Source: World Atlas, 2017

Table 33. Non-Cash Transactions and ATM and PoS Availability in India and Similar Countries

Country	Non-cash Payments Transactions by Non-banks per Capita per Annum	ATMs per 1,00,000 Adults	No. of Pay Points per Million People
India	11	19.71	1080
China	26	81.42	16602
Mexico	32	50.7	7189
South Africa	70	69.28	7267
Brazil	142	113.99	25241
UK	355	131.58	30078
Singapore	728	60.11	31096

Source: 1. GoI, 2017j
2. IMF, 2016

Table 34: Phone, Internet and ATM Availability in India

Telephone subscribers (in millions)	1151.78
Tele density (%)	89.9
Internet subscribers (in millions)	391.5
No. of Internet subscribers per 100 population	30.56
No. of Internet subscribers per 100 population (rural)	13.08
No. of Internet subscribers per 100 population (urban)	68.86
Number of ATMs	205860
Number of PoS devices	1767733

Source: GoI, 2017k and RBI, 2017f
Note: Data as on December 2016

Graph 36: Currency-GDP Ratio

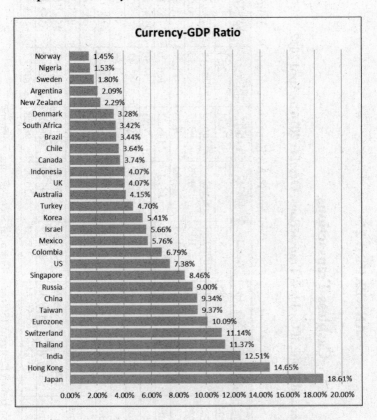

Source: Rogoff, 2017. Graph at scholar.harvard.edu/files/rogoff/files/ curse_fig_3.4_currency_to_gdp_ratio.xlsx. Accessed 3 July 2017

ANNEXURE 24

Cashless Transactions

Table 35: Absolute Number and Value of Cashless Transactions, October 2016 to April 2017

(Volume in Millions and Value in Rs Billion)

		Oct-16	Nov-16	Dec-16	Jan-17	Feb-17	Mar-17	Apr-17
RTGS	Volume	9.01	7.88	8.84	9.33	9.11	12.54	9.54
	Value	97554.34	101894.49	110980.33	100602.54	95266.75	154094.85	111743.70
ECS	Volume	1.77	1.04	1.16	0.96	0.87	1.15	0.68
	Value	18.59	9.27	14.39	11.94	9.35	11.24	10.89
NEFT	Volume	133.21	123.05	166.31	164.19	148.21	186.70	143.17
	Value	9504.50	8807.88	11537.63	11355.08	10877.91	16294.50	12156.17
IMPS	Volume	42.09	36.17	52.78	62.42	59.75	67.41	65.08
	Value	343.57	324.81	431.92	491.25	482.21	564.68	562.06
Credit Card	Volume	89.49	98.31	116.46	113.24	95.35	108.10	107.06
	Value	302.42	266.99	312.37	328.62	288.95	336.20	333.76
Debit Card	Volume	942.65	797.82	1045.93	1040.97	944.32	981.28	928.32
	Value	2767.23	1556.26	1429.65	2006.48	2286.82	2616.45	2543.41
Prepaid Payment Instruments	Volume	126.90	169.32	261.09	295.80	280.02	342.09	352.23
	Value	60.22	50.74	97.70	110.01	96.28	106.77	103.71

Source: RBI, 2017a. Database on Indian Economy (Statistics-Financial Sector-Payment Systems)

Table 36: Growth Rate of Cashless Transactions by Value and Volume, October 2016 to November 2017

		Nov-16	Dec-16	Jan-17	Feb-17	Mar-17	Apr-17
RTGS	Volume	-12.56	12.26	5.54	-2.43	37.72	-23.89
	Value	4.45	8.92	-9.35	-5.30	61.75	-27.48
ECS	Volume	-41.48	11.89	-17.24	-9.37	32.18	-41.04
	Value	-50.12	55.16	-17.03	-21.69	20.21	-3.11
NEFT	Volume	-7.63	35.16	-1.27	-9.73	25.98	-23.32
	Value	-7.33	30.99	-1.58	-4.20	49.79	-25.40
IMPS	Volume	-14.06	45.92	18.27	-4.28	12.83	-3.46
	Value	-5.46	32.98	13.74	-1.84	17.10	-0.46
Credit Card	Volume	9.87	18.46	-2.76	-15.80	13.37	-0.96
	Value	-11.72	17.00	5.20	-12.07	16.35	-0.73
Debit Card	Volume	-15.36	31.10	-0.47	-9.28	3.91	-5.40
	Value	-43.76	-8.14	40.35	13.97	14.41	-2.79
Prepaid Payment Instruments	Volume	33.42	54.20	13.29	-5.33	22.17	2.96
	Value	-15.73	92.53	12.60	-12.48	10.90	-2.87

Source: RBI, 2017a. Database on Indian Economy (Statistics–Financial Sector–Payment Systems)

Graph 37: Growth Rates in Volume of Cashless Transactions, October 2016 to April 2017

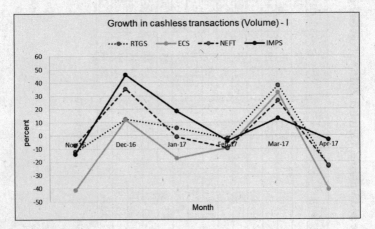

Source: Table 36

Graph 38: Growth Rates in Volume of Cashless Transactions, October 2016 to April 2017

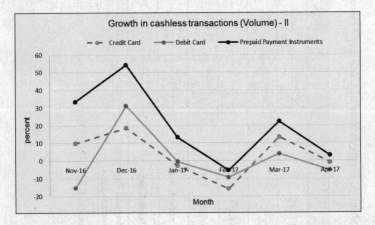

Source: Table 36

Graph 39: Growth Rates in Value of Cashless Transactions, October 2016 to April 2017

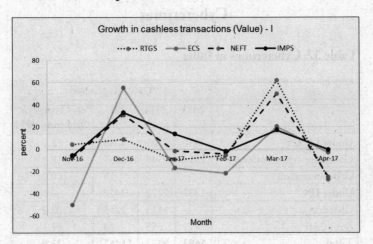

Source: Table 36

Graph 40: Growth Rates in Value of Cashless Transactions, October 2016 to April 2017

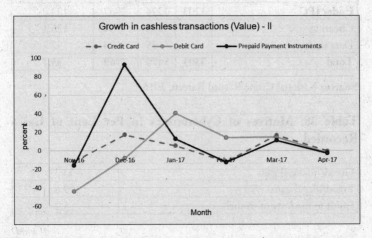

Source: Table 36

ANNEXURE 25

Cybercrimes

Table 37: Cybercrimes in India

	Cases Registered			
	2013	2014	2015	% Change in 2015 from 2014
Under IT Act	4356	7201	8045	11.7
Computer-related offences	2516	5548	6567	18.4
Cyber-terrorism	-	5	13	160.0
Under IPC	1337	2272	3422	50.6
Cheating	-	1115	2255	102.2
Data theft	-	55	84	52.7
Total	**5693**	**9473**	**11467**	**21.0**
	Persons arrested			
Under IT Act	2098	4246	5102	20.2
Computer-related offences	1011	3131	4217	34.7
Cyber-terrorism	-	0	3	-
Under IPC	1203	1224	2867	134.2
Cheating	-	335	754	125.1
Data theft	-	55	84	52.7
Total	**3301**	**5470**	**7969**	**45.7**

Source: National Crime Record Bureau, 2016

Table 38: Motives of Cybercrimes in Per Cent of Cases Recorded

Greed/financial gain	33.3
Fraud/illegal gain	9.6
Insult to modesty of women	5.2

(Contd)

Sexual exploitation	5.1
Causing disrepute	3.3

Source: National Crime Record Bureau, 2016

Table 39: Cybersecurity-related Incidents and Websites Hacked

Year	Cybersecurity Incidents Observed	Websites Hacked	Govt Websites Hacked
2013	41319	28481	189
2015	44679	32323	155
2015	49455	27205	164
2016	39730*	33147	199

Source: Lok Sabha, 2016b, 2017a and 2017b
* Till October 2016

Table 40: Major Cybercrime Cases in 2016

1. **Indian debit card hacking:** As many as 32 lakh debit cards belonging to various Indian banks were compromised earlier this year resulting in the loss of Rs 1.3 crore in fraudulent transactions, as per NPCI.
2. **Bangladesh bank hack:** One of the largest financial crimes executed online took place in early February when $81 million of Bangladesh's money was siphoned off by unknown hackers, reportedly to the Philippines, Sri Lanka and other parts of Asia.
3. **Philippines voter data leak:** Hackers divulged personal information of voters, including fingerprint data and passport information of 70 million voters.
4. **Yahoo data theft:** In December 2016, Yahoo said one billion accounts were compromised. User names, email addresses, date of birth, passwords, phone numbers and security questions were all leaked.

5. **Oracle MICROS hack:** A Russian hacker group, notorious for hacking bank websites, broke into the computer network of Oracle, compromising their MICROS PoS credit card payment systems. MICROS is among the top three PoS vendors globally.

Source: Christopher, 2016